BOB FULTON

"My Career My Life"

for 43 years

"The VOICE"

of the

Gamecocks

Dedication

This book is dedicated to
Gamecock fans everywhere!

Copyright © 2007 ICP, LLC

Published in Lexington, South Carolina
By ICP, LLC

Manufactured in the United States of America by Wentworth Printing, West Columbia, South Carolina

FIRST EDITION

Library of Congress Catologing-in-Publication-Data

Fulton, Bob 1920-
   BOB FULTON "My career My life" "THE VOICE" of the Gamecocks
   Tells the stories of his experiences that led him to a life as the most admired
   and beloved Sportscaster in South Carolina. / by Bob Fulton
     p. cm.
   ISBN # *978-1-4276-2746-9*. (alk-paper)
    1. Fulton, Bob 1920- 2.Sportscasters-United States-Biography
   3. South Carolina's Fighting Gamecocks (Football Team) –History
   I. Fulton II.Title-
   11U48333W58721945. 2007

Bob in the Announcers booth at Williams-Brice

Head Coach Steve Spurrier
University of South Carolina

~FOREWORD~

Anyone who knows me understands my love of history. When Jerri and I vacation we often make a point to stop at historic sites. My affection for sports history, and particularly football, is even greater.

Writers and fans sometimes marvel at my recall of scores and situations. Being able to recount games and remember scores always has come natural to me, and I think it has to do with having an appreciation for how each game, each season plays into the history of a program and the sport.

When I arrived at South Carolina in November of 2004 I immediately began to research and learn the history of our school's football program. What I learned right away was that there is no better source of information than Bob Fulton, who has lived Carolina athletics for a great deal of his long and wonderful life.

Whether it was wanting to know more about Carolina's 1969 Atlantic Coast Conference championship or to learn the stories of our retired football jerseys, time and again I was told that Bob Fulton could tell me everything I need to know.

As I understand he long ago earned the label "The Voice" among Gamecock fans and I certainly respect that. To me, though, he always will be Mr. Fulton. He merits that kind of title because he is as solid a representative of our fine university as anyone.

Through his 43 years as play-by-play announcer for Carolina athletics, Mr. Fulton has used his eyes and voice to tell a compelling tale on USC's athletic fields. Carolina fans should forever be grateful to have had such a professional radio announcer serve as their eyes for more than four decades.

In this book, Mr. Fulton uses his sharp recall of detail and innate ability to tell a story to bring back to life the many outstanding and memorable moments in Carolina athletics history.

His book has helped me gain a greater appreciation of Carolina's football history, but as you probably know I am a fan of all Carolina sports. Now I better understand why Carolina fans are so fond of Frank McGuire's basketball glory years and how fortunate the Gamecock Nation has been to have one outstanding baseball coach after another.

Beyond Carolina, I found it fascinating that Mr. Fulton once re-created professional baseball games, sitting in a studio to announce a game that was played many miles away. His chapter on sports broadcasting should serve as a tutorial for all students bent on joining that field.

Many times I have invited Mr. Fulton to stop by my office at Williams-Brice Stadium. Those times when we do talk I find him to be a virtual walking encyclopedia of Carolina athletics, and with my love of history that serves me just fine.

All Carolina fans should enjoy this book as much as I do my friendship with Mr. Fulton.

Steve Spurrier

~TABLE OF CONTENTS~

~ACKNOWLEDGMENT~

I realize that my broadcasting career that covered 53 years would not have achieved any measure of success and personal satisfaction, were it not for the kindness and support of many people.

At the risk of overlooking some who made important contributions to my career, I wish to say thanks, first of all, to members of my broadcasting teams that served me so well through the years – Analyst: Tommy Suggs, my right arm for 21 years, Todd Ellis, Don Williams, Jimmy Powell, Casey Manning, Mick Mixon, the late Johnny Evans, Bill Drake, the late Joe Petty, Hub Blankenship, Bobby Roberts, Bill Routh and Bill McCarthy; Producers: Clark Newsome, Liz McMillan, Tom Stevens, and Host Communications Company; Engineers: Homer Fesperman, Burt Smith, Carol Senn, John George and Jeff Flanders; Spotters and Statisticians: John and Cliff Terry – both of whom have passed away, Charles Irick, Dan Radacovich, David Spence, Mick Mixon, and Jim Corbett. And a special thanks to Julian Gibbons and Ree Hart, for not only their assistance on the broadcasts but also for their friendship and support over the years.

A special thanks to three people, long-time friends of mine, who contributed so much to Carolina athletics:

Ginger Rigdon – for thirty years, a secretary in the athletic department, most of that time spent in the basketball office;

The late Jim Price – who for over 25 years was head trainer for our teams;

Sarge Frye – who kept the playing fields looking better than any in the country – win or lose! Sarge Frye is gone but missed by all of us.

A special thanks to Dr. Charlie Crews and R.J. Moore, who are role models for Carolina fans.

My thanks and appreciations also to:

Tom Price, Kerry Tharp and Brian Binette of the USC Sports Information Department, and Steve Leak, who is now associate director of media relations;

Randy Herald, who traveled many years to shoot video for our TV shows.

Athletics Director Eric Hyman and the athletics directors who preceded him, and Dr. John Moore – a valuable department member for many years.

Former USC President Dr. John Palms and his successor Dr. Andrew Sorenson.

To all the coaches, players, and most of all, the wonderful Gamecock fans, who have made it all a great experience for me – one I will never forget.

To all the media people, who have been most kind to me.

To my wife Carol and Don's wife Betty – thanks for your patience and support.

To my lifelong friend, Don Barton, without whose help the original edition of my book – *Hi Everybody! This is Bob Fulton* - would not have been written.

To the indispensable Paul Streeter and to Wally Mullinax who played an important part in the writing and distribution of this book.

To Emily White who for 41 Years has been the Secretary to all the Football coaches and AD's of Carolina and a great help to me and many others.

To Ron Morris, my close friend, and my wife Carol for the encouragement and advice they gave me in getting this book put together.

~*INTRODUCTION*~

This book is really two books in one. You may recall the 1996 book "Hi Everybody This is Bob Fulton," which was co-written by my friend Don Barton and was a best seller in South Carolina for 16 weeks. Well, I have edited, updated and added a considerable amount of material to that book, and I trust you will find the new version interesting and entertaining.

This book is a story of my life and career, from boyhood to retirement. Believe me; it covers a lot of years.

Most people only know me as the voice of South Carolina athletics for 43 years, so I thought this book could better tell of my many travels over the years. It covers my growing up during the great depression, the real struggle of earning a college degree and the most unusual way in which I got my start in radio broadcasting.

Along the way, I not only was a newscaster and disc jockey, but also covered wrestling, horse racing, boxing and ice hockey. I also crossed into the coaching ranks for awhile, forever earning me the right to second-guess all coaches during my broadcast career.

I once opened a broadcast school and even purchased a diner in downtown Little Rock, Arkansas. Neither proved profitable. To get into the radio play-by-play field of broadcasting I had to lie about my resume.

In reading this book you also will learn about the long-ago art of re-creating baseball games, and about how I once was nearly sucked into a gambling ring through those re-creations.

Along the way I sat in the same Mutual Broadcast booth with Al Helfer, Dizzy Dean and Buddy Blattner to call Major League Baseball games. That was being at the top of my profession, but I had the same love for broadcasting then as I did when re-creating Dixie Youth baseball games in the Columbia area.

At USC, I survived thirteen athletics directors, ten basketball coaches, nine football coaches and ten university presidents.

The people I have watched perform on athletic fields, met in person or been associated with reads like a Hall of Fame in athletic circles. They include Ty Cobb, Lefty Grove, Hank Iba, Bud Wilkinson, Bobby Richardson, Walter Alston, Harry Carry, Ernie Harwell, Bill Veeck, Red Barber, Vin Scully, Bob Feller and Mel Ott.

So, find an easy chair and get comfortable as I take you down memory lane. I trust you will enjoy the read.

~VOICE OF THE GAMECOCKS~
(FOOTBALL)

When I came to Columbia in 1952 my contract was to do baseball, and nothing was assured beyond that. Then WNOK acquired the rights to originate the University of South Carolina football games, so Moody McElveen asked me if I wanted to stay.

Living in the same town for several years had its appeal, and I jumped at the chance. I never had a situation before where professional baseball and college sports were located in the same place.

Prior to coming to Columbia the only thing I had heard about the University of South Carolina involved the Big Thursday game with Clemson. Because no other games were played on that day, it received good coverage in newspapers around the country, so I was aware of the rivalry.

It also introduced me to one of my all time favorite people, Rex Enright, who was head coach and athletics director at Carolina. Rex was great to work with. He was of the old school of football coaches, but well ahead of his time in the area of public relations.

The worst thing I ever heard said about Rex was, "He's too good for his own good." This was before college coaches were earning megabucks. Big salaries, shoe contracts, football camps, TV shows and commercials. Rex did have a Sunday TV show, for which he received a suit of clothes each week from a men's clothing store. The suit always ended up in the closet of one of the assistant coaches.

Enright had played football at Notre Dame under the immortal Knute Rockne and was a contemporary of the famous "Four Horsemen." While playing professionally at Green Bay, he earned a law degree from Notre Dame, but football stadiums had more appeal to him than courtrooms.

Enright enjoyed good rapport with people in the community, but more importantly, he developed strong friendships with Rut Osborne, chairman of the Board of Trustees, and Sol Blatt, Jr., chairman of the committee on athletics and son of the Speaker of the House of Representatives.

Those ties provided some job security, but just as valuable was Enright's mastery of arch rival Clemson in the Big Thursday series. In the ten games following World War II Carolina lost to Clemson only twice, and nothing could bring him closer to the hearts of Carolina fans than beating the Tigers.

THE 1952 SEASON

My first official look at a Carolina football team took place on the night of September 20, when the Gamecocks opened their season with a 33-0 win over Wofford, a small Methodist institution located in Spartanburg, South Carolina. The capacity of Carolina Stadium was then 34,000, but it was little more than half full for that game.

My first Big Thursday game was somewhat of a letdown, although the Gamecocks won it by a score of 6-0. I had become accustomed to the wide open football they were playing in the Southwest Conference in that era, when Doak Walker was lighting up the scoreboard for Southern Methodist, and Bobby Layne was leading the Texas Longhorns into the end zones.

There was little else to get excited about in my first season behind the Gamecock mike, but following the Clemson game was one of the most remarkable games I witnessed

Bob Fulton "My Career My Life"

in my 55 years of reporting sports. It took place on November 1 at Norfolk, Virginia. Carolina was matched against Virginia in a Shriner-sponsored event called the Oyster Bowl, and this one was a pearl!

Virginia, coached by Art Guepe, had a powerful team and had lost only one game. They were heavily favored in the Oyster Bowl, which was to be televised by a Norfolk station and would be the third time in history that the Gamecocks had played before TV cameras.

For three quarters this game followed the script, and Virginia's dominance was really greater than the 14-0 lead the Cavaliers held with seven minutes remaining in the fourth quarter.

That is when lightning struck the Cavaliers. When second unit quarterback Dick Balka completed a couple of passes to move the Gamecocks into Virginia territory, some of the spectators had already headed for the parking lot to beat the traffic.

Virginia fans grew somewhat nervous when Balka fired a 26-yard touchdown pass to Clyde "Mule" Bennett, cutting the Cavalier advantage to 14-7, as Jim Jarrett added the extra point.

Jarrett's squib kickoff bounced crazily at the Virginia six-yard line, and Carolina's Bob Korn dived on it to give his team possession. Halfback Mike Caskey crashed into the end zone three plays later, and Jarrett's conversion made it a tie ball game, 14-14.

The next kickoff was a disaster for Virginia, too, as they were penalized for clipping on the return and had the ball on the Cavalier seven-yard line. On the next play Virginia quarterback Charlie Harding was knocked loose from the ball in a jarring tackle by Gene Witt, and Bob King recovered the ball in the end zone to give the Gamecocks a 21-14 lead.

All of this occurred while only a minute and 45 seconds ticked off the scoreboard clock. If there has ever been a college game in which three touchdowns were scored in less time than that, I've never heard about it.

That victory enabled Carolina to break even for the season and also give me a .500 mark for my broadcasting career with the Gamecock football team. I would never have guessed that 42 years later, entering my final season, that it would still be exactly .500!

THE 1953 SEASON

History was made after the 1952 season, when seven of the schools that were members of the Southern Conference pulled out to form the Atlantic Coast Conference. Rex Enright of Carolina and Eddie Cameron of Duke were the two key figures in this move, and Dr. Jim Penney, Carolina's faculty chairman of athletics, was named the league's first president.

The Southern Conference was unwieldy with too many members. Included were South Carolina, Clemson, North Carolina, North Carolina State, Duke, Wake Forest, Furman, The Citadel, Davidson, Virginia Tech, Virginia Military, Maryland, George Washington, William and Mary and, at one time, Washington and Lee.

Virginia joined the seven schools that exited the Southern, and one of the nation's premier athletic leagues was born.

After a few seasons with the Gamecocks I would come to expect a major highlight each year, such as the stunning win in the Oyster Bowl. The 1953 season was no exception.

A routine loss to Duke opened the campaign, but the Gamecocks continued their mastery of Clemson, 14-7, on Big Thursday. The season was going well for Carolina, particularly when they defeated North Carolina, 18-0, for the first time since 1944.

The real test of the caliber of this Gamecock team would come the following week against an undefeated West Virginia team at Morgantown, West Virginia. The Mountaineers were led by a super quarterback named Fred Wyant, while Johnny Gramling was setting records as a Gamecock quarterback.

The game was an exciting one, and Carolina held a 20-14 lead late in the fourth quarter, but the Mountaineers were driving and were in Gamecock territory, poised for the winning touchdown. I can still see Clyde Bennett dropping back into the flat, going high in the air to tip a Wyant pass, and then cradling it to his chest for a game saving interception.

When the Mountaineers were moving in their final drive, fog had engulfed the stadium to the point that Enright had difficulty seeing the scoreboard clock at the end of the field. He grabbed one of the managers by the arm and said, "Son, go find out what the time is."

The young man hastened off and returned in a few moments, as Enright nervously said, "Okay, what is it?" The manager gulped and said, in all seriousness, "It's a quarter till four!"

After that game the Gamecocks enjoyed their first-ever ranking in the Associated Press poll at 15th, a position they improved on by demolishing Wofford the next week. However, the bubble burst and the ranking disappeared when Carolina was upset, 19-13, by Wake Forest in the final game of the season at Charlotte. The Gamecocks had a golden opportunity to win that game, as they had a first down at the Deacon one-yard line in the fourth quarter. Four tries into the line netted nothing, and Carolina's fate was sealed.

The 7-3 record was still the best to date posted by the Gamecocks in the post-war era. They also had a shot at the second bowl bid in the school's history, as the Sun Bowl in El Paso, Texas contacted Enright about playing there. However, the bowl did not enjoy the prestige it gained in later years, and Carolina declined the invitation.

THE 1954 SEASON
When the 1954 season opened I was still doing baseball for Mutual, so I couldn't broadcast the Gamecocks' opener with a powerful Army team at West Point on September 25. And what a shame that was!

Army, coached by Earl Blaik, was a great team with national championship potential. They had excellent personnel, led by halfback Pete Dawkins, who would end up winning the Heisman Trophy. The Gamecocks were expecting good things, although they had lost several of the stars of their fine 1953 squad.

On the day of the game, as I alluded to in an earlier chapter, I was broadcasting my final game for Mutual at Ebbets field, home of the Brooklyn Dodgers. I was getting ready to board a plane at La Guardia field and asked someone if they knew how the South Carolina-Army game came out, and they said they thought South Carolina won.

That was hard for me to believe, so I bought an early edition of the Sunday paper, and sure enough, there was the score: South Carolina 34, Army 20. I bought another paper to make sure the score was correct. It was, and this was a great way to start the football season, and for me to end my major league baseball career.

Carolina never did fulfill the expectations created by that big upset, but it did propel them to a winning season of six wins and four losses. Today that type of record gets you into a post-season bowl, but this was long before the bowl explosion.

Although the win over Army was the annual piece de resistance for the Gamecocks, the season did provide another win over Clemson in a game that had a hectic finish.

6

Carolina was leading Clemson late in the fourth quarter, but the Tigers had moved into Gamecock territory and completed a pass that put them in scoring territory. However, Ray Moore, one of the officials from Columbia, threw a "flag" on the play. He had detected a Tiger interior lineman downfield before the ball was thrown. The play was nullified, and the Tigers were moved back to around midfield. On the next play Carolina quarterback Mackie Prickett intercepted a Clemson pass, and the Gamecocks ran out the clock.

After the game Clemson Coach Frank Howard encountered Moore, questioned his call on the crucial penalty and added, "I'll look at the film tomorrow, and, buddy, you had better be right!"

Moore spent a sleepless night and was on hand the next day at the company that processed the Carolina game film. He anxiously viewed the fourth quarter to confirm his call. The lineman was downfield, and Moore's call was correct.

THE 1955 SEASON

The 1955 season for Carolina was significant for only one reason. It was the final one for Rex Enright, who retired with the longest tenure - 15 seasons - in the school's history.

Enright was in declining health, and the days of being able to handle the duties of head coach of a major sport plus the job as athletics director were numbered at all schools. Clemson was having improved success in football, having played in several post-season bowl games within recent years, and that grated on the nerves of ambitious Carolina fans.

It appeared that the season would never end, and going into the final game against Virginia at Charlottesville, the Gamecocks had beaten only Wofford and Furman, while losing their first game since 1948 to Clemson.

Virginia didn't have a great team, but they offered an interesting player - a fullback by the name of Jim Bakhtiar. He was the son of a Shapur Bakhtiar, who later became prime minister of Iran. A powerful runner, Bakhtiar was nicknamed "The Pounding Persian," and that probably helped him to gain a position on the All-Atlantic Coast Conference team.

At that game against Virginia was Warren Giese, an assistant to Jim Tatum at Maryland and already the speculative successor to Enright.

The Gamecocks allowed Enright to go out on a winning note by beating the Cavaliers, 19-13, thanks to a 95-yard punt return by Carl Brazell in the fourth quarter.

As an indication of Rex's relationship with officials was an incident near the end of the game that could have been crucial for the Gamecocks. Time was running out, but the Gamecocks had possession of the ball deep in their own territory.

The most casual fan could tell you that the strategy in that circumstance is to keep the ball on the ground and the clock running. Quite often the referee will stand near the offensive huddle in order to get an idea of what to expect, and this was the case, as Carolina broke for the line of scrimmage.

The referee blew his whistle, called time and put his arm around the shoulders of the Gamecock quarterback. "Son, I think you've got a problem with your shoulder pads," he told the young man. Then he led him to the sideline to where Enright was standing.

He drew Enright aside and said, "Rex, you didn't want him to call a pass play, did you?"

"Of course not," was Enright's reply.

So Rex got the kid straightened out, he went back onto the field, called the right play, and Carolina ran out the clock to claim the victory.

A 3-6 record is not the way Enright would have chosen to end his career as a football coach, but he could take with him a number of accomplishments, including moving the Gamecocks into a higher level of competition than they were accustomed to prior to his coming to Carolina.

The Board of Trustees allowed him to select his successor and subsequently named the athletic center that was nearing completion on Rosewood Drive, "The Rex Enright Athletic Center," nicknamed the "Roundhouse" because of its circular design.

THE 1956 SEASON

To succeed him as head coach, Rex Enright settled on Warren Giese, a former Oklahoma player who was young, energetic, ambitious, and who was given a lot of credit for his contributions to Maryland's national prominence under Jim Tatum. He was top assistant on a staff that produced three undefeated teams at College Park.

Several members of Enright's staff had to double-up as coaches of other sports. Weems Baskin was head track coach, Ted Petoskey was head baseball coach, and Ernie Lawhorne coached the golf team.

Giese brought with him from Maryland a football philosophy that was ultra conservative. The offense depended almost entirely on a running attack, with the forward pass used only in case of emergency. His attitude toward the aerial game was that when you put the ball in the air, three things can happen, and two of them are bad.

His ground game was even conservative, depending on short runs to eke out first downs and consume time. It was described as "four yards and a cloud of dust." Detractors called it dull football that would drive the fans away.

Giese reasoned that as long as you win, the fans don't care how you do it - they prefer a dull win over an exciting loss.

Giese's debut was an unimpressive win over Wofford, but a week later he was walking on water. Carolina's 7-0 victory over Duke was the school's first over the Blue Devils since 1931, when Billy Laval was running his "crazy quilt" offense for the Gamecocks. You couldn't find a Gamecock fan anywhere who called that one-touchdown game boring.

The week after beating Duke the Gamecocks played Miami on a Friday night in the Orange Bowl, and it was a hot, steamy night. The Hurricanes won it, 14-6, but the Gamecocks had still played well, and it did nothing to take the edge off of the Duke victory.

Carolina's only touchdown was scored by Heyward King, a halfback from Lake City, South Carolina. The touchdown came on a ten-yard run to the goal line on the opposite side of the field from our radio booth, which was on top of the Orange Bowl press box - a mile away from a poorly lighted field.

Our spotter pointed to fullback Don Johnson, whose jersey number was 33, when it was actually King, number 23, who made the touchdown.

Although THE STATE newspaper had someone covering the game, they listened to my broadcast of out-of-town night games for stories in their early edition. Therefore, the story that went to Lake City had Johnson scoring, instead of their home town boy.

The following week, in his column, explained why the error had been made in that edition, giving me full credit for the mistake. They had never given me credit for all of the other games they had taken from my broadcasts!

A few weeks later Giese faced his former boss, Jim Tatum, who had taken the head job at North Carolina, his alma mater. When the Gamecocks blanked the Tar Heels, 14-0, in Columbia, the Carolina faithful were becoming convinced that their messiah had arrived. Now, they developed something new to worry about - another school luring away this rising star.

The Board of Trustees acted to head-off such a possibility by placing Giese on academic status - that of a full professor. Therefore the coach had job security, as long as he was not guilty of misconduct. He no longer needed a contract, because he was assured of a job of some type at the University of South Carolina.

Losing to Clemson, 7-0, on Big Thursday was attributed to bad luck, because the Gamecocks had a chance to tie late in the game but fumbled the ball into the end zone, and a Tiger pounced on it for a harmless touchback.

The Gamecocks still had a chance at the ACC title late in the season but were upset by North Carolina State in Raleigh.

As an indication of how seriously Giese took the forward pass, during the ten-game 1956 season, starting quarterback Mackie Prickett attempted a total of 44, completing 15, including two that went for touchdowns. That wouldn't even have been a good game for Steve Taneyhill when he was a Gamecock senior in 1995.

The bottom line was a record of seven wins and only three losses, which would have commanded a major bowl bid in the 1990s.

THE 1957 SEASON

Carolina fans were dragged back into reality before the 1957 was over, although the third game of the season lulled them temporarily to illusions of grandeur. The good news of this year was created in Austin, Texas, where Carolina met the Texas Longhorns in the only game ever played between these two institutions.

Texas was a perennial power in the Southwest Conference, had a bright new head coach in Darrell Royal and was heavily favored to dispatch Giese's ground forces.

King Dixon put the Gamecocks out front on the opening kickoff by returning it 98 yards for a touchdown, suffering a mild case of diarrhea en route and having to proceed directly to the dressing room for a partial uniform change. Texas put a further damper on that exciting beginning by mounting a 21-7 lead going into the fourth quarter.

Thanks to a couple of pathetic punts by Texas and heroics by the halfback tandem of Dixon and Alex Hawkins, the Gamecocks staged a sensational comeback and won the game by a score of 27 to 21.

Clemson again deflated the USC bubble with a 13-0 Big Thursday win, and North Carolina's Tatum avenged his 1956 loss to Giese with a 28-6 drubbing.

The season did provide one of the greatest football games I ever had the pleasure to broadcast. North Carolina State brought its ACC championship team into Carolina Stadium on the afternoon of November 23, and the game was a classic.

For Carolina it was an atypical offensive performance, as the Gamecocks put 26 points on the scoreboard, but so did the Wolfpack, and that's the way it was going into the final seconds of the game. State was in possession of the ball around midfield, with time remaining for only one play.

A long Wolfpack pass was intercepted by Hawkins, who returned it to deep in State territory, as time ran out. However, there was a yellow flag lying on the damp turf of Carolina Stadium in the vicinity of where Hawkins made the interception. Pass interference was called against The Hawk, a penalty was marked off, and State had one more shot at breaking the 26-26 deadlock.

All-America halfback Dick Christy had scored all four Wolfpack touchdowns and both extra points, so Coach Earle Edwards took the position that Christy could do no wrong on this particular night. Although Christy, a senior, had never attempted a field goal, Edwards decided to let him have a shot at one from 36 yards out. The kick split the uprights, and the Wolfpack had denied Carolina a winning season.

THE 1958 SEASON

In two games against Clemson a Giese-coached team had failed to put a point on the scoreboard, and such things as that don't set well with Gamecock fans. After I arrived in Columbia it took little time for me to grasp the importance of the Big Thursday game. It took Giese a little longer.

When he arrived at Carolina he shrugged off the Gamecock-Tiger meeting as "just another game," citing other ACC rivalries as just as important. After two losses to the Tigers, he had learned how seriously Carolina fans took this game. The loser of this battle has to live for a year within close contact with cousins, brothers, sisters, neighbors, friends and co-workers who pull for the other team, and they are constantly reminded of victories by the other team.

This year Clemson scored early in the game, and the Gamecock following braced themselves for more of the same. Finally, Giese's team crossed into the promised-land, and Tiger Coach Frank Howard, tipped his felt hat to Giese. Howard tipped it three more times before the game was over, pronounced his bald head sunburned and conceded a 26-6 loss to Carolina. It was Clemson's only loss of the season, adding satisfaction for Giese.

Earlier in the season Carolina had been a victim of Army's surprise "Lonesome End" offense at West Point and was blown out, 45-8. That was not indicative of the strength of this Carolina team, however, because it ended the season, winning seven of ten games, and earned a ranking of 15th in the Associated Press poll. It was the first time ever that Carolina had ended the season with a ranking.

It would have been higher, had not the Gamecocks lost a 10-6 verdict at Maryland in a game that they should have won. Late in the fourth quarter the Gamecock punter got a low snap from center, tried to run it out of the end zone and was downed on the one-yard line. If he had just stayed in the end zone and dropped to one knee for a safety, Carolina could have won the game by a 6-5 score. As it was, the Terps took it in to win the game.

Two 7-3 seasons in three years continued the positive attitude toward Giese, although Jake Penland, sports editor of THE STATE newspaper had become disenchanted with him the previous year and was going out of the way to point out any negative he could find. Penland pronounced the Carolina's pass-less offense too dull and made a big deal out of any opponent who used the aerial game to defeat the Gamecocks.

This feud would ultimately contribute to the demise of Giese as Gamecock coach.

THE 1959 SEASON

Of the 437 University of South Carolina football games I broadcast, one of the most impressive performances was turned in by the Gamecocks on October 3, 1959 in Columbia. Carolina had beaten Duke and Furman in their first two games, but Georgia, led by quarterback Francis Tarkenton, owned wins over Alabama and Vanderbilt.

The Gamecocks manhandled the Bulldogs, 30-14, and did it with only two forward pass attempts, completing those for a total of ten yards. Phil Lavoie scored three of the Carolina touchdowns in a grinding ground attack, while the Gamecock defense held Georgia to only 38 rushing yards. I remember that Ed Pitts, Carolina's all-ACC tackle, played one of the best defensive games I've ever seen in that game.

10

The magnitude of this accomplishment wasn't realized at the time, but it turned out to be the Bulldogs' only loss during the regular season, and they moved on to defeat Missouri in the Orange Bowl.

That was the season's peak, and the valley was reached on October 22, when the final Big Thursday game was played. Clemson had won the off-the-field battle to convert the game to a home-and-home basis and eventually move it to the end of the season, where it now stands.

Sadly for the Gamecocks, who mustered only 118 yards of offense and lost four fumbles, the Tigers closed out this storied event with a 27-0 victory.

THE 1960 SEASON

The 1960 Carolina highlights film was short. They had only three victories - over North Carolina, Wake Forest and Virginia.

In their first three games the Gamecocks were outscored, 90-12, and Penland's column in THE STATE placed great emphasis on the dominance by Gamecock opponents in the passing game. Many Gamecock fans were becoming convinced that USC football was a bit dull and were growing weary of the Penland-Giese feud.

It seemed that unusual things occurred when Carolina played at Maryland, and this season was no exception. When the two teams took the field for pre-game warm-ups, I looked down and couldn't tell which was which. Both had on red jerseys. This would be an impossible situation for me - everybody looked alike!

Then it was assumed that the home team would always wear white jerseys to avoid such situations, but Maryland hadn't bought that assumption and dressed in red, whether innocently or for psychological reasons. The result was that the Terps had to change to their white jerseys, and the game was played. Maryland won that battle, 15-0.

Carolina not only had the dubious distinction of losing the final Big Thursday game in 1959, but they were defeated, 12-2, amid all of the hoopla over the first Carolina-Clemson game to be played in Clemson's Memorial Stadium. That did nothing for Giese's job security.

Although the team finished strong, beating Wake Forest, 41-20, and Virginia, 26-0, it wasn't enough to convince the University Board of Trustees that the school's football future lay with Giese. So, with one fell swoop, the Board orchestrated Giese's retirement from his football coaching duties and the hiring of former assistant Marvin Bass to replace him. Bass had left the USC staff the previous year to become an assistant coach to Bobby Dodd at Georgia Tech.

In January of 1960 Rex Enright had died, following a long illness, Giese added the title of Director of Athletics, and he would continue in that capacity.

When Bass suddenly replaced Giese I was probably the last one to know it, and it was rather embarrassing. I was down at Houston, Texas, to broadcast the Bluebonnet Bowl, and Bo Hagan, head football coach at Rice Institute, invited me to lunch. Bo had been a quarterback under Rex Enright at Carolina in the late forties, and most coaches like the prospect of returning to their alma mater to coach.

At lunch Bo asked me if I thought Giese would be replaced, because rumors were flying. I went to great lengths to tell him that it might be possible but that I wasn't sure.

The night before the game I was at the Bluebonnet Bowl banquet, and Hagan came over to where I was sitting. He said, "Well, Bob, I can tell you who's going to be the head coach at Carolina.

I said, "Who?" and he answered, "They just announced that Marvin Bass will be the new head coach."

I felt rather foolish, because earlier that day I had told Bo that I just didn't have any idea. That perhaps they wouldn't make a change right now.

That was an early lesson for me to expect the unexpected at the University!

THE 1961 SEASON

The job at Carolina was not Marvin Bass' first experience as a head coach. He held that position at his alma mater, William and Mary, in 1951 and compiled a 7-3 record. He then went to assistant coach positions with the Washington Redskins, then North Carolina, then South Carolina, becoming an add-on member of Giese's staff.

While covering Arkansas football, I watched Marvin as he was playing for William and Mary against the Razorbacks. William and Mary had a very strong team, and it was Marvin who was the anchor of their offensive and defensive line. He was a tremendous football player.

Marvin was considered Giese's number one assistant and the person on the staff that the players could relate to and go to for counsel. He was responsible for the Gamecocks' defense, which was their strong point during the first four Giese years.

Probably because of Carolina's style of play under Giese and his problems with public relations, recruiting had suffered for several years. Hence, Bass' first Carolina team lacked in talent, and it showed.

Bass did win his first coaching encounter with Clemson's Frank Howard, beating the Tigers, 21-14, in Columbia. However, this was not a good Clemson team, and the game had lost some of the mystique that was present in the Big Thursday years. Still a win over Clemson is a win over Clemson and is not to be downplayed under any circumstances.

During Bass' first year Giese had continued in his role as athletics director, but the trustees felt that this responsibility would be better placed in the hands of Bass. So the school returned to its policy of having the head football coach serve in the dual capacity. Giese was transferred to the Physical Education Department, assuming a new role of college professor.

THE 1962 SEASON

One of the best things about Bass' first year at Carolina was the recruitment of Dan Reeves, who was entering the fourth decade of his distinguished career in the National Football League, where he played for the Dallas Cowboys and served as assistant coach to Dan Reeves at Denver.

Reeves played on the 1961 freshman team and became the Gamecock starter in the first game of his sophomore season. Dan was one of my favorite Carolina players of all time. He was highly intelligent, fiercely competitive, a serious student of football and a positive thinker.

Although there were talented players here and there on the Gamecock squads on which he played, Dan didn't have the supporting cast to make Carolina a consistent winner. He did have the satisfaction of breaking most of the career passing records for the Gamecocks.

There were no marquee victories for the Gamecocks this season, although they did manage a 7-7 tie with Vince Dooley's first team at Georgia, which eventually defeated Texas Tech in the Sun Bowl. Close losses were more prevalent, including heartbreakers to Maryland, North Carolina and Clemson by less than a touchdown.

12

I'll never forget the game we played against the University of Detroit up there in mid-November. It snowed all day, and when we got to the stadium we found out that there wasn't room for us in the press box, so we went to the top of the roof. They told us that there were a couple of tents up there, and we could work out of those!

We positioned the broadcast crew in one tent and our engineer, Homer Fesperman, in the other. We had to cut a hole in out tent so that we could see Homer to get our cues. Johnny Evans was working with me on the network then, and we looked at each other as if to say, "What in the world are we doing here?"

To add to the fun, the scoreboard clock wasn't working, so we didn't have a clue as to the time, and snow had obliterated the lines and yard markers, so it was a guessing game all the way. Why in the world they scheduled a game AT NIGHT that late in the season in Michigan, I'll never know. I've never worked a game under worse conditions.

I told the broadcast crew before we went on the air, "Anybody can work in good weather. This is a test to see what we can do in weather like this." Thankfully, it was the final exam, and I believe we passed.

Carolina won the game, 26-13, and Reeves played especially well. Dan was involved in all four Gamecock touchdowns, scoring two and passing for two. With the score tied, Dan called a change-up at the line of scrimmage, when Detroit's defense was slanting, found no one over center and went 44 yards up the middle for a touchdown.

The bottom line on the season was four wins, five losses and a tie.

THE 1963 SEASON
Probably the less said about the 1963 season, the better.

Dan Reeves spent the better part of the season nursing both eye and knee injuries and was not a great contributor to the Carolina offense.

Our only bright spot was a 21-13 victory over Maryland in the second game of the season. The Gamecocks did manage a tie with Virginia.

However, this team did make history in a tragic sort of way. The Gamecocks were scheduled to play Clemson on November 23 in Columbia, but on the preceding day President John F. Kennedy was assassinated in Dallas, Texas. The Saturday morning of the game, Jerry Johnston who handled the agency in New York which represented Texico – which was the sole sponsor of all Carolina games – called me from New York. He asked me what I thought we should do as to when the game would be played. I told him I would call the University and let them make the decision. They told me that it would be up to the agency in New York. I called Jerry Johnston back and told him it was his decision and he promptly informed me that it would be my decision. So, the only time I though it made sense to play it would be Thanksgiving Thursday on the following week. It was first time, the Clemson – Carolina game was played in the stadium which was not completely full because many fans were away celebrating the Thanksgiving holidays. The game was post-poned, as was practically every event of any kind scheduled for that weekend across the country.

Clemson won the game, 24-20, which was the Gamecocks' eighth straight game without a win.

THE 1964 SEASON
Two ties in their first three games tasted almost like victories, as the Gamecocks stretched their consecutive games without a win to eleven. The streak reached 15,

entering the eighth game of the season against The Citadel. The Bulldogs hadn't been on the Carolina schedule since 1954, and they couldn't have come back on at a better time.

Discouraged Gamecock fans were staying away from Carolina Stadium in droves, and a mere 19,000 turned out for the renewal of this intra-state rivalry. The Gamecocks ended their winless skein by edging the Bulldogs, 17-14, but any kind of win at this point brought welcomed relief to Bass and his squad.

Dan Reeves was still bothered by leg problems, but he was much more productive during the season than he had been the previous year. A week after The Citadel win, he led Carolina to another one. Dan's 69-yard touchdown pass play to Bobby Bryant, really a defensive back, seemed to give the Gamecocks a lift against the Deacons, and they won, 23-13, extending their winning streak to two.

Clemson was riding a two-game losing streak when Bass took his revived squad into Death Valley for the season finale. An early field goal by Clemson was looking like a game winner late in the fourth quarter, especially since Reeves had re-injured his leg and was out of the game.

With Jim Rogers at quarterback, the Gamecocks began a last-hope drive from deep in their own territory. They received great help from two 15 yard penalties against the Tigers, one for holding (that was the penalty then) and the other for a personal foul. A 45-yard pass from Rogers to J.R. Wilburn put the ball at the Clemson 15. Carolina could gain only two yards from there in two tries.

On third down Rogers dropped back to pass, couldn't find a receiver and scrambled his way into the end zone for a touchdown that gave Carolina a 7-3 win. It was another first for the Gamecocks - their first win at Clemson since the game began alternating in 1960.

Bass had only a 3-5-2 record to show for his fourth year at Carolina, but he felt that the "three" would give his team momentum going into the next season. Bass was a likable and popular man personally, but impatient fans were hungry for a winner, and most of them didn't share Bass' optimism.

THE 1965 AND 1966 SEASONS (AT GEORGIA TECH)

When Warren Giese was head coach I always did the Sunday television show with him, and this was important income for me. This show was produced by WIS-TV and was done "live," instead of being recorded, as they do now.

I continued to do the Sunday show with Marvin Bass through the 1964 season. Then WIS-TV said that they wanted to use the station's sports announcer on the show, which would leave me out in the cold.

Meanwhile, Georgia Tech contacted me about becoming the play-by-play announcer for the Yellow Jackets' radio network. It paid substantially more than I was getting, and Georgia Tech was a national power under Bobby Dodd. The offer was attractive, but I liked doing Carolina games and that's where my heart lay. I met with Bass and told him about the offer but that I would turn it down, if I could continue to do the Sunday TV show.

Marvin got back in touch and said that he tried, but he couldn't get WIS-TV to change their mind. So, off to Tech I went.

I had been recommended for the job by Johnny Evans, who had worked with me on the Gamecock network but had moved to Charlotte. Tech had contacted WBT for a recommendation, and Evans told them about me. WGST in Atlanta called me for an audition tape, I sent it, they liked it, and I got the job.

14

The two years I spent doing Tech football was a great experience and provided me a close-up look at one of football's coaching legends. In his college days Dodd had led the University of Tennessee football teams to 27 victories, only one loss and two ties during his varsity seasons, 1928 to 1930.

After serving 14 years as the top assistant to William Alexander at Tech, Dodd was chosen to succeed his boss in 1945. Talk about stability in an athletics department - Dodd was only the third head football coach in the school's history!

In 22 seasons Dodd's teams won 165 games, lost 64 and had eight ties, while winning nine of 13 bowl games the Yellow Jackets experienced under his guidance. It was purely a coincidence, but when I decided to return to doing Carolina football after the 1966 season, Dodd retired from coaching, and that was also his final season at Tech. He retained his position as athletics director.

As an individual Dodd was sort of a loner. He would sit by himself on the airplane when we were traveling, and you would never see him at the team's hotel headquarters. He was well liked by the sports media people, but he really only cared about the national media. Guess he figured the ATLANTA JOURNAL would look after his publicity in that area.

The first time I had any personal contact with Dodd was when I made my first road trip with the team. We played Vanderbilt at Nashville, and it was a disaster for Tech, because the game ended in a tie. That was the Georgia Tech equivalent to Carolina losing to The Citadel.

After we arrived at Nashville, on Friday, Dodd told me, "I want you to have breakfast with me tomorrow morning. We're going to have a special guest."

The guest turned out to be a delightful lady - Minnie Pearl - who was a star of the "Grand Ole Opry" there for many years. She even wore her famous bonnet with the price tag still hanging from it, and she played the role for us very well and to our delight.

Minnie had been a close friend of Dodd for many years, and both of them had strong Tennessee ties.

That was the only time I ever saw Coach Dodd outside of Atlanta.

Dodd had the reputation of making football fun, and that was no myth. His practice sessions were comparatively light. He never wanted to "leave the game on the practice field." Looking at his record, you can see that this philosophy was successful. His assistants handled the practice sessions, but once a game started, Dodd was definitely in charge.

From my standpoint, I knew that the coach was keeping up with what I was doing. He listened to the tape of every game, and only once did he acknowledge it. I got a nice letter from him about a broadcast, but he never questioned anything I said.

However, I did receive a most meaningful compliment from Dodd. After the 1966 season he offered me a ten-year contract to broadcast the Tech games and that is unusual in this volatile business.

While I was doing Tech football - and I still made my home in Columbia - I made and renewed some friendships. I got to know Jim Carlen and Richard Bell, both of whom were on the Tech staff and later came to Carolina, and former Gamecock assistant Jesse Berry was also an assistant there. The Tech freshman coach, Jack Flegg, later served on the Carolina staff.

Clemson was one rival that Tech had in common with Carolina, and the Dodd-Frank Howard match-up was a contrast in personalities and coaching styles.

In 1965 the Yellow Jackets were playing the Tigers in Atlanta. It was difficult to get Tech to play away from Grant Field, because Dodd loved that friendly atmosphere and the big crowds his teams drew.

The Jackets got off to a great start against Clemson and led, 21-0, at the end of the first quarter. Howard later said that he looked up at the scoreboard and thought, "My God, we're going to lose this game eighty-four to nothing!" The Tigers pulled themselves together and lost the game by only 38-6.

In 1966 Howard's Tigers were much more competitive, losing a 13-12 squeaker in Atlanta. The Tigers actually had the lead late in the game, but the Yellow Jackets put on a long drive to score the winning touchdown. However, Clemson came back with a long drive of its own, and was in Tech territory when Tech held and took over on downs.

Early the next week Howard reviewed the game film and saw something the game officials failed to detect. During most of the Tigers' last ditch drive, the Jackets had 12 players on the field. Howard blew his top, but it was too late to do anything about it.

Tech always played its games in the afternoon. I don't believe they even had lights at Grant Field then. This allowed me to come back to Columbia in time to watch Carolina play, when it was a night game.

The Gamecocks had their best season under Bass in 1965, breaking even at 5-5 and tying with Duke for the Atlantic Coast Conference championship. A thrilling 17-16 victory over Clemson enabled the Gamecocks to accomplish that, and it gave Marvin Bass a 3-2 edge in his coaching rivalry with Frank Howard. Tech was not playing that day, so I was able to be present for the Carolina-Clemson game. My heart was still with Carolina, but, I must say, that after watching Southeastern Conference football, games involving ACC teams appeared to be in slow motion.

While I was doing games for Georgia Tech, Bob Shelley, sports director at WMRB in Greenville handled the play-by-play for Carolina, and I understand that he did a very good job.

If I had to miss a Carolina football season, 1966 was a good one to miss. Paul Dietzel had become head coach of the Gamecocks when Marvin Bass resigned to accept the head coaching job with Montreal of the new Continental Football League. The Gamecocks were halfway through spring practice when Bass resigned, and Ralph Floyd was "acting head coach" until Dietzel came aboard.

Dietzel had only one victory to show for the 1966 season, a 31-21 verdict over North Carolina State at Raleigh, and his debut against Clemson was a 35-10 loss in what was now known as "Death Valley."

THE 1967 SEASON

Prior to the 1967 football season I had to make another career decision. As I mentioned earlier, Dodd had offered me a ten-year deal at Tech, and that network paid well, and I also was offered the job of doing the Georgia network, which was sponsored by Texaco. Earlier I had worked for Texaco when that company sponsored the Gamecock Network.

A third factor was involved when Paul Dietzel contacted me about coming back to do Carolina games. Paul will go down as one of the all-time positive thinkers, and he is a very persuasive individual. He was handsome - had that Pepsodent smile - and carried that mystique of having won a national championship at LSU (1960). He could have sold sand to Saudi Arabia.

Dietzel had come to Carolina from Army, where he had previously served as an assistant to Earl Blaik, on whose staff he was serving when Carolina pulled its stunning upset over the Cadets in 1954. Dietzel was an idea man, as demonstrated by his creation of the "Chinese Bandits" at LSU in the early sixties. He took a group of borderline players, made them defensive specialists, nicknamed them and made them national celebrities.

When an opposing team was threatening on offense, Dietzel would send his "Bandits" to the rescue, as the band played their special oriental sounding "theme song." Dietzel had also created a new fight song for LSU, putting words to the popular song, "Hey, Look Me Over."

I met with Dietzel, and he told me that he wanted me back at Carolina and that, if I would return, he would give me (back) the Sunday TV show, plus a few other perks that made the situation attractive to me. I still would have been making more money at Tech, but the intangibles weighed heavily toward Carolina. Dietzel and I shook hands, and it was a done deal.

It was great to be back home and in Carolina Stadium, as the Gamecocks opened their second season under Dietzel. Fans were getting the fever again, as Carolina defeated Iowa State, North Carolina and Duke to go 3-0, their best start since 1959. Incidentally, Dietzel "owned" the North Carolina Tar Heels, winning all five games he coached against them. Maybe Duke should have hired him!

After that start there were no big wins, but the season was a great improvement over 1966, with five wins and five losses. One of those losses was to Clemson, 23-12, Dietzel's second straight to the Tigers.

When Dietzel faced Alabama in Tuscaloosa he was working at a slight handicap. The previous week he had twisted his knee in practice, had to undergo surgery and operated from a wheel chair during the game. The Tide won it, 17-0.

One of the Carolina assistants in 1967 was Lou Holtz, at that time one of the nation's high profile coaches and head man at Notre Dame. Holtz had been hired by Bass in February of 1966, having previously served as an assistant at the University of Connecticut.

Holtz loves to tell the story of his first interview with his new boss when Dietzel arrived shortly after Lou came to Carolina. Lou said that Dietzel was evaluating the holdover members of the staff and when he reached the end of his review, he offered some advice. Lou recalls that Dietzel said that he was going to give him some helpful advice, and that was to get out of coaching, because he wasn't suited for it.

However, Holtz did not heed that suggestion and served two years at Carolina before moving on to head coaching jobs at William and Mary, North Carolina State, Arkansas, Minnesota and Notre Dame, with a one-year stand as coach of the New York Jets.

Constantly aware of image, Dietzel had been bothered by the appearance and use of the Gamecock logo used in various graphics. He said the graphic Gamecock was not what he would like and that the use of it was not being controlled properly.

So he had a new Gamecock designed, registered and restricted its use to those approved by the University athletics department. It was still in use in 1996.

THE 1968 SEASON

As has been so often the case, there was one spectacular happening during the Gamecock season in 1968. It took place at Chapel Hill on September 28, following Carolina's season-opening loss to Duke.

The first three quarters were disastrous for the Gamecocks, who seemed to be unable to do anything right. They couldn't even score after Don Bailey returned a kickoff 90 yards to the North Carolina ten. It was one of those days that had Carolina fans heading for the parking lot early.

Thanks to heroics by South Carolina quarterback Tommy Suggs, a sophomore, and fullback Warren Muir, plus some miscues by the Tar Heels, the Gamecocks fought back to pull within ten points at 27-15. Muir scored from close-in and Suggs passed to Rudy Holloman for a two-point conversion that made it 27-25.

With just a couple of minutes remaining, Suggs climaxed a 61-yard drive by running it in for the winning touchdown from four yards out, and the Gamecocks claimed a 32-27 "miracle" victory. Many of the Carolina fans had come to the game on buses, and when the game was so one-sided going into the fourth quarter, they decided to head for home.

They were listening to the game on the radio, and when Carolina started its comeback they turned around and headed back for the stadium, and some of them made it back in time to see the great finish.

Dietzel's wife, Anne, had become ill and had to leave the stands for a while, but she felt much better when she returned and saw that her husband's team was right back in the game.

The Gamecocks blew chances for a winning season by allowing Georgia to come back from a two-touchdown deficit to beat the Gamecocks, 21-20, and Carolina lost a muddy 21-19 decision at Maryland, when a deflected Suggs pass wound up in the hands of a Terp defender, who returned it for the winning score.

The ending of this 4-6 season was positive. The Gamecocks won their first-ever game in Clemson's Death Valley when Tyler Hellams returned a punt 73 yards for the game's only touchdown – Gamecock, 7-4.

Dietzel was always doing his job as athletic director, and the project of the year 1968 was the completion of a new complex of dormitories to house athletes, and it was immediately nicknamed, "The Roost." Paul figured that this would give him an advantage in recruiting, keep the players together under one roof where they could be better supervised and improve morale and spirit with first class living conditions. This was a far cry from the antiquated Preston Dormitory, where the football players dwelled when I first came to Carolina.

Even when things weren't going well on the football field, Dietzel could always come up with something else to intrigue the fans. On November 16 of this year, on a rainy night in which Virginia Tech was beating Carolina, 17-6, in Carolina Stadium, Dietzel had a surprise for the faithful.

He had the band introduce a new fight song, "The Fighting Gamecocks Lead the Way." The Gamecocks weren't leading anywhere that year, but this was another Dietzel innovation. He had prompted band director Jim Pritchard to obtain rights to the tune, "Step to the Rear," from the Broadway musical, "How Now Dow Jones." The tune was written by Elmer Bernstein, but Dietzel added his original words, and a song was born.

It was a catchy addition to the Gamecock scene and helped to soothe the pain of a losing season.

THE 1969 SEASON

When Dietzel took over the coaching reins at Carolina in 1966 he listed his goals, including the Atlantic Coast Conference championship and a post-season bowl game. The time was right in 1969, because the number of bowls was on the increase, and ACC football was on the decrease. In 1968 only one ACC team, North Carolina State, had compiled a winning record, and that was 6-4.

The Gamecocks took full advantage of the circumstances, winning seven of ten games, with all three losses being non-conference, to Georgia, Tennessee and Florida State. The latter did nothing for Carolina's national prestige, but they were king bee in the ACC.

The most dramatic win took place at Blacksburg, Virginia, on October 18, when the Gamecocks faced Virginia Tech. The Gobblers threatened to dash Carolina's bowl ambitions by scoring a go-ahead touchdown with only a minute remaining in the game. They missed the extra point and held a 16-14 lead. Suggs did a masterful job of utilizing sideline passes to conserve precious seconds. With Carolina in possession of the ball at the Virginia Tech 30, only 17 seconds were showing on the scoreboard clock.

Billy DuPre, the smallest player on the Gamecock squad, became the biggest by kicking a 47-yard field goal, tying a school record and giving Carolina a 17-16 victory. The kick looked like a dying sea gull, and I didn't think it would make it, but it barely cleared the upright, and the Virginia Tech players just collapsed on the field.

The Carolina coaches' booth was located next to ours, and we noticed a commotion there that appeared to be more crisis than celebration. Assistant coach Scooter Purvis was experiencing what appeared to be a heart attack. He was flown back to Columbia in a private plane, but it was determined that he had merely hyperventilated and was perfectly fine.

Although it was a loss, probably the best game played by the Gamecocks that season was against Tennessee at Knoxville. This was a Volunteer team that lost only one game during the regular season.

The Vols scored twice in the final three minutes to turn a one-point ball game into a 29-14 victory.

Carolina had devised a spread offense that was highly successful in moving the ball against Tennessee. Later I was in Dietzel's office when he received a telephone call from Alabama Coach Bear Bryant. Paul had been one of Bryant's assistants at Kentucky in 1951 and 1952.

He had heard about the spread offense that Dietzel had developed and wanted every detail of it, and I sat there for a long time while Paul dictated it to Bryant's secretary. Bryant planned to use it against Tennessee in their game early in the 1970 season.

I couldn't help but recall that conversation when I saw the outcome of the game. The Volunteers clobbered the Crimson Tide, 24-0!

The week after the game at Knoxville, Carolina went to Winston-Salem to play Wake Forest in a game that could clinch the ACC championship for the Gamecocks. Carolina won the game, but the memorable thing for me was that I had my worst ever case of flu. On top of that, it was snowing in Winston-Salem, and I didn't know whether I could talk, much less broadcast a football game for nearly three hours.

I went on the air, and I was absolutely terrible. People who listened to the broadcast, couldn't tell who it was, and some called stations carrying the game to ask where I was. They would say, "That couldn't be Bob Fulton. It doesn't sound anything like him." I stuck it out, however, and finished the game.

The Gamecocks' season-ending victory over Clemson, 27-13, in Columbia was not necessary for them to win the ACC, but it was essential to calling this a championship team and earning a bid to the Peach Bowl.

A new post-season event - the Peach Bowl - had been created in Atlanta, and Carolina was invited to play West Virginia in the inaugural event. The Mountaineers were coached by Jim Carlen, who would become the Gamecocks' head man a few years later.

It was a rainy, muddy night in Atlanta, Carolina's passing game was practically nullified, and West Virginia's ground-oriented offense plodded to a 14-3 victory.

Overall it was a highly satisfying season for Dietzel. He had achieved two goals, the ACC championship and a bowl, and his program was apparently on the rise.

Ironically, after winning Carolina's first outright ACC championship, going undefeated in conference games, Dietzel continued to push the school's withdrawal from the league, because of his dissatisfaction with higher admission standards than required by the NCAA. This placed ACC teams at a disadvantage in competing on a national basis.

In the spring of 1970 Carolina carried out its threat and officially withdrew.

The Gamecocks couldn't have left on a higher note, because after the football team won all of its conference games the Gamecock basketball team went through its 14 regular-season ACC games without losing. The school was now an "independent" and ready to benefit from whatever advantages that provided.

THE 1970 SEASON

Expectations were at an all-time high for Carolina, because of their fine 1969 team and of the fact that 34 lettermen from that team returned, including at least one in all of the 22 starting positions. National magazines gave the Gamecocks high rankings.

The NCAA had approved an increase in the number of games that a school could schedule during the regular season, and Carolina had added Georgia Tech for the season-opener in Atlanta. The Yellow Jackets were coached by Bud Carson, who once served as an assistant at Carolina. This was my first visit to Grant Field since my final broadcast there in 1965.

A large contingent of Gamecock fans was among the sellout crowd at Grant Field, and they came back with a letdown feeling. Tech won the game, 23-20, but Carolina did show potential, with Tommy Suggs in his senior year at quarterback. The Gamecocks also had one of the finest kickoff return men I've ever seen - Dickie Harris. Harris had blazing speed and demonstrated it by winning the ACC 440-yard dash in the ACC championship track meet.

The Gamecocks were 3-1-1 after their first five games, but that preceded a streak of five losses to Maryland, Florida State, Georgia, Tennessee and Duke. Carolina put points on the scoreboard in record numbers, but they couldn't stop anyone. For example, they scored 34 against Georgia but lost the game, 52-34, and later they were outscored by Duke, 42-38.

If the Gamecocks had played all season like they did against Tennessee in Columbia on November 7, they would have been nationally ranked. The Volunteers lost but one game that year, to Auburn, but had the scare of their lives in Carolina Stadium.

Carolina held an 18-17 lead and apparently had the game in the bag when they intercepted a Tennessee pass at the Carolina one-yard line. The Gamecocks needed a first down to run out the clock but didn't make it and had to punt. That was the chance Tennessee needed and set-up a winning 31-yard field goal by surprising a pass-wary Gamecock defense with a 22-yard gain on a draw play. The winning points came on a field goal with only 15 seconds remaining on the clock and the big crowd was in a state of shock.

That gave the Gamecocks a record of four wins, six losses and a tie.

There is nothing that will ease the pain of a losing season like ending it with a victory over Clemson. The Gamecocks did just that, 38-32, in Clemson Memorial Stadium, and it gave Suggs the satisfaction of quarterbacking his third straight win over the Tigers. Four, if you include Sugg's freshman year, in which the Biddies beat the Cubs.

THE 1971 SEASON
Doak Campbell Stadium, home of the Florida State Seminoles, was not one of the classier places to broadcast a football game back in the early seventies. The Seminoles were a budding football power, even before Bobby Bowden arrived on the scene.

Yet their stadium was still in the dark ages, giving all the appearances of an overgrown high school arena, with poor facilities. However, the Seminoles took advantage of it for a great home field advantage. Of course, this stadium has grown with the Seminole program and has been expanded and improved to a first class facility.

We played down there in the seventh game of the 1971 season before a packed house of 30,000. On Florida State's first play from scrimmage they lined up with two quarterbacks in the backfield. I yelled out, "They're gonna throw the ball."

The quarterback under center pitched out to the other, and he fired the ball downfield as far as he could throw it. He didn't complete it, but pass interference was called on the Gamecocks; the Seminoles were recipients of a 45-yard penalty (to the spot of the foul) and took it in for an early touchdown.

That was the beginning of a 49-18 rout that ended a four-game Carolina winning streak and threw a damper on rising bowl hopes.

The season produced two high points. The first came in the season's opener, when the Gamecocks lured Georgia Tech to Columbia for the first time in history. That resulted in a 24-7 win for Carolina before a record 54,842 spectators in enlarged Carolina Stadium.

A new upper deck had been added on the west side of the stadium, along with a new press box, plus Dietzel's pride and joy, Astroturf on the playing field.

The Gamecocks ended a 6-5 season and a three-game winning streak against Clemson by losing, 17-7, in Columbia.

In this game Dietzel made a bold move by moving defensive back Dickie Harris, who led the world in kickoff return yardage, into the offensive backfield. He worried that at 164 pounds his ace kick returner couldn't endure the punishment received by full-time ball carriers. Dietzel had a point, because in the first quarter, after a 20-yard run, Harris sprained an ankle and was ineffective the rest of the game.

THE 1972 SEASON
The Rev. Ed Young, now pastor of Houston's Second Baptist Church, which has the largest membership in America, I believe, was pastor at First Baptist Church in Columbia in the early 1970s. Historians remember this church as the site at which South Carolina legislators met to make their official decision for the state to secede from the Union in December 1860.

Dietzel was a faithful member of First Baptist, and Young became the football team's unofficial chaplain. The Gamecock coach reciprocated by delivering a sermon from that church's pulpit one Sunday. Dietzel would have made a great preacher himself, made no qualms about his faith in Jesus Christ and promoted the Fellowship of Christian Athletes.

Young followed the Gamecocks with a passion, including many of the road trips, when they did not interfere with his church commitments. Young, like Dietzel, was a positive thinker.

The preacher was present during the latter part of the season when the Gamecocks played North Carolina State at Raleigh. This was Lou Holtz's first year as head coach, and he had already established his interview style by stating, "I think we'll be able to move the football - forward, I hope!"

Holtz had immediately revived the State football team, which was definitely moving the football forward and scoring mega points. They were winning big and were definite favorites over visiting Carolina.

On the morning of the game I saw Ed Young at the hotel, and he was his usual upbeat self. He said, "Bob, we're going to win today. I've looked in those players' eyes, and they are ready!"

I said, "Preacher, I've looked into the State football brochure, and we're gonna lose!"

The brochure won out over the eyes, because the Wolfpack pounded the Gamecocks, 42-24. Later in the season when it appeared that State would play Florida State in the Peach Bowl, Holtz came to Columbia to scout the Seminoles against South Carolina. He said he had heard rumors that Dietzel might be giving up the coaching duties at Carolina in the near future and that he would very much like to have the job, if it came open. "If you can help me, I would appreciate it" he said.

Now that Carolina was an "independent," there were new teams appearing on the schedule, replacing some of the ACC schools. Mississippi, Miami of Ohio (Dietzel's alma mater), Memphis State and Appalachian State were among the newcomers. Carolina hadn't played Mississippi since 1947, and the Rebels came into Columbia following a 1971 season that produced ten victories, including a 41-18 win over Georgia Tech in the Peach Bowl.

It was not a pretty game for Carolina. The Gamecocks made only one first down in what had to be their worst offensive performance I witnessed in my 41 years of broadcasting their games. Carolina's total offense was 51 yards.

Dietzel revised his offense, and the Gamecocks were more productive in statistics, if not victories, during the rest of the season.

Their peak came on November 18, when Florida State brought its 7-3 record and Peach Bowl hopes into what had been re-named Williams-Brice Stadium. The Brice family of Sumter had donated several million dollars toward the stadium expansion.

The Gamecocks and Seminoles were tied at 21 points each, but Carolina had reached the Florida State 21-yard line with 1:28 remaining in the game. Dietzel decided to replace his regular field goal kicker, who had missed two earlier tries, with freshman Bobby Marino. The freshman responded with a kick that split the uprights, and Carolina had pulled a 24-21 upset, denying the Seminoles a bowl bid.

In the final game of that year at Clemson, snow was falling when the teams took the field, and it was just a generally nasty day. So it was for the Gamecocks through three-plus quarters, and Clemson held a 7-0 lead. In the last five minutes Jay Lynn Hodgin scored for Carolina, after a 67-yard screen pass from Bill Troup to Eddie Muldrow had put the ball at the Tiger three.

Dietzel decided to go for a two-point conversion, it failed, and the Gamecocks had spent another frustrating afternoon in Death Valley, losing by a 7-6 score.

One bright spot in the season was the emergence of freshman Jeff Grantz in the latter part of the season as Carolina's quarterback of the future.

THE 1973 SEASON

Any doubt that the Gamecocks had something special in quarterback Jeff Grantz was removed during the 1973 season. Jeff was the most productive quarterback the Gamecocks ever had as a combination runner and passer.

He had been recruited by South Carolina over North Carolina, because Dietzel told him he could also play shortstop in baseball.

Grantz engineered a 7-4 season, and it could have been a great one, if Miami hadn't upset the Gamecocks, 13-11, and the Gamecocks could have held off a last-minute LSU touchdown that resulted in a 33-29 Carolina loss.

Grantz injured an ankle in the LSU game and was on the bench when Holtz's North Carolina State Wolfpack massacred the Gamecocks, 56-35, in one of the all-time great shootouts in Williams-Brice Stadium. The Gamecocks did discover another quarterback, freshman Ron Bass, in the game.

It was Bass who helped the Gamecocks run up 52 points against Florida State at Tallahassee and that was the most ever scored against a Seminole team at that time.

The season ended on a high note, as Carolina defeated Clemson, 32-20. Dietzel had felt assured, that if his team beat Clemson and Georgia Tech beat Georgia, the Gamecocks would be invited to play in the Peach Bowl. However, Georgia beat Tech and played Maryland in the bowl game, leaving a disappointed Dietzel to ponder what might have been.

This was also the year that Tommy Suggs joined me as the analyst on the radio network. I was fortunate to have him as the color/analyst for twenty-one years.

I first heard of Tommy when he was leading his Lamar High School team to a state championship. When he decided to come to Carolina it was a great day for the Gamecocks. Suggs was an outstanding quarterback – a fine team leader – and throughout his college career, set many performance records, some of which still stand. Tommy led the Gamecocks to the 1969 Peach Bowl and was named Most Valuable Player in the 1970 Blue/Gray All Star Classic.

Following his playing career, he was named to the S.C. Athletic Hall of Fame and the USC Hall of Fame. While he played at Carolina, he made my job easier. It was exciting to see him pull one game after another out of the fire. So in the early 70's when I was looking for someone to work with me, the choice was easy.

During our twenty-one years together he brought knowledge, excitement and humor to the broadcast booth. No matter whom I would meet they would always discuss the broadcasts in terms of "Bob and Tommy".

Tommy joined me and began to adapt to his role on the broadcast team. He learned one lesson very early. We played our opener at Houston, Texas, and Tommy was in the middle of his pre-game comments, when it came time for the playing of the national anthem. I gave Tommy a hand signal to stop talking.

He read that part correctly, but he said, "We're going to pause now for a commercial, while they play the national anthem!" During the commercial I reminded Tommy that he was right - we do pause - but it is out of respect for the national anthem. Not for a commercial.

Tommy did add a lot to our broadcasts, because he knew the game, had played quarterback and could explain to the listeners such things as change-ups at the line of scrimmage, rationale behind calling plays and generally supplement my description of what was taking place. I thought we could develop into a good team.

When Todd Ellis came on board several years later, we had the expertise of two outstanding Gamecock signal callers, both of whom remain part of the Gamecock Network. Todd is a very successful lawyer, but if he chose to devote himself full/time to broadcasting, I am sure he could do quite well.

THE 1974 SEASON

The Carolina fans and coaching staff were somewhat optimistic, as the 1974 season approached, although there had been some grumbling about the progress of Dietzel's program for a couple of years. People were beginning to say that he was a great athletics director, but, perhaps, it was too much for him to handle two jobs.

When Dietzel came to Carolina in 1966, Frank McGuire was beginning to convert it to a "basketball school." Dietzel's program was not passing the test of comparison with the national prominence the school was enjoying on the basketball court.

When the Gamecocks opened the season by losing, 35-20, to just an average Georgia Tech team, Dietzel detractors became more vocal. But as Dietzel so often said, "One game does not a season make."

The Gamecocks still had their home opener coming up with Duke on September 21. And guess who the Duke head coach was. Mike McGee, the former Blue Devil All-America lineman, was in his fifth year at the helm.

Duke defeated the Gamecocks, 20-14, and most of the 46,000 fans in attendance departed the stadium in a not-so-happy frame of mind.

Before we went on the air that day University trustee Mike Mungo came by the booth and said to me, "There's something you ought to know."

He told me that Dietzel planned to resign after the game and that he might even do it on the post-game show with me. I spent the entire game thinking about what I would say, and I thought that someone else would take over the team for the remainder of the season.

That wasn't the case. Dietzel did announce his decision to resign on our show, and you could hear horns honking all over the parking lots and nearby streets leading away from the stadium. Dietzel explained that his resignation would take place as of the end of the season and that he would continue in his position of director of athletics. As usual, Paul handled it with class and finesse, as if this was what he had been looking forward to all his life.

So he stayed on as coach for the rest of the year, and that made it somewhat difficult for the assistants, particularly in the area of recruiting. It was hard to get a good high school player interested in coming to a school that didn't even know who its head coach would be.

Philosophically or realistically, Dietzel often made the remark that "football isn't the most important thing in my life." He would then position football in relationship to family and his religious faith.

Paul was reminded of the importance of a football game on November 14, 1970, when Carolina had lost a heartbreaking 42-38 decision to Duke in Columbia. It was a game that was important to Dietzel's season, and he was devastated by the close defeat.

He called me to tell me that he just couldn't do the show and to go on without him.

During the game I had heard the news that the entire Marshall University football team, its coaches and some fans had been killed in an airplane crash that day.

I said, "Paul, I want to tell you something. We only lost a football game, but the entire Marshall football team and staff lost their lives today, when their plane crashed going into the Huntington airport."

Paul thought for a moment and whispered, "I'm sure sorry to hear that."

A few moments later he was doing the post-game show with me in his usual professional style.

After our five opening losses we played Mississippi at Oxford, and the team was feeling awfully low. I'll have to give Ed Young, the Baptist minister, a lot of credit on this one. He spoke to the team before the game, and it was like he was inviting them to come down to the altar and be saved. It paid off.

The Gamecocks went out and beat Ole Miss on a late field goal, 10-7, and it was like manna from Heaven. After the field goal, I turned to Tommy during a break and said, "Tommy, let's try to get some people out to the airport to meet the team when they get back to Columbia."

Tommy said, "I'll try, but we won't get anybody out there." We must have been convincing, because when the plane landed at the Columbia airport there was a pretty good number of people to greet them.

Dietzel ended his final season at Carolina by winning four of the last six games. It would have been a great ending, if he could have beaten Clemson at Clemson, but that was not in the cards. The Tigers had one of their better performances under Red Parker, winning by a score of 39-21.

That ended a nine-year tenure for Paul Dietzel, and the bottom line was that he left the football program at Carolina in much better shape than it was when he arrived. The Gamecocks had improved practice facilities, built great living quarters for athletes and an enlarged stadium. Fan support had increased a great deal, and the Gamecock Club was growing rapidly. Dietzel had raised the sights of the program and had the University "thinking big" in terms of its potential.

Personally, I found him a pleasure to work with. He was responsible for my return to do Carolina football, and I will always remember him for that. Since his departure I have continued to have contacts with him from time to time and consider him to be a good friend.

THE 1975 SEASON

The usual raft of rumors floated around Columbia concerning who would be chosen as the successor to Dietzel as Carolina's head football coach. The "reliable sources" contended that Bud Wilkinson, the retired Oklahoma coach, was going to un-retire and take the job, while others were certain that it would be Lou Holtz. Also mentioned were Ara Parseghian (Notre Dame) and several others who had allegedly already made down payments on homes in Spring Valley. Or was it Wildewood?

One person who was interested in the job and made no bones about it was Mooney Player of Columbia. Mooney was a highly successful high school coach at Lower Richland and had an unorthodox, but colorful, approach to football. I knew Mooney well, and you couldn't help but like him. He knew how to relate to people, especially football players.

A search committee was appointed for the responsibility of selecting a coach, and their path led to Lubbock, Texas, where Jim Carlen was having good success with his Texas Tech Red Raiders. He got the Carolina job, and the other coaches disappeared from Spring Valley. Or was it Wildewood?

I had known Carlen when I was broadcasting Georgia Tech football, and he was an assistant coach there. I renewed acquaintances when Carolina played his West Virginia team in the first Peach Bowl. Incidentally, remember who succeeded Carlen at West Virginia? It was Bobby Bowden, who had now moved on to Florida State.

In an unusual move Carolina's trustees had sent the secretary of the board, Dr. George Curry, a delightful Englishman, for their first contact with Carlen at Lubbock. Then Jim came to Columbia, gave an impressive interview and was given the job.

Carlen hit the ground running in Columbia, and there was no doubt that he was here. He was definitely a hands-on coach in everything. He brought six or seven members of his Texas Tech staff with him and kept several of the members of the final Dietzel staff.

Carlen was what you call "up front." Some people called it "abrupt." Whatever you called it, you had no difficulty knowing where Carlen stood.

Jim began making believers out of a lot of people by winning five of his first six games, losing only to Georgia by a 28-20 score at Athens. It didn't hurt that his quarterback, Jeff Grantz, was having a Heisman Trophy-like year.

When Carlen held his first spring practice Grantz was playing baseball and was only a figure on film, as far as the football coaches were concerned. Therefore Ron Bass was the quarterback by forfeit at the end of spring practice. Before fall practice began, a sports reporter asked Carlen about Grantz's potential as a star of national significance.

Carlen's reply was, "All I know about Jeff Grantz is that he's a good baseball player."

Carlen did inherit some good players and potential stars from the Dietzel recruiting efforts, but none of them were prominent enough to make the cover of the media guide. I don't know what the significance was, but the cover featured a full color photograph of a kneeling Jim Carlen, surrounded by seven female cheerleaders. Perhaps it meant that we would have something to cheer about.

Well, we did! Grantz had a record breaking season, finishing high in the Heisman voting, and Carolina had its first two thousand-yard rushers in the same backfield. They were Kevin Long and Clarence Williams.

Carolina had gained the attention of bowl scouts in an upset of 18th ranked Baylor and kept their attention when Grantz hit Phil Logan with a game-winning touchdown pass with 22 seconds left in the game with Mississippi at Oxford.

Consecutive losses to LSU and North Carolina State didn't do a lot of damage to Carolina's bowl hopes, but an upset to Appalachian State the following week in Columbia did. The Mountaineers outscored the Gamecocks, 39-34, and I remember Carlen saying, "We didn't play very well defensively," which was a candidate for "understatement of the year."

The bowl picture brightened when the Gamecocks outscored Wake Forest, 37-26, and a victory over Clemson would make post-season a probability.

Carolina and Jeff Grantz were at their best for the Tigers in Columbia, winning 56-20, and scoring the most points ever by either team in this series. The Gamecocks scored every time they had the ball, but it was the last one that enraged Clemson Coach Red Parker.

In the fourth quarter Carolina held a 49-20 lead and had the ball in a fourth-and-goal situation at the Tiger 20. Grantz then hit split end Stevie Stephens in the corner of the end zone for a touchdown.

Parker insisted that Carlen was running up the score, while the Gamecock coach reasoned that it would have been more of an insult to try a field goal. The Tigers vowed revenge.

Several months later I was traveling to a Carolina baseball game in the car with Grantz, and he was recalling that situation. I asked Jeff how he felt when he threw that touchdown pass to make the score that big.

He smiled and said, "I'm just glad I'm not coming back next year!"

Carolina received a bid to play Miami of Ohio in the Tangerine Bowl at Orlando, Florida, a bowl that is now called the Citrus Bowl and is played in a newer and larger stadium than the one that existed then.

Miami's defense was too strong for Carolina, and the Gamecocks were on the short end of a 20-7 score. The Gamecocks had now failed to win a bowl game in three tries, and almost 20 years later I was beginning to think that I would never broadcast a bowl win for them.

Even at that, Carlen was riding high in the eyes and hearts of Carolina fans, and I was beginning to believe that he could have a long future in Columbia. But I've been wrong before!

THE 1976 SEASON

When Carolina played Notre Dame for the first time ever on October 23 in Williams-Brice Stadium, I could look to the right of my broadcast booth and see the President of the United States. Gerald Ford was on the campaign trail in his re-election bid against Jimmy Carter, and his stop in Columbia took place on the same weekend as the game.

At the time James Edwards was South Carolina's governor and the first Republican to hold that office since reconstruction days that followed the War Between the States. Ford was guest in his box, which was to the right of me in the press box.

The Gamecocks put on a good show for the President, rallying from ten points by the Irish in the first quarter to trail by only a 13-6 margin late in the fourth quarter. The Gamecocks were moving deep into Notre Dame territory when the longtime timekeeper for Carolina games, Bully Farr, was caught in a pile-up on the sideline and was shaken up. This caused about a 15 minute delay in the game, and I'm afraid that it gave the Carolina players too much time to think about what they were in a position to accomplish. They had an excellent chance to tie or defeat one of the great programs in the history of college football.

When play was resumed Carolina continued their march toward the Irish goal line, but a pass interception at the 15-yard line dashed the Gamecock hopes.

Carolina had a 5-2 record entering that game, and had they been successful against Notre Dame that would have placed them in the national rankings, because they beat North Carolina State, 27-7, at Raleigh and would have had great momentum to take them into their final two games.

Even though they were upset by Wake Forest, 10-7, thanks to five fumbles and a blocked punt, they could still get back into the bowl picture by beating Clemson. That didn't happen.

Clemson was still burning over the 56-20 loss in Columbia the previous season and particularly over the Gamecocks' last touchdown. A record crowd for Clemson Memorial Stadium, 54,000, saw an inspired team frustrate the favored Gamecocks, 28-9, and that ended any possibility of a bowl. Still the Gamecocks finished with six wins against five losses, the second straight winning season for Carlen.

Although I wasn't doing the Sunday TV show with Carlen, I still interviewed him on the radio network following the games. I found out early on that you didn't put words in his mouth. In fact, if you came out with an observation about the game, chances are that he would contradict you, which made me feel real good. By now I had learned to simply pose a question to Carlen and let him have his say, and he did. Particularly after a loss, he would guess what was going through the minds of the fans and try to answer questions that weren't even asked.

It wasn't that I didn't get along with Jim, because I did and thought that he was an excellent coach. It's just that you have to figure out the style of whatever coach you're talking to and fit into that. That's something I gained a lot of experience in doing at Carolina!

THE 1977 SEASON

In the 1970s the media and public weren't caught up in the recruiting hysteria that exists today. Blue chip recruits are treated like national celebrities, with daily reports on what they are thinking, which way they are leaning and whether or not they have made a high enough grade on the Standard Aptitude Test.

In the spring of 1977, when George Rogers committed himself to attending the University of South Carolina, there was no press conference held for the announcement, and I don't recall that there was even a story in the newspapers about it. A lot of schools were contending for this running back from Duluth, Georgia.

George simply told Jim Carlen that he'd come here, they shook hands, signed a simple piece of paper, and that was it. Rogers came to Carolina because he liked the way Carlen talked to him. No big promises, no incentives and no pie in the sky. Rogers didn't then and doesn't now think in terms of "what's in it for me?" He has always been unaffected by any honors or material gains that came his way.

Otherwise 1977 wasn't that good to Carolina, because it experienced Carlen's first losing season, 5-7. The season did produce one of the most exciting Carolina-Clemson games in history, even if it did end in a Gamecock defeat.

It was the first Gamecock-Tiger game to be televised, as ABC-TV added the game to its schedule with a 4 p.m. starting time, which meant that it would also be the first game in the series played under lights. It was a good one.

Carolina overcame a Clemson lead when Ron Bass threw a 40-yard touchdown pass, giving the Gamecocks a 27-24 advantage with only 1:48 remaining in the game. Carolina players celebrated on the sidelines, pulling up their jerseys to expose t-shirts with the imprint, "No cigar!" That was in response to the practice by new Tiger head coach Charley Pell of handing out cigars after a Clemson victory. Incidentally, Clemson had already been invited to play in the Gator Bowl against Pittsburgh, but a loss to Carolina would surely put a damper on that.

The Tigers responded like champions, as their quarterback, Steve Fuller, used the clock well and engineered them down to the Gamecock 20 with 48 seconds still showing on the clock. From there he lofted a pass to a leaping Jerry Butler in the end zone, and Clemson had saved the game, 31-27.

Although Carolina's record was now 5-6, the Gamecocks still had their version of a bowl game coming up, as they were beneficiaries of the NCCA's allowance of a 12th game, if that game was with the University of Hawaii in Hawaii. And the trip was a bonus for the players and the fans that followed the team

It's no secret that Carolina lost, 24-7, in a game in which they looked as if the Gamecocks were just going through the motions. It's very difficult to win at Hawaii, because when you get there it's really hard to focus on the game. A lot of fans go along, and it's party time.

The home team has so many advantages because of the general atmosphere for the visitors.

I think there was just too much surf riding! I got ready to leave the hotel to go to Aloha Stadium and looked out of the window to the beach. There were still about ten football players on the beach, and they couldn't have been thinking about the game.

When you play football in Hawaii, the visiting team is allowed to bring along one of the officials for the game, and Carlen invited Weldon Waites of Columbia. He had officiated in the ACC for many years and was a good official, whom I knew pretty well.

When we got to Hawaii Weldon told me, "Don't worry, I'll take care of you guys as well as I possibly can." And he did.

At one point in the game there was a measurement for a first down, and Weldon gave Carolina about two feet on the spot and a first down they really hadn't earned. Later in the game Hawaii threw what appeared to be a touchdown pass, but Waites threw a flag and called offensive pass interference against the receiver. That is something that is rarely called.

After the game Weldon asked me, "Okay, did I pay for my trip?"

I said, "I guess you did." He just laughed.

THE 1978 SEASON

There were two games worth remembering during the 1978 season. The first took place on September 30 and was Carolina's fourth game of the season. Georgia's Bulldogs were the opposition, and this was the only game that Georgia lost during the regular season. They were defeated by Stanford in the Bluebonnet Bowl.

An overflow crowd of 56,500 witnessed the emergence of George Rogers as a back of national prominence. George carried the ball 29 times for 128 yards, as the Gamecocks dominated the Bulldogs, 27-10, and helped to develop the rivalry between the two schools. The series had been one-sided in the past, and Carolina had not beaten the Bulldogs since that great game in 1959.

The Gamecocks cooled off the following week against Georgia Tech in Atlanta, 6-3, but even then Rogers had 148 yards in 21 carries, his third straight game of over 100 yards. The next week, against Ohio University, Rogers suffered a shoulder separation that would keep him out of action for two games, but he still finished the season with over a thousand yards.

The other game worth remembering produced one of the most spectacular plays I ever witnessed as a Carolina broadcaster. With about 22 seconds left in the game, Carolina had the ball on its own 20-yard line, trailing Mississippi by a score of 17-10 in Williams Brice Stadium.

I can see it now. Quarterback Garry Harper dropped back to pass, as split end Horace Smith sprinted down the left sideline. Harper threw the ball probably as far as his arm would allow, and it was perfect. Smith caught it right behind a Rebel defender and outran him into the end zone. Only nine seconds were left when he crossed the goal.

Carolina still faced the decision of whether or not to go for one extra point and accept a tie. You couldn't have blamed Carlen for making that call, because the Gamecocks had fought back from a 17-0 deficit in the fourth quarter. Carlen didn't hesitate, he called a Harper-to-Zion McKinney pass, and it worked perfectly for the two-point conversion. Carolina had pulled out a miracle victory and saved their season.

That enabled Carolina to break even for the season at 5-5.

Rogers did recover enough from his shoulder injury to come back to rush for 237 yards in a win over Wake Forest and 128 yards in a year ending loss to Clemson. In the last game Rogers had to leave when he re-injured his shoulder, which required surgery during the off season.

THE 1979 SEASON

Against North Carolina in the 1979 season's opener at Chapel Hill, George Rogers played his first game at tailback. His backfield running mate, Johnny Wright had suffered a knee injury in the pre-season and was lost for the year, so George was switched from the fullback position he had played during his freshman and sophomore years.

The Tar Heels blasted Carolina, 28-0, and Rogers gained only 97 yards, a poor day for him, so it was obvious that he was doing something wrong. What they told George was to not run at defenders, as he was doing at fullback, but to pick his holes and "run to daylight." George learned fast, and two games later, against Duke, he started a string of 100-yard-plus games that continued through the end of his collegiate career.

He led the Gamecocks to the first eight-win season in their history, and it should have been even better.

At South Bend, Indiana, the Gamecocks held a 17-3 lead over Notre Dame late in the third quarter, but late in the fourth period the Irish had trimmed the lead to 17-10. Carolina faced a fourth-and-two situation around the Notre Dame 40-yard line but decided to punt, rather than have Rogers try for a game-ending first down. The punt sailed into the end zone, and the Irish had new life.

They took full advantage of it, driving the length of the field for a touchdown, with 42 seconds remaining. A two-point conversion gave the Irish an 18-17 victory and denied Carolina a marquee win that would have placed them high in the national ratings. Rogers did nothing to damage his image, gaining 113 yards to stay in contention for the NCAA rushing title. He would eventually finish second to Charles White, the Heisman Trophy recipient from Southern California.

When we played North Carolina State at home the following week, Rogers delivered one of the hardest blows I've ever seen by a running back. He broke through the line, had his momentum up, and two Wolfpack defensive backs converged on him. Rogers didn't try to avoid them, but just turned up the afterburners and met them both head on. He split the two defenders, laid both of them out on the field and completed his route to the end zone. They had to help both Wolfpack players off the field!

Carolina's eighth win came against Clemson in Columbia, as Carolina won, 13-9, on a Harper-to-Ben Cornett pass at the end of the first half and two Eddie Leopard field goals. That was Danny Ford's first season as Clemson's head coach.

Carolina was invited to play in the Hall of Fame Bowl in Birmingham, maintaining the school's winless record in bowls by losing to Missouri, 24-14. The Carolina team didn't win, but the fans caught the attention of bowl officials everywhere by turning up 30,000 strong in Birmingham. From that point forward this encouraged bowls in the Southeast to give Carolina a good look, anytime they warranted it.

The season produced another first for Carolina, as Rogers became the first Gamecock to be named to the Associated Press All-America first team. Several Gamecocks had previously made the AP second team, including center Lou Sossamon in 1942, center Bryant Meeks in 1947, defensive back Norris Mullis in 1952 and quarterback Jeff Grantz in 1975.

Carlen was riding high, in spite of ruffling some feathers among high ranking Gamecocks with his abrupt manner. He was rewarded for producing the school's first eight-win season with a contract extension.

Several years' earlier relationships inside the athletics department had not been going well, with two strong personalities heading up the two major sport programs. Frank McGuire was still putting out winning teams in basketball.

That's when the administration decided to make Carlen, athletics director for football, McGuire, athletics director for basketball, Bo Hagan, athletics director for, what they then called, minor sports, and Dr. James Morris, a business professor, assistant to the president in the matter of athletics. Dr. James Holderman was president at the time, and it was as if he had four athletics directors on his hands!

That arrangement eventually evaporated without fanfare, and the Gamecocks ended up with one non-coach athletics director a few years later.

THE 1980 SEASON

Of all the years I broadcast Carolina football, I consider 1980 to be the most exciting in the matter of big happenings. It began with great expectations and with Rogers being mentioned in the pre-season magazines as a legitimate Heisman Trophy candidate. To win the Heisman, a player almost has to be "nominated" in pre-season or early season otherwise he doesn't stand much of a chance. George had gotten past the primary and into the general election.

As everybody knew George won the coveted award, led the nation in rushing and was named to every All-America team. He broke all of Carolina's rushing records and was the first pick in the National Football League draft, by New Orleans, and was the league's Rookie of the Year.

The Heisman Trophy stands as easily the top honor won by a University of South Carolina athlete or team.

Carolina was fortunate to be playing a high-profile schedule and even more fortunate to be playing very well in the key games.

We went to Southern California in the third game of the year, and the Trojans were ranked fourth in the polls at the time. The Gamecocks lost the game, 23-13, but were impressive, and Rogers gained 141 yards, including a 34-yard touchdown run. The West Coast media gave high marks to George.

Probably the greatest win in Carolina history came the following week at Ann Arbor, Michigan. Before the largest crowd, 104,213, ever to see a Gamecock team play, Carolina upset Michigan. The Gamecocks at one time trailed the Wolverines, 14-3, but short touchdown runs by Rogers and Johnny Wright put the Gamecocks in the lead. They thwarted a late Michigan threat to leave Ann Arbor with a record of three wins and a loss.

Rogers added 142 yards to his rushing total and was now in the lead for the NCAA title in that category. I believe Marcus Allen of Southern Cal was his biggest competition.

Michigan won the Big Ten championship that season and defeated Washington in the Rose Bowl.

A month later Carolina played what is no doubt the most publicized game in the school's history. The Gamecocks took a 6-1 record into Athens, Georgia, to meet the undefeated Georgia Bulldogs. It was a nationally televised game featuring two top ten teams and two of the leading candidates for the Heisman Trophy, Rogers of Carolina and Herschel Walker of Georgia.

The game was not the offensive battle that the media hype projected, but it lived up to its billing in excitement. The Bulldogs won it, 13-10, and continued unbeaten the rest of the season and post-season. Vince Dooley's Dogs were voted National Champions in the polls.

In the battle of the backs, Rogers held his own, gaining 168 yards. Rogers later was named the winner of the Heisman Trophy.

The final game of the season at Clemson was a disappointment, as the Tigers upset the Gamecocks, 27-6, keeping Rogers out of their end zone for the fourth straight year. However, George gained 168 yards to sew-up the national rushing title and keep his name on the top of the Heisman list.

Before the Clemson game the Gamecocks had already been invited to play Pittsburgh in the Gator Bowl at Jacksonville, Florida. Linebacker Hugh Green of the Panthers was the runner-up to Rogers in the Heisman voting and was determined to show sports writers that they had made the wrong choice. Neither Rogers nor Green had a particularly great game, although George did gain 113 yards to be named the game's top offensive performer.

Rogers might have been given the award on sentiment and reputation, because Pittsburgh quarterback Dan Marino played a game that showed the record crowd (72,000) that he was becoming one of the nation's best.

Carlen's personality was now being interpreted as "up front," rather than "abrupt and he received another contract extension. Things were looking good for Jim, because McGuire was gone, and he was now THE athletics director. He had it all.

However, it seemed like Jim went out of his way sometimes to do, let's say thoughtless, things that didn't ingratiate him to people. An example was when he and Rogers returned from the Heisman trophy announcement in New York and there were several thousand fans at the Columbia Airport to greet their returning heroes. Carlen rushed Rogers through the crowd and straight to a waiting bus that carted them away without as much as a "thank you for coming."

Perhaps winners can get away with things like that, but the rule is that, sooner or later, those things catch up with you.

THE 1981 SEASON

I'm not one to dwell on negatives, but the thing that really sticks in my mind about the 1981 season was the fifth game in which the Gamecocks met Pittsburgh, the team that had beaten them in the Gator Bowl the previous year. Dan Marino had a field day, throwing five touchdown passes, but that's not what I, or a lot of Carolina fans, remember.

This went down as the day ABC-TV "pulled the plug." I still hear Carolina fans mention that occasionally.

The network chose this game to televise, because it was an intersectional match-up of two teams who were having good seasons. However, Marino made it a rout in the first half, when the Panthers ran up a 28-0 lead, and Carolina had done nothing to indicate that it would get any closer. ABC, fearing that even the Pittsburgh fans would become bored with this fiasco, made the decision to switch to "a more competitive game." So they "pulled the plug" on the Gamecocks.

However, after falling behind by 35 points early in the second half, the Gamecocks staged a furious comeback, scoring 28 points, while holding the Panthers to one more touchdown. Gordon Beckham, who would make news a couple of weeks later, threw three touchdown passes for Carolina, and the final score was a more respectable, 42-28.

Bob Fulton "My Career My Life"

Beckham had his career day two weeks later, when Carolina played third-ranked North Carolina in Chapel Hill. Gordon completed 16 of 17 passes for 195 yards to lead the Gamecocks in a blowout of the Tar Heels, 31-13. Beckham had 14 straight completions at one point in the game, and that was a new Gamecock record.

That victory breathed new life into the Gamecock season, and after beating North Carolina State the following week, Carlen's team was right back in the bowl picture. The word was that, if they defeated Pacific the next week, they would receive an invitation to play in the Peach Bowl.

The Tigers defeated the highly favored Gamecocks, 23-21, with the actual margin of victory coming on a safety in the first quarter, when they blocked a Carolina punt out of the end zone.

I don't know whether the shocker against Pacific had anything to do with it, but it preceded a collapse by the Gamecocks. Clemson pounded the Gamecocks in Columbia, 29-13, and adding salt to the wounds was the fact that this propelled Clemson to the number one ranking in the polls. The Tigers later defeated Nebraska in the Orange Bowl to clinch the national championship.

To make matters worse the Gamecocks went on a joy ride to Hawaii and lost to the University of Hawaii, 33-10. In justice to the team, it should be pointed out that their starting quarterback, Beckham, broke his hand in practice the preceding week and missed the game.

Relationships between Carlen and University President Holderman weren't too rosy at that time, and Carlen was no longer the conquering hero. That's all Holderman needed, and he called Carlen and told him that he was through. I've often wondered if that would have happened, if the Gamecocks had won the game with Pacific and played in the Peach Bowl.

After a much-publicized legal battle, the University settled a contract dispute with Carlen, who left with a sizeable nest egg. Jim eventually ended up at Hilton Head, where he operated a business and, a couple of years ago, became a volunteer coach of a high school team.

THE 1982 SEASON
First there was Enright, then Giese, then Bass, then Carlen. Now I was getting ready to start a relationship with a new head football coach.

First there had to be an athletics director to hire a coach, because when Carlen left, that position became vacant. Holderman settled on Bob Marcum, who had served as athletics director at the University of Kansas for the three previous years.

Marcum's first order of business was to hire a football coach, however. He found one down the hall at the Roundhouse. Marcum's choice was Richard Bell, who had been assistant head coach and defensive coordinator for Carlen for seven years and previously served on Carlen's staffs at West Virginia and Texas Tech.

Bell is one of the finest people I have ever met, and our acquaintance stretched back to when he was playing for Arkansas and later at Georgia Tech, when I was broadcasting games there, and he was on Bobby Dodd's staff. That's where he first knew Carlen.

Bell was a popular choice among Carolina fans, and it allowed Marcum to concentrate on getting settled in Columbia, rather than running around the country looking for a football coach.

It is always difficult for an assistant coach to move up and become the boss of his former peers on the staff - from one of the boys to king of the hill. Whether that was a problem for Bell, I don't know, because he did have the support and respect of the other assistants.

Bell's start was good enough, as his team defeated Pacific, 41-6, in his first game and downed Richmond, 30-10, the next week. The competition was stiffer the rest of the season, and he won only two more games, over Cincinnati and Navy, and neither were very strong teams.

If you could point to one game that contributed most to Bell's demise, it would be the loss to Furman on October 16 in Columbia. Late in the fourth quarter the Gamecocks scored to go ahead, 23-21, but they couldn't stop the Paladins, who drove the better part of the field to push over a touchdown and win, 28-23. It was a devastating loss for Carolina fans, and 30-point losses that followed, to North Carolina State and Florida State, didn't help matters. A final 24-6 defeat to Clemson ended the season - and Bell's career as Carolina's head coach.

After the loss to State at Raleigh, some of the Carolina players were standing around outside the dressing room and they were laughing and kidding around. Marcum was one of the people who saw this, and that didn't set well with him at all. At the time I wondered if Bell's days were numbered.

As it turned out, they were. Marcum did an evaluation of Bell's performance and reached the conclusion that he needed to get rid of four assistant coaches. He gave Richard the choice: fire these four men or you will be fired yourself. Knowing Richard and his loyal nature, I could have predicted the response. Bell stuck by his friends and paid the price.

THE 1983 SEASON

Hopefully, Joe Morrison would be the lucky number seven in my broadcasts of South Carolina football. He became the seventh head coach for me to work with since coming to Carolina in 1952.

Morrison was the consummate professional, having spent 14 years playing for the New York Giants in the National Football League. There he played several positions and played them well enough that the team retired his jersey number 40.

Joe had ten years of experience as a head coach prior to being selected by Bob Marcum to head the Gamecocks program. He was at the University of Tennessee at Chattanooga for seven years and the University of New Mexico for three.

It didn't take much persuasion for Morrison to leave New Mexico. His 1982 team had won ten games while losing only one, and would have been rewarded with a bowl bid at almost any school in the country - but not New Mexico. They didn't draw flies at their home games, so how would they bring a big following to a bowl game?

So Morrison was on his way to become the new savior of the Gamecocks, and, as usual, enthusiasm increased among the Carolina faithful. Eternally optimistic, Gamecock fans had a feeling that this time we've got it right. That's what I've always admired about Carolina fans - they can find a silver lining in the darkest of clouds.

Morrison's first Carolina team was just good enough to inspire hope. The bright moments were victories over Duke, Southern Cal and North Carolina State. True, those teams were far short of being national powers, but the games had some significance. Duke and State were ACC teams, and the Gamecocks' 31-17 home win over the Wolfpack was televised nationally. Against State, Morrison brought his team out in all garnet uniforms to see if that would help the Gamecocks break a two-game losing streak. They had lost to Notre Dame and LSU.

The ever matter-of-fact Morrison explained that, with the game being on Homecoming Day and all that, "It was something to do." Making a big to-do over uniforms would have been completely out of character with Morrison, but he did take note of the reaction of the fans.

Carolina demolished Southern Cal, 38-14, in their finest performance of the year and evened the "series" between the two schools at one game each.

I don't remember what color the Gamecocks wore in a loss to Florida State at Tallahassee, but I doubt if any combination could have helped against Bobby Bowden's Seminoles.

Carolina beat Navy the following week to even its record at 5-5, giving Morrison a chance to have a winning season in his debut with the Gamecocks, if he could beat Clemson in Columbia. This Clemson team under Danny Ford had lost only one game and tied one, but they were not headed for a bowl, because they were on NCAA probation.

This time Morrison tried a uniform of all black jerseys and pants, with the usual garnet helmets. The Gamecocks played a respectable game against the heavily favored Tigers, and this may have planted a seed in Morrison's mind. "Maybe there's something to this all-black combination." All of a sudden it was "the good guys" who wore black hats!

It hadn't escaped the attention of Carolina fans that Coach Joe wore all-black - cap, t-shirt and trousers. When asked why he wore this he wryly answered, "Because it was clean and it fit!"

Joe also learned something about Gamecock fans. They liked to be dressed in keeping with their coach's attire. Black caps and shirts began selling like crazy at stores that sold such stuff, and this became a new source of income for the coach who became the owner of the license.

Williams-Brice Stadium could now seat well over 70,000, and the new enthusiasm of Gamecock fans resulted in seven of the school's all-time largest home crowds during the season. Over 74,000 attended the games with Clemson, Notre Dame, Southern Cal and North Carolina.

Despite the 5-6 record Morrison had indicated to the fans in one season that the Gamecocks were on the rise.

I had done the Jim Carlen Sunday TV show during his final few seasons at Carolina, but it seemed about the only things that changed as often as coaches at the University was the host of the coach's television show. I was again on the outside looking in, as Jim Forest, who had been in that position before as WIS-TV's sports director, was back in the chair as an "independent sportscaster."

I did have a good relationship with Morrison and found him to be most cooperative in my dealings with him. Joe was sort of a loner and kept a low profile, outside of the public appearances he made because of his position.

THE 1984 SEASON

There was nothing in the opening game against The Citadel to indicate to even the most optimistic Carolina fan that this would become their best-ever season. The Gamecocks were highly favored over a Bulldog team that had won only three games the previous year, but with less than two minutes remaining, they were locked in a 24-24 struggle.

I couldn't help but think back over the past years, in which Carolina had a history of pulling big upsets and, at other times, being victims of upsets of equal size. A tie isn't a loss, but in games with teams of The Citadel's stature, a tie is a loss in the eyes of the fans.

Bob Fulton "My Career My Life"

Then this Gamecock team did what became a trademark of their season by scoring on a 40-yard halfback option pass, Quinton Lewis to Chris Wade, with 1:02 remaining to win the game, 31-24. Even that wasn't enough to reveal anything special about this team.

A 21-0 win over Duke was nothing to get excited about, and a 2-0 start for a Gamecock team was not that common. The stage for the season was set the following week, when the Gamecocks defeated Georgia, 17-10, in Williams- Brice Stadium, because this was a very good Georgia team. THE PLAY in the game came in the fourth quarter and with the score tied at 10-all. Back-up quarterback Mike Hold, a junior college trans- fer playing his first season here, avoided onrushing tacklers and lofted a bomb to Ira Hillary, who was finally chased down at the Georgia six. Hold scored three plays later, and the 17-10 victory was clinched.

Nobody had even noticed that Hold was around during the Gamecocks' first two games, so they were sent thumbing through their programs to see who this guy was. Those of us in the press box were just as surprised that he turned out to be the hero of one of the Gamecocks' biggest wins in several years.

When the Gamecocks routed Kansas State the next week, they caught the attention of those who voted in the various polls, jumping from nowhere to 17th. At 4-0, Gamecock fans began wondering when the bubble would burst. It wouldn't be soon, because Carolina romped over Pittsburgh, 45-21, the next week for their first win in three tries against the Panthers. Morrison's veer offense was making believers out of Carolina fans and the poll- sters, who voted them ever closer to the top ten.

Through their first four games the Gamecocks had begun to establish a pattern. Allen Mitchell would start the game at quarterback, and Hold would come in later to relieve him. Mike was the hero at South Bend, Indiana on the afternoon of October 20, when the Gamecocks finally defeated a Notre Dame team in football. Carolina was trail- ing the Irish, 26-22, with nine minutes remaining in the game, when Hold couldn't find a receiver open and scrambled 33 yards for a go-ahead touchdown.

Carolina scored another TD to put the game out of reach, and it didn't matter that the Irish narrowed the final score to 36-32. That victory resulted in a ninth place ranking for the Gamecocks in the polls, and the 6-0 mark was inspiring bowl talk.

After beating East Carolina, the Gamecocks had to go on the road again, facing North Carolina State in Raleigh. With Hold again coming off the bench to lead a rally, the Gamecocks needed 25 fourth- quarter points to beat the Wolfpack, 35-28.

A week later Carolina faced 11-th ranked Florida State at home. This game drew national attention and a decision by ABC to televise it coast to coast. The Gamecocks were unbeaten, while Bobby Bowden's Seminoles had lost only Auburn, and that was by one point.

The play of the day came on the second half kickoff, when Carolina's Raynard Brown bent low to pick up the ball on his one-yard line, cut to his left and sprinted 99 yards to the Seminole end zone. That gave Carolina a 24-7 lead, and the Gamecocks extended it to 38-7 with two more third quarter scores. Neither the Seminoles, ABC-TV, nor the Carolina fans could believe this was happening. Florida State scored 19 unan- swered points to narrow the final score to 38-26, but the Gamecocks had made believers out of the nation's football population. Incidentally, two members of the Florida State coaching staff were Art Baker, who later became director of the Carolina Gamecock Club, and Brad Scott, who came to the Gamecocks as head coach in 1994.

Therefore, when the Gamecocks went to Annapolis the following Saturday to play Navy, they were ranked number two - the highest ranking then or since by a Carolina team.

36

Dreams of an unbeaten season vanished, when the Middies arose from the football doldrums to upset the Gamecocks, 38-21, and it was no fluke. They simply outplayed the Gamecocks from start to finish.

Quite frankly, losing to Navy was not a big surprise to me. Carolina was the heavy favorite, but I've always said, "Never play a service team when they're playing their final home game." That's what Navy was doing, and they hadn't had a good season.

One thing about playing one of the service academies, you always get great effort. They never let down, and they are well disciplined.

The day before the game I spoke to the Spartanburg Touchdown Club, and I told them that I was worried about the Navy game, because it would be a spot for a letdown before playing Clemson. They all laughed at me. I thought we were going to win, but I knew it could be a problem. We scored too easily to begin with, and then they came back and scored, and we weren't in the ball game after that.

Around the hotel prior to the game, Carolina fans weren't talking about Navy. They were discussing which major bowl the Gamecocks would accept, and how we could have an unbeaten record by beating Clemson. All that speculation was leading up to the possibility of the Gamecocks playing for the national championship. And they would have been.

Now they had to face Clemson in Death Valley, and the Tigers needed a victory to make it another good year for Danny Ford.   Ironically, Clemson had been beaten, 41-23, at Maryland on the same day Carolina was upset by Navy. The two teams met at the Washington National Airport, as they both prepared for the long trip back to South Carolina.

The game with Clemson was one of the more exciting ones in the series, with Carolina winning it by a 22-21 score. They did it by coming from behind, just as they had done on several other occasions during the season.

With seven minutes remaining in the game, Carolina trailed by a 21-12 score, but Scott Hagler's 41 yard field goal narrowed it to 21-15. With only three minutes remaining, Carolina had the ball at its own 16-yard line, and it appeared that the "Black Magic" season would end in mourning.

Once more, Mike Hold had a little magic left, guiding the Gamecocks downfield and conserving the clock. With less than a minute showing on the scoreboard clock, Hold scrambled eight yards to the Tiger three, and a penalty moved it to the one. Then Hold pushed his way into the end zone behind a surging Gamecock line, and it was a tie game. Hagler's extra point sewed-up the win for Carolina, and "Black Magic" was back.

The Gamecocks had one final chance to make this a truly great season, facing Oklahoma State in the Gator Bowl on December 28. The usual huge following of Gamecock fans enabled the Gator Bowl to set another attendance record, 82,138. For 58 minutes and 56 seconds it appeared that Carolina had broken the bowl jinx, leading the Cowboys, 14-13. A 57-yard pass from Hold to Hillary had given the Gamecocks the lead in the third quarter.

But with 1:04 remaining in the game, Oklahoma State climaxed an 88-yard drive by scoring on a 25-yard pass play. The fifth straight bowl loss by the Gamecocks was full of "ifs," but the result was the same. Of some consolation was the fact that Carolina was ranked as the 11th best team in the nation in the final polls, their highest finish ever.

Looking back over the games of 1984, in which the Gamecocks finished with a 10-2 record - best in the school's history - one can only think about what might have been. So close but yet so far.

Bob Fulton "My Career My Life"

THE 1985 SEASON

Although expectations were high, because of the great success in 1984, it must be remembered that a large number of seniors who had been the leaders of that team had now departed. They had been recruits of Jim Carlen in 1981, following George Rogers' Heisman Trophy season. With coach firings taking place after the 1981 and 1982 seasons, recruiting suffered, and Morrison hadn't had the necessary time to build his own recruiting program.

The Gamecocks did avoid a scare, such as they had in 1984, in the opener with The Citadel, winning , 56-17, before a crowd of 73,500 in Columbia. The size of that turnout for a game of this significance demonstrated the excitement that had been generated by the previous season.

This was not a season to remember for Carolina, as the Gamecocks finished with five wins and six losses and were blown-out in several games. Yet it had its moments and several new players that created hope for the future.

Sterling Sharpe, the wide receiver who later set NFL records at Green Bay, saw his first real action this season and indicated that he had the potential for greatness. Another newcomer was Todd Ellis, the all-everything quarterback from Greensboro, North Carolina, who was sitting out the season as a redshirt. I had a role in recruiting Todd, and I'll talk about that in my chapter about the coaches with whom I worked.

On the other hand, the Gamecocks didn't need any help recruiting Sharpe, because no other Division I school was interested in this player from tiny Glennville, Georgia. Of course, Georgia has always been a fertile recruiting area for Carolina. That state contributed Dan Reeves, George Rogers and several other great ones.

The second game of the season was nothing extra. The Gamecocks trailed Appalachian State, 7-0, at the end of the first quarter and had to struggle before edging the Mountaineers, 20-13. The interesting sidelight to this game was that Sparky Woods was in his second year as head coach at Appalachian State. Neither I nor anyone else would have speculated that, four years later, he would be head coach of the Gamecocks.

The next three games brought revenge for three of Carolina's 1984 victims, as Michigan won, 34-3, in Columbia, Georgia prevailed, 35-21, in Athens, and Pittsburgh's 42-7 win at Pittsburgh was a complete turnaround from their rout at the hands of the Gamecocks in Columbia a year earlier.

In a game that Carolina wanted to forget, a play that is still featured in football highlight films took place. In a play that originated at the Carolina 20 in the second quarter, Mike Hold went back to pass, couldn't find a receiver and zig-zagged around for what seemed to be an eternity in the backfield. He finally went to his right, avoided another Panther, and then released a ball that appeared to be up for grabs. In fact it was.

Both Carolina and Pittsburgh players fought for the ball just past midfield, it ricocheted off a Panther, and the Gamecocks' Raynard Brown caught it in stride. Nobody could catch Raynard, and the Gamecocks completed a spectacular 80-yard touchdown play. Add the 99-yard kickoff return against Florida State in 1984, and Raynard had a good start on his own highlights film.

All you could say about the rest of the season was "more revenge," and the Gamecocks were on the positive side of that only once. They defeated Navy, 34-31, but that couldn't remove the sting of what the Middies did to the Gamecocks in 1984.

North Carolina State, Florida State and Clemson downed Carolina, bringing to six the number of 1984 Gamecock victims who reversed the result this season.

Carolina appeared to have the game with North Carolina State in the bag, with less than two minutes remaining in the game and the Wolfpack at their own 25, trailing by three points. A State receiver took a relatively short pass up the middle, shook off a couple of Gamecocks who appeared to have easy shots at him, and completed the 75-yard trip to the winning touchdown. However, if you think that was heartbreak, it was nothing compared to the finish of the Gamecock-Wolfpack battle in 1986.

THE 1986 SEASON

Nothing is permanent in football as Carolina's veer offense was abandoned in 1986, being replaced by the exciting "run and shoot." This offense, installed during spring practice, features only one running back, with the emphasis on pass receivers, who were spread across the field.

The "run and shoot" was installed to utilize the talents of Todd Ellis, the gifted quarterback who had red-shirted the previous year. It also showcased the exceptional abilities of Sterling Sharpe, who would combine with Ellis to rewrite the Carolina passing and receiving record book. It took awhile for this offense to settle in, and the Gamecocks' more impressive games this season were close losses, rather than victories.

A national television audience watched the Miami Hurricanes thwart the Gamecocks, 34-14, in Columbia, as Heisman Trophy winner Vinny Testaverde launched his team toward an unbeaten (11-0) season. They lost the national championship game to Penn State in the Fiesta Bowl.

Ellis matched Testaverde in pass completions and yardage, but he was intercepted four times by the Hurricanes.

In a season that produced only three victories and two ties, two games against national powers proved that the Gamecocks could compete with the best.

Against Georgia in Williams-Brice Stadium, Carolina was trailing, 31-26, with less than two minutes remaining, but the Gamecocks had driven inside the Bulldog 20. Ellis fired a pass to Sharpe at the goal line, but the ball was deflected and fell into the arms of a Georgia defender, denying our bid for an upset.

Fate delivered an almost identical blow to the Gamecocks the following week on the same field, when Nebraska's Cornhuskers came to Columbia for the first time ever. Again Carolina had a chance to win at the end, with the ball inside the Cornhusker 20 and less than a minute on the clock. Ellis' pass was intercepted with 38 seconds left, and another golden opportunity had been lost, as Nebraska won, 30-21.

As if that were not heartbreak enough, what happened to the Gamecocks in Raleigh two weeks later shouldn't happen to anybody - or any team. The Wolfpack won the game, 23-22, on a 33-yard last play pass that will remain controversial in the minds and hearts of Carolina supporters.

It was a loss that was hard to take. Carolina had the lead and seemingly could run out the clock, as they had the ball with little time left. But the guy keeping the clock was doing a real good job for State, stopping it, even when there was no reason to stop it. Even so, Carolina stopped the Wolfpack on what was to be the final play of the game, but the Gamecocks were ruled offside, and State was given another chance at the Gamecock 33.

State quarterback Erik Kramer threw a "Hail Mary" pass into a crowd of players in the end zone, and a Wolfpack receiver came down with the ball for a winning touchdown.

There was obvious pass interference in the end zone. The film showed a State player pushing a Carolina defender out of the way, before catching the ball. The official covering the play pulled a flag out of his pocket, but then he decided not to call it. I guess he realized he was in Raleigh and put the flag back. The touchdown was allowed and State had defeated the Gamecocks "at the buzzer" for the third time in my broadcasting career with Carolina. Remember the Dick Christy field goal in 1957?

But if the clock had been handled properly in the 1986 game, State would never have had the ball at the end.

There was still room for one more heartbreaker that year. Against Clemson at Clemson, Carolina had a chance to break a 21-21 tie with 25 seconds remaining. However, Scott Hagler missed a 41-yard field goal attempt, and the game ended in a tie. Hagler had made a number of field goals of that length during the season, but he simply miss-hit that one.

The bright spots of the season were the 3,020 passing yards by Ellis and 1,106 yards in receptions by Sharpe, both new school records. And there was more to come.

THE 1987 SEASON

The 1987 Carolina season was a broadcaster's dream. Ellis and Sharpe provided the Gamecocks with two of the nation's most exciting players. I really think that Sharpe proved that he was worthy of the Heisman Trophy, but it went to Tim Brown of Notre Dame. Sterling did exactly the same things Brown did - catch passes and return kicks - but he did them better. Brown played for Notre Dame, however, and that's a big advantage.

This Gamecock team lit up the scoreboard and outscored the opposition by 200 points, an average of almost three touchdowns per game. They won all seven of their home games and were invited to play in the Gator Bowl for the fourth time. It was a fun year, and I really had some great games to broadcast.

In what has now become a Carolina rivalry that ranks second only to the Clemson game, Georgia edged the Gamecocks, 13-6, in Athens. That was the only defensive battle of that year. Even so, Ellis passed for 306 yards, and Sharpe had 11 catches.

The following week at Nebraska, Carolina had the second-ranked Cornhuskers on the ropes going into the fourth quarter, leading 21-13. Ellis' 80-yard touchdown pass to Sharpe was the longest ever.

In the fourth quarter the Cornhuskers changed quarterbacks and went to a running game that produced a 94-yard touchdown march that pulled them within a point. They soon recovered a fumble deep in Carolina territory and moved to the winning touchdown. A late field goal made the final score, 30-21.

Carolina ran up big scores against Virginia Tech, Virginia and East Carolina, before "welcoming" the now despised North Carolina State Wolfpack to Williams-Brice. The Gamecocks demolished the Wolfpack, 48-0, holding them to minus thirteen yards rushing and only 49 passing.

By this time Harold Green, a sophomore running back who now plays in the NFL for Cincinnati, was making his presence felt, supplementing the Ellis-Sharpe passing attack.

Carolina ran its winning streak to six by defeating Clemson, 20-7, in Columbia, before a national ESPN television audience.

In a game that was moved to the end of the season, December 5, Carolina moved into Miami for another nationally-televised and highly publicized game against the sec-ond-ranked Hurricanes. This Miami team later defeated Oklahoma in the Orange Bowl to claim the national championship.

Late in the game Carolina had the ball around midfield and a chance to drive for a winning touchdown, but the drive fizzled, following hostilities that broke out between the teams. In this confrontation Ellis was clobbered in the back by a Miami player in full view of everyone, with the possible exception of the officials.

Regardless, to play the national champions and lose by a 20-16 score on their home field was an accomplishment for Morrison's young men. And I say "Morrison's young men," because that is the way Joe always referred to them, rather than "kids" or "boys".

This earned the Gamecocks, ranked ninth in the polls, a return to the Gator Bowl to meet seventh-ranked Louisiana State. It was not a pretty game for Ellis or the Gamecocks. Todd passed for 304 yards but was intercepted four times.

The result was a 30-13 LSU victory, and the frustrated Gamecocks had lost their seventh bowl game without a victory.

The Gamecocks finished the season at 8-4 and were ranked 15th in the final AP rankings.

In spite of a few disappointments, it was a good year for me as a play-by-play announcer, because every game that Carolina lost was competitive, and most of the wins were comparatively easy.

And it didn't hurt to see Ellis and Sharpe become the school's all-time best in passing and receiving statistics, even if they did replace my good friends, Tommy Suggs and Freddie Zeigler in that respect. Suggs, who was the analyst on the network, accepted this philosophically, but I'm sure it's hard to see your name erased from the record books. As they say, "Records are made to be broken."

THE 1988 SEASON

Early in 1988 University President Jim Holderman decided it was time for a change in athletics directors at the University. There were some things he didn't like about the man he had brought here to give stability to the overall program. Bob Marcum had to go.

One of the problems relating to the football program was increasing talk and symptoms of a steroid problem with some of the players. Supervision of this area was, of course, one of Marcum's responsibilities, and Holderman obviously didn't give him high marks there. Often, when you're in charge, there are two deadly sins. One is knowing and not doing something about it, and the other is not knowing.

Marcum denied any knowledge of the steroid problem, but he was gone, amidst the usual contractual disputes. Ironically, when Marcum fired Richard Bell he said that the school didn't have to honor the remainder of his contract, because he was being fired for what amounted to insubordination. Failing to fire four coaches as ordered. Bell won that argument and financial settlement.

With the office of athletics director vacant, Holderman made Columbia attorney Johnny Gregory, former Gamecock wide receiver, acting athletics director, and his main duty was to find a new AD. His recommendation was Dick Bestwick, an assistant AD at the University of Georgia and assistant football coach at Carolina under Marvin Bass in 1965. Holderman accepted the choice, and I was now involved with the eleventh athletics director during my years at Carolina.

Bestwick didn't make it through the football season, resigning at the midpoint because of "health reasons." His immediate replacement was King Dixon, who was in the early months of his duties as director of the USC Alumni Association. Dixon had retired as a lieutenant colonel in the Marine Corps a few years earlier, serving as vice president of a bank in his hometown of Laurens, before returning to his alma mater.

Dixon had a great image with Gamecock fans, having been a star football player, Phi Beta Kappa student and recipient of the Algernon Sydney Sullivan award as the outstanding member of his graduating class of 1959.

Ellis engineered the Gamecocks to their most impressive start in history - six straight wins. North Carolina, Western Carolina and East Carolina were routine victims in Williams-Brice Stadium, then came the big one. This time the Gamecocks played before a national television audience via WTBS "Superstition." The guest was Georgia, which had opened with consecutive wins over Tennessee, Texas Christian and Mississippi State.

The Gamecocks won it going away, 23-10, leading by 23-3 until late in the fourth period. Georgia's final touchdown was scored with 32 seconds left in the game.

Carolina dispatched Sparky Woods' Appalachian State team, 35-9, and he didn't dream that he would be walking the opposite sideline less than a year later. Then Carolina had to finally play away from home, and they were fortunate to escape with a 26-24 win over Virginia Tech at Blacksburg.

The closeness of that game didn't bother the people who vote in polls, because they had the Gamecocks ranked sixth the following Monday. This set the stage for Dixon's first game as athletics director, and it wasn't a pretty sight.

Carolina faced Georgia Tech in Atlanta, and this was billed as a mismatch, because the Yellow Jackets hadn't won a Division I football game within memory. They had beaten the University of Tennessee at Chattanooga in their opener of 1988, followed by four straight losses.

It was one of those days when Carolina could do nothing right, and the Yellow Jackets seemed to forget who they were. They, not Carolina, looked like the sixth ranked team, and Tech won the game by a 34-0 score.

Thank goodness, the Tech game wasn't televised, but the meeting with State's Wolfpack at Raleigh the following Saturday night was. ESPN was on hand for the affair, and it was a good outing for the Gamecocks. Both teams entered the game with 6-1 records, but the Gamecocks were the ones to reach seven wins.

Carolina not only survived the football game, 23-7, but also a battery of thrown objects from Wolfpack fans. Everything up to and including beer bottles were hurled toward the Gamecock bench following an Ellis to Eddie Miller touchdown pass in the fourth period. The Gamecocks had been receiving their share of verbal abuse during the game, and it even rankled the normally undemonstrative Ellis.

After Miller crossed the Wolfpack goal, Ellis turned toward the Wolfpack student section, went through the motion of drawing a couple of imaginary six-shooters and fired them toward the stands.

ESPN was back again the following week to televise the Gamecocks' game with fifth-ranked Florida State. The less said about this game, the better. Florida State led by 31-0 at the half, en route to a 59-0 rout, and I wonder if ESPN would have switched to "a more competitive game," as ABC had done in the 1981 Pittsburgh telecast, if there had been another game to switch to.

The Gamecocks closed their home season by beating Navy, but lost to Clemson at Clemson to end their season at eight wins and three losses.

Because of their great fan support, the Gamecocks were courted by several bowls, including the Gator, but the school opted for a change of scenery and accepted an invitation to play Indiana in the Liberty Bowl at Memphis, Tennessee.

The Liberty Bowl was a failure from every standpoint for Carolina, and that was a shame, because it was the last game that Joe Morrison would coach. It was a night game that was played three days after Christmas, and, take my word, it is cold that time of year on the banks of the Mississippi. Indiana further chilled the Gamecocks in a 34-10 disappointment. The game drew only 39,000, and the Gamecock fans who made the trip wondered why they went.

I remember Carolina followers venting their frustration near the end of the first half, when Indiana had already run up a 17-0 lead. With time running out, Carolina had the ball inside Indiana territory, and with just seconds left, they decided to kill the clock, rather than try for a long touchdown pass. The fans roared their disapproval. And Carolina was still winless in eight bowl games.

Morrison ended his six seasons at Carolina with a record of 39 wins, 28 defeats, two ties and three bowl games. He died of a heart attack on February 5, 1989 at the age of 57. The attack came while he was taking a shower after playing handball.

Coach Morrison was later memorialized in an impressive service in Williams-Brice Stadium, as his players and admirers lined the west sideline, where his black-clad figure had become so familiar.

THE 1989 SEASON

After Joe Morrison's death, the usual speculation about who would be selected as the new Gamecock coach dominated the radio talk shows around South Carolina. The decision was up to King Dixon, who had been athletics director only a few months. King's choice was Sparky Woods, whose Appalachian State teams had played in Williams-Brice Stadium on three occasions. Woods was sort of a low key individual, but he seemed to give all the right answers to questions at the press conference announcing his hiring.

Sparky inherited a solid squad from Morrison, including future NFL stars Harold Green, a running back, and Robert Brooks, wide receiver. Brooks has become famous for leaping into the arms of waiting Green Bay fans in the end zone seats, after scoring a touchdown. Todd Ellis was entering his senior season, so Sparky was loaded with offensive weapons.

Woods' debut in Williams-Brice was an unqualified success, as the Gamecocks defeated Duke, 27-21. This was a Duke team that won eight games during the season.

Although Ellis was still putting the ball in the air, Carolina was now placing more emphasis on the running game. For instance, Ellis passed for 192 yards against Duke, just a little more than Green's 162 yards rushing.

Carolina lost its third game of the season to West Virginia at Morgantown, but Woods enhanced his image with Gamecock followers by beating two rivals in the state of Georgia on consecutive weekends. They downed Georgia Tech, 21-10, in Columbia, and Georgia, 24-10, in Athens.

After Carolina downed East Carolina and Western Carolina, bringing its record to 5-1-1, bowl talk was swirling around Columbia. However, disaster struck on the third play of the game with North Carolina State on October 28 in Columbia. As Ellis released a pass, he was hit on his left knee by a Wolfpack tackler. The result was a torn medial collateral ligament, and Ellis' college football career was over.

For all intents and purposes, the Gamecock season was also over. Dickie DeMasi replaced Ellis at quarterback, but he had little experience and couldn't propel the offense as effectively as Ellis had. After losing to Florida State at Tallahassee, the Gamecocks did manage a 27-20 win over North Carolina at Chapel Hill, but that was a Tar Heel team that defeated VMI for its only victory.

A nationally televised (ESPN) collapse against Clemson, 45-0, brought a disappointing end to a season that had such promise at its midpoint. Losing to the Tigers by such a landslide margin was a bitter pill for Woods to swallow, and he vowed that nothing like that would ever happen again.

At 6-4-1, the Gamecocks were still bowl bait, and they received an invitation to play in the Independence Bowl at Shreveport, Louisiana. That opportunity was rejected, because it came during final exams, and the administration didn't want to schedule a game at that time.

From a professional standpoint, Woods and I didn't get off to the greatest start. College football had evolved into a situation that found head coaches becoming like franchises. They had radio shows, television shows, did commercials, licensed caps, marketed camps for youngsters, and so forth. The coach, not the school, received the bulk of the money from all these things. Having been at the University for 37 years, I felt that I had something to offer as host of Sparky's Sunday TV show.

Woods didn't see it that way, and brought in Jon Pritchett, a 22-year-old Appalachian State graduate, who had worked with Sparky the previous year. Let me tell you a rather amusing story about my first experience with Jon.

He came to me one day and told me they wanted to tape something with me and put it on the Woods TV show. So I went to WIS-TV to do the tape and I took my position on the studio set next to Pritchett.

He turned to me and said, "Do you like wine?"

I answered, "Yes. That's about the only thing I ever drink."

He said, "Well, I want you to be relaxed here. So just picture that you and I are sitting at some cafe, and we're drinking a glass of wine. And that will make you feel really relaxed."

I thought to myself, "I was doing television when your parents were in grade school." I didn't say anything to him - I went right along. But one of the cameramen with whom I had worked in the past, just broke out laughing.

We finished the taping, and I left. But I just couldn't believe what had happened in that studio - this 22-year-old telling me to relax and how to do an interview. I believe that Pritchett was later put on the athletics department payroll in some position to do with recruiting.

THE 1990 SEASON

Sparky Woods' second season at Carolina was rocking along well. The Gamecocks opened by beating Duke, North Carolina and Virginia Tech on consecutive weekends, before losing to Georgia Tech's co-national champions in Atlanta. After easily defeating East Carolina, 37-7, Carolina was again on the bowl track, with a breather against The Citadel coming up.

In Sparky's worst experience as Carolina's head coach, including the Clemson blowout, the Gamecocks lost to The Citadel in Columbia for the first time since 1919 - the year before I was born!

After struggling for most of this game, Carolina seemed to have survived, when we took a ten-point lead with eight minutes remaining. The Citadel kicked a field goal with 3:11 left, which was enough to make the Gamecocks nervous, but not panicky.

The Bulldogs executed a successful on-sides kick and drove for a winning touchdown, with 22 seconds remaining. The final score was 38-35. Losing to Clemson is irritating to Carolina fans, but losing to The Citadel is inexcusable.

That loss sent Carolina's season into a tailspin, with two straight losses, to North Carolina State at Raleigh and Florida State in Columbia. The Gamecocks rebounded to down Southern Illinois, but only 52,000 spectators turned out - the smallest home crowd in years.

Danny Ford had been ousted as Clemson's head coach, but his successor, Ken Hatfield, kept the Tigers' winning streak against the Gamecocks intact by a 24-15 score at Clemson.

As luck would have it, the Gamecocks still had a chance to salvage something from the season. A game with West Virginia which was originally scheduled for early season in Columbia, had been switched to Thanksgiving night, so that ESPN would have something to televise. It was a good game for the Gamecocks, who never trailed in a 29-10 victory to send their fans into the winter months on a positive note. It was the first time since 1973 that Carolina had won its final game of the year.

Again, with a 6-5 record, Carolina qualified for a bowl game, and, again, the Independence Bowl was forthcoming. And, again, the Gamecocks turned it down for the same reason they gave the preceding year.

Quite often at the University of South Carolina, what happens off the field - or out of the classroom - draws the most attention. Such was the case in 1990.

On May 30 Jim Holderman resigned as president, and Arthur Smith, the school's provost, was named interim president. He became the sixth president of the University since I began broadcasting here in 1952.

Although his presidency would last for less than a year, Smith participated in probably the most important project in the school's athletics history. That was culmination of the school's efforts to become a member of the Southeastern Conference, which was considering expanding from 10 to 12 teams. Smith and Athletics Director King Dixon continued the campaign initiated by Holderman and brought it to a successful end. The Gamecocks were voted into the league, along with Arkansas, which had withdrawn from the Southwest Conference.

The conference affiliation became effective with the 1991-92 basketball season, with 1992 scheduled as the first SEC football season. This ended Carolina's 22 years as a football independent, marking a quantum leap into the number one athletics conference in the country.

Less than a year after appointing Smith to the interim presidency, the University Board of Trustees selected Dr. John Palms to become the school's 26th "permanent" president, as of March 15, 1991. Palms, a graduate of The Citadel, was president of Georgia State University in Atlanta, prior to coming to Carolina.

THE 1991 SEASON

It was a bizarre beginning for Carolina's 1991 season. The Gamecocks held a 24-10 lead over the Duke Blue Devils, with 1:15 remaining in the game.

At that point Duke scored to narrow the gap to 24-16. All Carolina had to do was receive the kickoff and kill the clock - the same situation they faced against The Citadel a year earlier. Again the Gamecocks saw their opponent recover the expected on-sides kick, and Duke still had life.

The Blue Devils moved the ball close to the Gamecock goal but were penalized and, seemingly had one more play in which to get the ball into the end zone, because they were out of timeouts. A pass play ended with the receiver being downed on the Carolina five, and the Gamecocks thought that they had the game won. For some unknown reason an official stopped the clock, with three seconds still showing. Duke had not made a first down on the play.

Protests from the Carolina sideline were ignored, and Duke scored on the last play of the game to pull within two. A two-point conversion was good, and the game ended in a 24-24 tie. What a way to start the season. I felt that the officials really blew this one, and I never did hear a satisfactory reason. But the score will stand forever.

It seemed that the Gamecocks never recovered psychologically from that blow, although they defeated Virginia Tech, but lost to East Carolina and were tied, 12-12, by Louisiana Tech. The latter game was a perfect example of how a team can "snatch defeat" from the jaws of victory." This time the Gamecocks snatched a tie, but it felt like a loss, because of the team they were playing and how they were tied.

Carolina scored a touchdown with 3:10 remaining in the game to overcome a 7-6 Tech lead. Ahead by 12-7, the Gamecocks tried for a two-point conversion, which was the correct call to make under those circumstances. Execution was the problem, because a Bulldog defender intercepted Bobby Fuller's pass and returned it 100 yards to give Louisiana Tech the two points, narrowing Carolina's lead to 12-9.

Tech faced a 4th-and-22 situation on their final position and completed a 31-yard pass that kept the drive alive and ended up with a 38-yard field goal that tied the game with just two seconds left. How many times had I seen things like that happen to Carolina. When you're broadcasting something like that, it is awfully difficult to handle.

You know you're delivering terrible news to listeners who are just dying at their radios, and you wonder if, perhaps, they think it's your fault! I remembered reading in ancient history books how the Greeks would execute the messengers who brought bad news from the battlefield.

Carolina made a slight comeback in a 23-14 win over Georgia Tech, but that was followed by consecutive losses to North Carolina State, 38-21, and Florida State, 38-10. The first loss to North Carolina since 1983 and Woods' fourth straight loss to Clemson, 41-24, in Columbia finished out the season.

It was Woods' first losing season - 3-6-2 - at Carolina, but it wouldn't be his last. Looming over the horizon were the formidable foes of the SEC.

THE 1992 SEASON

The 1992 season for Carolina was historic on two counts. First, it would be their first football season in the Southeastern Conference. Second, it marked the 100th anniversary of football at the University. The latter was greeted with an outburst of indifference from the Columbia media, as if they were embarrassed that it was mentioned.

Anyhow, the University arranged enough hoopla to observe this anniversary, and it no doubt served its purpose. It would have been much better, if the football team had cooperated in its performances.

There was another major event in my life prior to this centennial football season - I married Carol Robertson, whom I had met at a party at the Spring Valley Country Club in Columbia several years earlier. Carol lost her husband, Hank, who died of a massive coronary in March of 1971, after watching Carolina edge North Carolina for the ACC basketball championship. Carol was left to raise their five children – the youngest of whom was four months old. She managed to send all of them to college, and I seriously doubt that there are many other women who could have accomplished that. Carol has three sons, two daughters and four grandchildren. We were married in the Rutledge Chapel at the University, and she was already thoroughly indoctrinated as a Gamecock supporter.

Bob Fulton "My Career My Life"

Carolina's opponent in its SEC debut was Georgia, which was the first official opponent the Gamecocks faced back in the 1890s, when it all began. When the teams prepared to kickoff on September 5, the SEC television network was on hand, as were a record 75,000 fans in Williams-Brice Stadium.

After the expected pre-game ceremonies, observing both a century of football and entrance into the conference, the two teams had at it.

The Gamecocks started well and held a 6-0 halftime lead, but that was it for the day. Georgia scored 28 unanswered points in the second half, ripping off huge hunks of yardage on the ground, as Gamecock tacklers fell by the wayside.

The following week they faced a team that had a worse beginning than the Gamecocks experienced against Georgia. The Arkansas Razorbacks lost their opener to The Citadel, 10-3, in Fayetteville, resulting in the immediate dismissal of head coach Jack Crowe. His ultimate successor would be former Clemson coach Danny Ford.

An Arkansas offense that could manage only three points against The Citadel, exploded for 45 against Carolina, which could muster only a last-quarter touchdown.

Meanwhile, Sparky was playing musical chairs with his quarterbacks, alternating Wright Mitchell and Blake Williamson. Nothing seemed to work. So, after losing to East Carolina and Kentucky, Woods was ready to try anything. Trailing Alabama, 38-0, at the half in Tuscaloosa, Woods inserted an untried but highly confident freshman named Steve Taneyhill.

Steve completed ten of 17 passes for 135 yards, leading them to their only touchdown and prompting Gamecock fans to believe that maybe he wasn't just mouthing-off when he attended Carolina's spring practice game. He came down from Altoona, Pennsylvania, where he had been a highly recruited high school star, took a look at the Gamecocks and predicted that he would be the starting quarterback as a freshman. It turned out that he was absolutely correct.

The Gamecocks had an open date between the Alabama game and their home game against 15th ranked Mississippi State. That allowed time for some dramatics off the field.

On Monday preceding the game, news broke that the Carolina football squad had revolted, demanding that their head coach resign. Various interpretations of what happened at a squad meeting that day were aired and written about, and it was hard to select the most accurate one. However, it did indicate that there was unrest in the Carolina camp and that Sparky had a morale problem on his hands at the very best.

Whether it was a meeting of the minds that caused it or the insertion of Taneyhill as starting quarterback or a combination of the two - nobody will ever know - but the result was a turnaround of the Gamecock season.

Taneyhill passed for two touchdowns in a 21-6 upset of Mississippi State, led the Gamecocks in a comeback win at Vanderbilt and had two more touchdown passes when they upset 16th ranked Tennessee, 24-23, in Columbia. Gamecock fans loved Taneyhill, earrings, ponytail and all. The love affair heated up when the Gamecocks fought Florida's SEC runner-ups to a standstill before losing, 14-9.

Taneyhill established himself as a folk hero, when he went into Clemson's Death Valley, led the Gamecocks to a 24-13 win and autographed the Tiger paw in the center of the playing field, following one of his two touchdown passes.

A record of five wins and six losses is not something to celebrate, but after that dismal start, it seemed like a national championship to Gamecock fans. It was something to pin their hopes on. They had survived a season in the SEC and ended a four-game losing streak against Clemson.

THE 1993 SEASON

Another changing of the guard had taken place at Carolina following the 1993 football season. President John Palms had decided to move King Dixon into an administrative position in the president's office, and bring in an athletics director of his choice. Remember, it was Jim Holderman who had given the job to Dixon.

Palms went to California and hired Mike McGee, the athletics director at Southern Cal, and whom Carolina fans remembered as the football coach at Duke during the 1970s. He had been an All-America lineman for the Blue Devils in 1959.

As you may recall, McGee was coach of the Duke team that defeated Carolina on the night that Paul Dietzel announced his resignation. McGee assumed his position on January 1, 1993.

He had to be impressed with the football coach he had inherited, after the opening game at Athens, Georgia. The ending of that game is a part of Gamecock folklore, and the description of it by my counterpart on the Georgia network, Larry Munson, was played many times on Columbia radio stations during the months that followed.

The play that gave the Gamecocks a 23-21 victory came with two seconds left in the fourth quarter. It sounded like something that usually happened to Carolina.

Georgia had taken a 21-17 lead by scoring two touchdowns in the fourth period, setting the stage for a final Carolina drive. Steve Taneyhill engineered the Gamecocks touchdown drive, as the Gamecocks ran out of timeouts and were almost out of time, period. The Gamecocks reached the Georgia two, but the Bulldogs stopped a running play at the one, with fewer than ten seconds showing on the scoreboard.

"Lay down you Dogs!" Munson screamed into his microphone, as Taneyhill rushed to get off a final play. Steve managed to hand the ball to a diving Brandon Bennett, who soared into the end zone at the two-second mark. That finish was as dramatic as any I ever witnessed at Carolina - or anywhere else.

Munson was a good friend of mine, and we usually had lunch together when our teams played each other. Before this game I told Larry that I thought Carolina had a good chance to win, and he gave me sort of a funny look. On his pre-game show, which was heard by a lot of Carolina fans en route to the stadium, Munson said, "Bob Fulton says he thinks Carolina has a chance to win. Can you believe that?"

I've reminded Larry of that a number of times since.

On that last play we had also had our moments in the booth. When Bennett went over the pile, Tommy Suggs announced the touchdown before I had a chance, and you could hear it on the air. Also, our producer, Liz McMillan, didn't realize that she had a microphone in front of her, and she was screeching with joy. They could hear it in ESPN's booth, and they said they could hear a sound like someone strangling a squirrel. I've never heard a squirrel being strangled, but now I know what it sounds like!

Sadly, that wasn't typical of the Gamecock season, which had begun with speculation over Sparky Woods' future at Carolina. The rest of the season would do nothing for Woods' job security.

The Gamecocks won only three more games, beating Vanderbilt and two non-conference opponents, Louisiana Tech and East Carolina.

The Gamecocks blew a fourth-quarter 17-7 lead and lost to Kentucky, 21-17, held a 26-23 lead over Florida in a 37-26 loss, and saw Clemson come back from a 13-3 halftime deficit to win, 16-13.

48

The real downer of the season was a 55-3 loss to Tennessee at Knoxville. Taneyhill completed only six passes for 47 yards in that game, demonstrating the futility of the Carolina effort.

Carolina's record read 4-7 overall and 1-7 in the SEC, giving McGee something to think about for the weeks that followed. Speculation that the AD would probably give Woods another year to turn things around proved to be unfounded. McGee decided that Carolina's football future would be better placed in someone else's hands, and Woods was on his way

THE 1994 SEASON

Since my career at Carolina began in 1952, the school had changed head football coaches on seven occasions, five of the replacements had come to the University with previous experience as a head coach. Neither Warren Giese nor Richard Bell had been in the top job before.

Fans didn't have a clue as to which approach McGee would take, because he was very good at keeping things to himself. The usual leaks "from sources close to the University" had been successfully plugged, so that Mike could talk to prospects with some degree of confidentiality.

McGee decided to go the route of hiring an assistant coach from a topflight program, and what better place to look than Florida State, undefeated and perennial contender for the national championship under Bobby Bowden. Florida State scored points in bushel quantities with its run and shoot offense. Although the old football adage is, "Offense sells tickets, but defense wins games," the Seminole offense seemed to be pretty good at both.

McGee gave the job to Brad Scott, the 39-year-old offensive coordinator of the Seminoles. He was young, personable, hard-working, good at recruiting, and possessor of a good knowledge of the game. How could you miss?

Brad had some unfinished business before leaving Florida State, and that was to help prepare the Seminoles for their national championship game against Nebraska in the Orange Bowl. FSU won that game, 18-17, and Scott headed to Columbia with his championship ring.

Scott brought with him three other members of the Seminole staff, which gave him a good core group to install his system. This prompted Carolina fans to start thinking about a program comparable to that of Florida State, but an important part of a football program is recruiting. To be another Florida State, a team has to have players of Florida State quality. Nobody knows that better than Brad Scott, and he made it clear that recruiting would be his number one challenge.

When Scott took the job in December of 1993, I hadn't made the decision that 1994 would be my last year on the Gamecock networks. But when I arrived at that conclusion in the spring, it established a special connection between me and the Gamecock coach and a contrast with the situation when I came to Carolina.

In 1952 I was a young guy starting out with a football program headed by an aging coach, Rex Enright. Now I was a sports announcer, getting up in years and on the way out, while Scott was the young head coach, on the way in. Nobody wanted Brad to experience instant success more than I did, because this was my last shot, and I wanted it to be a good one.

This was the 17th change in football and basketball coaches that I had witnessed during my 42 years with Carolina, and I had a good relationship with all the coaches. I knew some better than others, depending on their personalities, but I never tried to force myself on them. When they first came to town, I didn't go rushing over and say, "Here I am. I'm your play-by-play man." I let the contact take its natural course, and I hope that they appreciated it.

Brad was one of our more personable coaches to come here, and he developed good relationships with the media

It was brought to my attention that in my 40 years of broadcasting Carolina football games - I spent two years at Georgia Tech - the Gamecocks had won 206, lost 206 and tied 13. Pleasantly, I remember many more of the victories than defeats. However, this season would decide my final record, and Brad would determine whether I went out a winner or a loser! I reminded him of that several times, but little did I know that it would depend on the final game of my football broadcasting career.

One of Scott's first accomplishments at Carolina impressed people. He motivated Steve Taneyhill to get a haircut, and this attracted newspaper and TV cameras from all around. This was symbolic that Scott was "in charge," even when it came to dealing with Carolina's flamboyant quarterback hero. Steve seemed to like this new type of discipline, and he would benefit from it.

Scott unveiled his first Carolina team on the night of September 3, 1994 in Williams-Brice Stadium, and Georgia was the opponent. The game was decided by two plays - both long pass completions by Bulldog quarterback Eric Zeier to receiver Hason Graham. Graham got behind the Gamecock secondary on a 77-yarder in the first period and, again, for a 63-yard TD in the third. That was the difference in a 24-21 Bulldog win.

A win would have been desirable, but the Gamecocks showed potential. They just needed to avoid breakdowns, such as those that occurred on the two long pass plays.

Things looked much brighter when Carolina won its next four games. They defeated Arkansas and Louisiana Tech in Columbia, and then did something that a Carolina team hadn't done since 1973 - win two consecutive weekends on the road. They won over Kentucky at Lexington and defeated LSU at Baton Rouge to give them a 4-1 start.

Then the bubble burst. Carolina's offense rolled up 477 yards of total offense and 42 points, but the defense couldn't stop anything, as East Carolina upset the Gamecocks, 56-42, in Columbia. Taneyhill had completed a record 39 passes in 58 attempts for 451 yards, but the Pirates offset that with 621 yards of total offense.

It bothered me that this was reminiscent of so many years in the past, when Carolina would win some games they were supposed to lose, then turn around and lose games they were supposed to win. Champions win the games they're supposed to win.

The Gamecocks claimed only one victory in their next four games, beating Vanderbilt but losing to Mississippi State, Tennessee and Florida. This sent them to their final game at Clemson with a 5-5 record. My record was now 211-211-13!

Prior to 1994 I don't think I ever gave much thought to retiring. That's something you don't think about when you're enjoying what you're doing. You don't think about such things as growing old, retiring, making out wills, arranging for long term care or purchasing cemetery lots. I felt sorry for people who had a job they probably didn't like, and they couldn't wait till their retirement day arrived. That's pretty good evidence that whatever they were doing all those years they didn't particularly enjoy, and that is a shame.

That was not the case with me. I had loved broadcasting, going into my final year, so it was difficult for me to come face to face with a decision that most people have to make, if they're lucky. Some have no control over that decision, because of health or other circumstances beyond their control. It was my good fortune to have a choice, and I gave it a great deal of thought. It was, without a doubt, the most difficult career decision I've

Bob Fulton "My Career My Life"

ever had to make. Many people in various fields have to make similar decisions. Timing is most important in practically everything we do in this world, and knowing when to stop is a matter of timing.

History is full of stories of people, particularly athletes, who waited too long to retire. They finally move on, and the world remembers them when they were in the valley, rather than on top of the mountain.

I had spent so many years in the business, and I was getting up in years. I also realized that one of the worst things anyone can do is to stay in a job or profession too long. People have a tendency to remember what you did last week or last month, but they forget what you did one, two, five or ten years ago.

So I thought I might at the end of the upcoming basketball season and then broadcast a few baseball games. I later decided to do a few baseball games, but for all intents and purposes my career at Carolina would end with my final basketball broadcast.

Therefore, when football season began, I thought it might be my last season and, if so, hoped that it would be a successful one. It would be my first experience with Brad Scott as head coach, and hopes ran high that he would bring with him his success as offensive coordinator for Florida State's 1993 national championship team. Ironically, at a school that had aspired for so many years to great things in athletics, I had broadcast 425 games and entered my final season dead even, having broadcast 206 victories, 206 defeats and 13 ties. That had included 18 seasons in which Carolina won more games than it lost, 18 losing seasons and five break-evens. That adds up to only 40 years, because I spent two years doing play-by-play for Georgia Tech.

When I started the 1994 season I began counting the games, realizing that when we came to the Clemson game, that one would be my final one as a broadcaster of football. The season went well for me and the Gamecocks. I tried to keep busy and not think too much about it. I had a lot of encouragements and a lot of nice things said to me, personally, publicly and in letters.

My final home broadcast was between Carolina and Tennessee, and the University was very good to me. They featured a full color photograph of me on the cover of the program and had a nice article, written by Tom Price, on the inside. At halftime I was honored on the field with a plaque, and they even had the band spell out F-U-L-T-O-N. I was somewhat disappointed that there was not a microphone down on the field, so that I could respond to the crowd's ovation by telling them how much I appreciated their support.

There are no better fans in the world than followers of the Gamecocks, and they displayed this after the game with their comments and requests for me to autograph programs. Even Tennessee fans asked me to sign programs. The only down side of the day was that Tennessee won the football game, 31-22.

After playing Florida at Gainesville, my football swan song was scheduled at Clemson, where the Gamecocks and Tigers would continue one of the nation's most colorful rivalries.

Early that week I received a phone call from someone in the Clemson athletics department and they said they wanted me to participate in a special ceremony honoring former Clemson football coach Frank Howard at halftime. I told them that I would be more than happy to be a part of that, because I had always liked Coach Howard and got along with him very well, in spite of the rivalry between the two institutions. Jim Phillips, the Clemson broadcaster, was to also participate at halftime.

The night before the game I received a call from Phillips, he invited me to a party at the home of one of the Clemson fans, and my wife, Carol, and I accepted. I began thinking about halftime of the game the next day and wondered, "Is this something I'm going to give someone, or is it something beyond that - for me?"

I asked Jim "Is this really something we're going to do for Coach Howard?"

He answered, "Yes, no doubt about it. I wouldn't lie to you." Then he added, "If you don't mind, wear a coat and tie to the game."

That in itself would be a rare occasion in my half century of broadcasting, because I made a practice of wearing a sport shirt for comfort, more than appearances.

Saturday was a picture-perfect day for football, and the largest crowd - 85,000 - in the history of South Carolina sports took advantage of it. The first half of the game was an exciting one, especially for Carolina fans, as the Gamecocks took a 14-7 lead at the half, thanks to a 14-yard run by Stanley Pritchett with 1:31 remaining.

I had momentarily forgotten about the halftime ceremony and was busy with statistics when someone from the Clemson athletics department came to the booth and said, "Bob, you need to get downstairs in a hurry, because we're going to make the presentation right away."

I walked down the concourse to the north end zone and started down the sideline. Then I saw my wife standing around the 50-yard line, and I didn't have to be a genius to figure out right away that this is something for me! When I got to midfield there was Jim Phillips, Cocky, the Carolina mascot, along with Clemson's Tiger mascot and some people from the Clemson athletics department. I put my arm around Jim and said, "I love you" and he said, "We love you too."

The public address announcer told the crowd that this was my final game at Clemson. Then Phillips presented to me a beautiful framing that included a photograph of me that appeared earlier in the GREENVILLE NEWS and a plaque with words of appreciation for what I had done for sports in the state of South Carolina. I also received a white Clemson football jersey with an orange number 43 for my years of broadcasting in the state.

That was followed by a ride for Carol and me around the stadium in a golf cart. The standing ovation by 85,000 people choked me up as much, or more, than the final basketball game, which I discussed at the first of this chapter.

To think, the vast majority of this crowd is made up of Clemson fans - our arch rivals - and they are doing this for me. It meant so much to Carol and me, and it's one of the moments in my life that I shall cherish forever. Its one thing to be honored by the home team, but this is enemy territory.

At the end of our excursion around the stadium, time for the second half kickoff was nearing, so I had to hurry back to the broadcast booth. While I was waiting for the elevator I heard a tremendous roar in the stadium, but I had no idea what had happened. When I arrived at the booth, Tommy Suggs, the network analyst, was doing the play-by-play, because I didn't make it back in time to start the half. I sat down and took over the play-by-play, with Clemson in possession of the ball. I glanced at the scoreboard, and it didn't look right. Carolina 21, Clemson 7. I couldn't have missed much of the second half action.

I turned to my spotter, Ree Hart, and said, "They've got the wrong score up there."

He said, "No they don't. Carolina scored."

I learned during the next timeout that on the second half kickoff Brandon Bennett started up the right sideline, and then threw a lateral to Reggie Richardson on the other side of the field. This caught the Tigers by surprise, and Richardson made it all the way to the Clemson six-yard line before tripping over a teammate. Bennett scored on the next play.

Bob Fulton "My Career My Life"

It came down to the final regular season football game of my career to say that I had experienced about everything in sports. And it had to be missing one of the most exciting plays in the history of this storied rivalry. But I wouldn't have traded the halftime experience to have seen it!

Even after the game, which Carolina won, 33-7, we were engulfed by fans, Carolina and Clemson, outside the stadium. We signed just about anything you could write on, from programs to ticket stubs to caps. A lot of pictures were taken, and this went on for about an hour. But I didn't mind it at all. It was the culmination of a great day in all respects.

As it turned out, the Clemson game was not my final football broadcast, because the victory by the Gamecocks earned them a bid to play West Virginia in the Carquest Bowl in Joe Robbie Stadium at Miami on New Year's Day. During the season I had kidded with Brad Scott about making it possible for me to go out as a winner. The win over Clemson had brought my career won-lost record at USC to 212 wins, 211 losses and 13 ties.

Therefore, against West Virginia in the Carquest Bowl, my winning mark would be in jeopardy. In fact, the Mountaineers were favored by the oddsmakers, and that would finish my career at break-even, right where I had started the season. This would definitely be my last football broadcast.

I didn't have a lot of time to think about the Carquest Bowl. New Year's Day fell on a Monday, and I had to broadcast the Carolina-Providence basketball game in Columbia the preceding Saturday afternoon. I couldn't leave for Miami at the same time as the large following of Gamecock fans and officials. Instead, I flew down Saturday night in a private plane piloted by Joe Byers.

When I arrived at Fort Lauderdale, there was a Christmas-like atmosphere around the hotel where the Gamecocks were staying. I was there in time to participate in some of the media hype on television and radio, and they made a big deal out of the fact that Carolina had never won a bowl game in eight previous tries.

The Gamecocks made certain that I would go out a winner by defeating West Virginia, 24-21, in a very exciting game, one of the best bowl games of the season. The celebration by Carolina fans was worthy of a national championship. The monkey was finally off our back.

I received a personal bonus, because CBS, which televised the game, sent a camera to our radio booth and put a minute or two of my broadcast on national television.

My daughter, Robin, in California had the TV on, but was in another room. She said that, all of a sudden she heard my voice, and it scared her. Robin dashed to the TV set in time to see my segment on CBS.

There wasn't much time for me to either celebrate the historic bowl win or to lament the end of my football broadcasting career. On Tuesday morning I flew to Oxford, Mississippi, where Carolina's basketball team played Mississippi that night. The game was featured on the SEC television network, and my friend Larry Conley the former Kentucky great, was one of the announcers. The TV people were nice enough to pick up a segment of my broadcast and, thanks to Larry; they did this on several other occasions during my last basketball season. That season seemed to be the fastest I ever experienced. Probably because I just didn't want it to end.

However, on March 4 the final game in Carolina Coliseum arrived, as the Gamecocks faced Tennessee. Unlike the surprise ceremony at the Carolina-Clemson football game, a plan to honor me at halftime of the game was announced in advance. The lights were turned off, as Carol and I were escorted to the center of the court by Athletics Director Mike McGee.

As we walked out, a spotlight made its way to the Coliseum rafters and settled on a basketball jersey hanging among those of Gamecock "retired jerseys." It had my name on it and under that, "The Voice." It was special in two respects. First, it was hanging next to the one honoring my friend Frank McGuire. And, too, it was the first time anyone other than a player or coach had been so honored. I received a framed replica of the jersey to keep among my mementoes.

It's a great honor to be "hanging" in the rafters with Grady Wallace, John Roche, Kevin Joyce, Alex English, Sheila Foster, Martha Parker, B.J. Mackie, and Coach McGuire.

Before I knew it I was at the countdown in Atlanta and at the end of my career as a football and basketball broadcaster for Carolina. Although I was getting somewhat depressed earlier and feeling that perhaps I should be staying on, I realized I had made the right choice.

Whether I liked it or not, this would be it.

I wanted it to be a good game for Carolina, but Auburn didn't allow that to happen.

THE FINAL GAME

How many countdowns had I heard during my 53 years of broadcasting sports? It's always the fans of the winning team counting off the final seconds of victory.

Ten, nine, eight, seven. This time it was the Auburn cheerleaders leading the count, concluding the Tigers' 81-66 victory over South Carolina in the first round of the Southeastern Conference basketball tournament in Atlanta's Georgia Dome on March 9, 1995. Mentally, I was counting with them. Six, five, four. Only to me it was the end of a 53-year journey that was shared with millions of others - fans, players, coaches, media associates, administrators, and, most emphatically, my family.

Finally, three, two, one. And the cheers of victorious fans resounded throughout the arena. Perhaps I should have stood up and cheered, too, because this was supposed to be more than the end of just another basketball game. It would mark the beginning of what I had been working for 53 years to achieve. A chance to relax, travel, pursues hobbies; spend time with family and friends. Now I could do things because I WANT to, not because I HAVE to.

It would have been better, had it been Carolina fans counting down to victory in my final broadcast. The only way that could have happened would have been for the Gamecocks to win the NCAA championship. Otherwise they would have to go out in defeat, and a Carolina win over Auburn would only have delayed the inevitable. So my broadcasting career came to an end with a loss for a team with which I had been associated for 43 years.

Of some consolation was the fact that, in my final broadcast in Carolina Coliseum, the Gamecocks had defeated Tennessee, 66-50. It would have been nice to bow out after that game, but the life of a broadcaster is dictated by schedules, and you don't stop short of the finish line.

One of my favorite quotes is a statement that George Brett made about ending his career. Brett was an all-star third baseman for the Kansas City Royals and three-time American league batting champion. He was a class act in every respect. When a reporter asked Brett what he wanted to do in his final at-bat before retiring, he gave this response: "I want to hit a routine grounder to second and run all out to first base, then get thrown out by a half step. I want to leave an example to the young guys that that's how you play the game - all out."

What a great attitude! Giving it everything he had on an infield out would be more important than circling the bases after hitting the ball over the fence. My final game was definitely not a home run, but I did have the satisfaction of knowing that I was just as prepared and trying just as hard in this final "time at bat" as I was in my first experience as a play-by-play announcer.

By building a sizeable lead and removing any doubt about the outcome of the game, Auburn allowed thoughts to creep into my mind. During the last ten minutes I began to think back over my career - particularly as a basketball broadcaster. Even though I loved doing football and baseball, basketball was what I enjoyed doing the most.

I had played and coached basketball, and that drew me closer to the game, which is more personal than football, because you can see the players up close. You can see their faces, the strain in their efforts and the emotions they feel - you become a part of the game.

I started thinking back over all the games I had done, and when the game was over I was feeling very uptight, yet letdown at the same time. As the seconds ticked off the clock, I was saying to myself, "This is it. You won't be doing any more basketball games. You've been doing them for 53 years, but you won't be doing any more."

The game ended and in a few moments, announcers and a camera crew from Jefferson Productions came over to my broadcast position. They were televising the SEC tournament and producing a feature on me to be shown at halftime of the championship game. They had taped a portion of the feature during our final home game in Columbia, but this was to be the wrap-up.

As the interview with me was set to begin, I looked up and saw Roy Kramer, Commissioner of the Southeastern Conference, approaching the table. This is a man who has done a magnificent job for the number one sports conference in America and for whom I have the greatest respect. As the camera rolled, Roy grabbed me by the arm and said, "Bob, I want to thank you on behalf of the Southeastern Conference for all the wonderful things you have done, not only for your school but for the conference as a whole."

I'll never forget that. In the comic strip, BLONDIE, Dagwood's boss, Mister Dithers, often said, "I hate to see a grown man cry." Well, so do I, especially when I am that grown man! But Roy Kramer's comments triggered tears, and I really had a hard time talking - something that had been earning me a living for 53 years. I had not wanted it to wind up this way, but it did. I broke down and had a very tough time saying anything, and all this time the camera was on me, and I knew this would be shown later.

I finally got a hold on myself, but even until the end of the broadcast and interview with Carolina Coach Eddie Fogler I was struggling. I have seen a tape of this and it was obvious that all was not well with me. At my worst moment Casey Manning, the analyst on Carolina basketball broadcasts, took over while people in the vicinity of the broadcast gathered around and made me feel much better.

In the final moments of that broadcast I had thought of so many things that hadn't crossed my mind in years. The first game I broadcast was in Little Rock, featuring the University of Arkansas playing the Phillips 66 team of the AAU. Of course, the 43 years of basketball at Carolina and especially the 16 years I spent with Coach Frank McGuire.

Many of the highlights of my basketball broadcasts through the years came back to me. Things I had not thought about for a long time. It was like a 53-year highlights film that flashed by in a matter of minutes. Thankfully, they were good memories. You tend to forget the bitter and remember the sweet.

I recall watching the telecast of the 1996 NCAA playoffs and seeing Coach Pete Carril's Princeton team eliminated by Mississippi State in Carril's final game as a coach.

As the camera followed him back to the dressing room you could see that he was crying, although he was noted for being a tough-as-nails coach. He hadn't been in the game as long as I had, so if he could cry, I didn't feel so bad about shedding a few tears when my career came to an end.

Actually the countdown on my career was more than those seconds ticking off the clock at the end of the Carolina-Auburn game. It had started months earlier in what seemed like an eternity in some respects, yet a very short run in others. The University, other colleges, the South Carolina community, friends and fans made this a special and exciting year for me.

Bob Fulton "My Career My Life"

~VOICE OF THE GAMECOCKS~
(BASKETBALL)

Basketball was not a big sport in South Carolina in 1952. Carolina's approach to the game was similar to that of many other schools in that era.

Frank Johnson was coach of the Gamecocks, a position he had held since 1940, with the exception of three years during World War II. Frank was also the freshman football coach until 1951, when he was relieved of those duties to become business manager for the athletics department.

Johnson was allowed a limited number of scholarships, but the Gamecocks were not in a position to compete with the blossoming basketball powers around the country. They did the best they could with what they had, and they competed very well with schools that placed the same type of emphasis on basketball. For instance, right after returning to Carolina after the war, Johnson's Gamecocks ran up a nine-game winning streak against Clemson, which placed even less emphasis on the sport.

Few of Carolina's games were broadcast before I came here, and the situation was not one to encourage stations to air the games. There was not that much interest in basketball, experienced play-by-play announcers were scarce, sponsors were hard to come by and the facilities were poor.

In my first basketball season here, 1952-53, I did some games for WNOK, and I also had to find sponsors. It was not an easy sell.

When they built the old Carolina field house in the late 1920s, they didn't have radio or television coverage in mind. My first broadcast was done from the top of the field house, where we roped off a few seats to create a radio booth. We could have shared a box of popcorn with fans!

I don't remember how many games I broadcast that first season, but I don't think any of them were away from home. It was a losing season, 11-13, for the Gamecocks, and they didn't qualify for the Southern Conference Championship tournament at Raleigh. There were so many schools in the conference that only the ones with the eight best records in conference games qualified for the event.

It was almost a foregone conclusion that Everett Case's North Carolina State team would win the tournament and qualify as the league's only representative in the small NCAA championship field. That was before Frank McGuire went to North Carolina.

My first season with Carolina was also the last year with the Southern Conference, because the Atlantic Coast Conference was formed in 1953, with Carolina becoming a charter member.

My most exciting broadcast in the 1952-53 season was when Furman came to town with Frank Selvy, who was national scoring champion that season and the next. Furman had routed the Gamecocks earlier.

Selvy got his points, but the Gamecocks played well as a team to offset his one-man show and won the game, 74-72. At the end, Jack "Spider" Neeley was the unlikely Carolina hero, controlling the ball, while Furman was desperately trying to gain possession and overcome Carolina's shaky lead.

During the next 42 years I would follow the Gamecocks through three conference affiliations and as independents. I would also see basketball emerge to challenge football in spectator interest.

EARLY YEARS IN THE ATLANTIC COAST CONFERENCE

The new conference set-up inspired a little more interest in basketball, but Carolina was still lagging behind North Carolina's "Big Four" of State, Duke, North Carolina and Wake Forest. Thanks to Clemson, the Gamecocks were able to register two ACC victories in their first year.

I did broadcast my first ACC tournament. I set up a small network in South Carolina, and I believe I also did Clemson's game in the tournament.

With the new conference set-up, North Carolina had hired Frank McGuire, who had taken his St. John's team to the NCAA championship game in 1952. This was done to make the Tar Heels competitive with Case's Wolfpack, but it also stirred up interest at other schools in the conference.

Carolina played Wake Forest, a team that had beaten them by 33 points less than two weeks before, but the Gamecocks played an inspired game. They lost to the Deacons, 58-57, in overtime but could hold their heads high by being competitive with a team that went to the finals, losing to State by two points.

It was obvious that the ACC was making a move to become one of the nation's strongest basketball tournaments, and that suited me just fine. As I said before, I really enjoyed broadcasting basketball more than any other sport, and this was right down my alley. It began to force the hands of all the conference teams to improve their basketball programs or be a have-not in a sport that was enjoying increased popularity.

The 1954-55 season wasn't a great improvement over the previous season. Carolina's only two conference wins were, again, over Clemson, and we were again eliminated in the first round of the tournament. As McGuire recalled after he came to South Carolina, his North Carolina teams always considered the Gamecocks to be "white meat," and so did the other Big Four schools.

The 1955-56 season was a little better for Carolina in the conference, where they had three wins and a "scare." They won their customary two games from Clemson and added a one-point win over Virginia. The "scare" came when they held McGuire's team, featuring Lennie Rosenbluth, to a 75-73 win in Columbia.

If you look in a modern day Carolina basketball media guide, you'll see that the record section says that the Gamecocks' first three teams in the ACC reached the tournament quarterfinals. In other words they got to the first round!

Although the 9-14 record didn't indicate it, there was a ray of hope on this Carolina team. Grady Wallace, who had led the nation's junior college scorers at Pikeville, Kentucky, had joined the team, along with his coach, Walt Hambrick, and teammate Bobby McCoy. Wallace was a wiry 6-4 forward with a great jump shot and unusual rebounding ability for a player his size. In his first season he set a new Carolina scoring record, with an average of 23.9 points per game. The flat projectory of his shots was in complete contrast to the arching shots that Frank Selvy used in setting national records at Furman.

So, after broadcasting four straight losing seasons for the Gamecocks, I would have some excitement to describe in the 1956-57 season. First of all, the Gamecocks beat somebody in the ACC besides Clemson and Virginia. They added Big Four members: State, Duke and Wake Forest to their list of victims, and had a chance to beat North Carolina, which won the national championship that season.

McGuire brought his Tar Heels into the Carolina field house and was fortunate to escape with a 90-86 overtime victory. That was typical of the Tar Heels' season.

Wallace was having a season that would gain him a place on the United Press All-America first team and the national scoring title. He wound up with 31.3 points per game. Grady is gone now and missed by all of us.

The Gamecocks finished strong by beating Duke in the first round of the ACC tournament and disposing of Maryland in the second round, matching them with North Carolina in the championship game. The Tar Heels won it, 95-75, but Carolina had gained a measure of respect in the conference.

This also perked—up interest in basketball in the Palmetto State, and selling sponsorships of basketball games was becoming easier than it had been in the past. With the increased interest came talk of building a new arena for basketball at Carolina, but for years to come, the University would graduate basketball players who came with the "promise" that they would be playing in the proposed coliseum.

Although the athletics director, Rex Enright, was a football coach at Carolina, he had coached basketball at Georgia and loved the game. He supported it as much as the department's limited funds would allow, but that was not enough to compete with the growing budgets at rival ACC schools.

END OF THE JOHNSON ERA

The 1957-58 season would prove to be the last for Johnson as coach, because he became the full-time business manager following that year. The only good news coming out of the season was that they again beat Clemson twice and handed Duke one of the three ACC losses it suffered that year. Carolina won only five of 24 games, and things would get worse before they would get better.

Walt Hambrick, who had served as Johnson's assistant for two seasons, moved up to the head coaching job, while Enright pondered the future of the basketball program and who would be the best person to direct it. Hambrick recruited a fine player of the future in Art Whisnant, but freshmen were not eligible to play on varsities, so that didn't help Walt in his one-year stand as head coach.

The Gamecocks finished 4-20, but that included a satisfying win at Clemson. However, the memorable game of that year ended in a loss. Against a State team that eventually won the ACC championship, Carolina almost pulled a miracle win in the first round of the tournament. With only five seconds left in the game, Carolina had a three point lead and possession of the ball at State's end of the court. All they had to do is get the ball in bounds, even if it was to the Wolfpack, get out of the way and win the game.

Instead, the Gamecocks threw a rainbow pass to the top of the key, and a Wolfpack player intercepted it. That would have been all right, but the player took a shot, made it and was fouled by a Gamecock on the shot. It's hard to figure what a player is thinking about when he does something like that. I guess the answer is, "He isn't."

Of course, there's that sports adage that says, "Good teams find a way to win, and poor teams find a way to lose." In terms of finding a way to lose, the Gamecocks had displayed a touch of genius in that tournament.

Anyhow, State won it in overtime, that was the season, and it was the end of Hambrick's stint as head coach. After that he devoted full time to his duties in the school's physical education department. He subsequently became head coach at Coastal Carolina, a regional campus of the University of South Carolina at Conway. Hambrick passed away several years ago.

BOB STEVENS – CONSTANT MOTION

For his next basketball coach, Enright went to East Lansing, Michigan, and hired Bob Stevens, an assistant coach in Michigan State's successful program under Forrest Anderson. The Spartans had won two Big Ten championships in the preceding three years, and Enright was hoping that Stevens could use the same system to revitalize the Gamecocks.

Stevens brought with him a "constant motion" offense that moved the ball quickly up the court and counted on getting off shots before the opposing team could get its defense in place. There was no shot clock in college basketball then, but if there had been, a Stevens's team would never have gotten close to violating it.

A prime example was a game with Miami at Miami. The Gamecocks scored 106 points and lost by one. And this was an era when scores seldom got above sixty or seventy points.

On defense Stevens was immovably devoted to the man-to-man, regardless of game situations. He never used a zone.

Wake Forest had a center named Len Chappell, and although he was not the seven-footer that is so common today, he was a great athlete and had a huge body that occupied a lot of space under the basket. Our smaller and less gifted players would try to defend him, and he had a field day against them. He played against Carolina six times, and in those games the Deacons scored over a hundred points twice and in the nineties twice. Stevens' teams had more trouble with Wake Forest than any other team in the conference. Len Chappell's son John later became a member of the Gamecock's team under Coach Odom.

Stevens' 10-16 overall record and 6-8 in the ACC looked great in comparison with what the Gamecocks had been experiencing in their earlier seasons in the league. Under his guidance, the Gamecocks accomplished something Gamecock fans had considered impossible. For a number of years Carolina and Clemson played two nights of games against North Carolina and North Carolina State in the Charlotte Coliseum. The two South Carolina teams would play the two North Carolina teams, and the Tar Heel State teams usually won.

But the 1959 event belonged to Carolina. On Friday night they beat State, 68-66, and upset McGuire's Tar Heels, 85-81, on Saturday night. In fact it gave Carolina a sweep of its two-games against the Wolfpack, a team they had beaten only once since the ACC was created.

Carolina also won a rare holiday tournament championship, defeating Richmond and Lafayette in the Richmond Invitational at Richmond, Virginia.

Stevens was likeable, enthusiastic and hard working, and this played well at the University. He had a master's degree from Michigan State, and this gave him academic credibility.

He also had a practice of playing loud music in the locker room before a game, and had his players beating on the lockers and generally raising a ruckus. This was supposed to get them fired up for the game. I could hear them all the way up to where I was doing my broadcast.

60

The 1960-61 season wasn't quite so kind to Stevens, although his team did win the Gulf South Classic at Shreveport, Louisiana by beating Louisiana Tech, Centenary and Mississippi.

Carolina's crowning achievement of the year was defeating North Carolina, 89-82, in Columbia. This was a Tar Heel team that featured marquee players such as Larry Brown, Doug Moe and York Larese. Donnie Walsh, who would be prominent in South Carolina a few years later, was also on that team.

The Gamecocks finished 9-17 overall and 2-12 in the ACC, beating Maryland, as well as North Carolina. They did defeat State, which had beaten them earlier in the season by 27 points, in the ACC tournament first round. Duke eliminated the Gamecocks the following night.

The sports writers who selected the ACC coach of the year must have considered it a great accomplishment to have a winning season at the University of South Carolina and break even in conference games. Stevens accomplished that in 1961-62 and received the honor over Bones McKinney, whose Wake Forest team won the ACC championship and had a ranking of seventh in the final UPI poll.

Stevens' teams seemed to play well in the Charlotte Coliseum. The Gamecocks always had a large following there, because it was a fun weekend for them - sort of a mini-tournament. It was also a big money game for Carolina and Clemson, because neither could sell many tickets for home games, even if somebody wanted them.

The 1962 games at Charlotte saw the Gamecocks battle a strong State team down to the final seconds, only to lose by one point, 76-75. The following night they avenged an earlier loss to Frank McGuire's North Carolina team at Chapel Hill, by defeating the Tar Heels, 97-82. That score is correct, 97-82.

Later the Gamecocks again beat McGuire's team, 57-55, in the first round of the ACC tournament, and that gave Stevens a record of four wins against three losses in his coaching match-up with the future Gamecock coach.

In this final year for Stevens, he also won both games against Clemson to even his record against the Tigers at three wins and three losses.

Stevens' 15-12 record impressed the University of Oklahoma as much as it did the ACC sports writers, because the Sooners made him an offer, and he accepted. This ended the "Stevens era" at Carolina, and the search was on for a new basketball coach. Incidentally, Bob Stevens coached at Oklahoma for five years and never had a winning season.

CHUCK NOE AND THE MONGOOSE

When Rex Enright was looking for a basketball coach, prior to hiring Bob Stevens, one of the more aggressive candidates was Chuck Noe, who held the top job at Virginia Tech and was doing very well. Although Noe had head coaching experience, Enright passed him over and chose Stevens, whose only experience was as an assistant.

When Stevens left, it was after Enright's death and Giese's departure from the athletics directorship, which was now held by Marvin Bass. Bass had coached in Virginia and knew Chuck, who had also been a head coach at Virginia Military Institute. Noe applied for the Carolina job again and was successful.

The Carolina basketball media guide led off the write-up on Noe with, "The University of South Carolina's mascot is a Gamecock, and Chuck Noe looks and acts like a fighting rooster."

You could say a lot of things about Chuck Noe, but the word "dull" would never be included. Chuck had a great basketball mind, but he was unorthodox. He didn't go strictly "by the book," because he could have written his own.

His career at Carolina lasted a season and a half, which tells you something right there. But it was one heck of a season-and-a-half to broadcast. By this time there was enough interest in basketball that we were traveling with the team to do games on the road. And what trips!

I remember a trip to Atlanta, where we played Georgia Tech. Tech had a great center named Rick Yunkus, and our center was a junior college transfer, Jim Fox.

When we got to our hotel, Noe called Fox over and said, "Jim, did you see that open air market we passed on the way in? Well, I want you to go down there and buy some garlic. Right before the game I want you to eat as much of it as you can stand. Then when the game starts, I want you to get right in Yunkus' face and breathe in it!" The entire Carolina team just fell on the floor laughing.

Jim obeyed his coach and breathed on Yunkus as hard as he could, but he needed more than garlic, because Tech won the game by 14 points.

ATLANTA JOURNAL sports editor Furman Bisher described the arrival of the Carolina basketball team as the "traveling circus," and Noe was in center ring.

Noe liked to get the students involved in the home games as much as possible, and every coach likes that home floor advantage. I think Chuck carried it to the extreme, and I'll give you a good example.

In January of 1963 Carolina played Duke in Columbia, and I believe Duke was ranked second in the polls at that time. I do know that they didn't lose a regular-season ACC team that year and won the conference championship.

If you ever attended a game in the Carolina Field House, you remember how noisy it could get in there, even with a small crowd. Often I couldn't hear my own voice in there, and it's loud enough.

On this night, Noe had positioned the band directly behind the Duke bench, putting it in a position to drown out anything that was said there. Bubas caught on to this in a hurry, so when a timeout was called, he took his players to the middle of the playing floor and had them huddle as close around him as possible, so that they could hear what he was saying.

He escaped from the band, but the Carolina cheerleaders were very mobile, and they took full advantage of it. They would race out on the floor and do a war dance around the Duke players, as they tried to concentrate on what Bubas was telling them.

Bubas must have made his points, because the Blue Devils won the game, 88-70. I was so embarrassed for the University that I wrote a letter of apology to Bubas. The home crowd should support their team, but it should be done within the bounds of good sportsmanship.

Chuck couldn't stand to lose, although he should have gotten accustomed to it at Carolina. I remember a game we lost by just a few points at Maryland in 1963, and Chuck was really upset about it.

Ronnie Collins, who was a fine player and was from Winnsboro, was on that team and having a good year. However, Noe didn't like the way he played defense in this particular game and got on Ronnie about it, after the game. Then he really blew up and hollered, "You're not traveling with this ball club. You're not going to travel with us until you learn to play defense!"

He left Ronnie up there, and he had to borrow money to get back to Columbia.

Collins was an all-around great athlete and was being recruited for his talents as a quarterback in football, as well as his basketball ability. In fact, there was some speculation as to which of Carolina's coaches would get him - basketball coach Bob Stevens or football coach Marvin Bass.

One of the best basketball officials I've known was Charlie Eckman, who did a lot of games in the ACC and other places in the East. I got to know Charlie pretty well, and we often talked when he was assigned to one of our games.

After officiating one of our games, Charlie came to me and said, "I want to talk to you." He then told me, "Bob, I honestly believe that your ball club is 'on' something."

I knew at the time the players were taking what they called "uppers" that were supplied by a doctor.

Charlie said, "I looked at some of those ballplayers during the game, and they looked right through me. I know that something is wrong."

I said, "Charlie, you're right, but just don't say anything about it."

Eventually the story came out, and it wasn't long before Chuck Noe was gone as head coach.

Based strictly on coaching, Noe was a good one. He used what was called the "mongoose" offense. Chuck had gotten it from Babe McCarthy, who was coaching at Mississippi State and had a good record of upsetting teams that had much better talent than his.

Bob Stevens had not left behind an abundance of talent, so Chuck felt he needed to compensate with strategy. The mongoose offense depended on quickness and patience that would result in a "back door" basket. It neutralized the "big man," both on offense and defense. As an example, Jim Fox, who was 6'9", and led the Gamecocks in scoring when he was a senior in Frank McGuire's first year, wasn't among the top five scorers for Carolina under Noe in 1963-64.

More often, 6'1" guard Jimmy Collins was playing in the middle, and he averaged 16.2 points per game that year.

The mongoose had its moments, but it couldn't make the Gamecocks consistent winners, and they finished 1962-63 with an overall record of 9-15, including 4-10 in the ACC. They did manage a double-overtime win over State in the North-South doubleheader at Charlotte, along with two wins over Virginia and one over Clemson.

Noe's teams broke even in their first 12 games of 1963-64, and three of those wins were over ACC teams Virginia, Maryland and State. However, during a gap in the schedule for the school's exam break, January 12 to January 25, the University zeroed in on Noe's health and personal problems and decided it was time for a change, even in mid season.

They gave the job of "acting head coach" to Dwane Morrison, who had been a star forward for Carolina in 1951 and 1952. Dwane had joined Noe's staff after a successful career as a high school coach in Anderson, South Carolina.

Jimmy Collins, who later managed four radio stations in Columbia, told me that, after Chuck Noe left, the players were no longer on pep pills, and nobody could get off the floor after that. He recalled going over to play Georgia in old Woodruff Hall at Athens, and they were soundly thrashed (112-90), because they no longer had the quickness or ability to get off the floor that they had earlier in the season.

Morrison did his best to steady the ship and even registered ACC victories over Clemson, State, Maryland and Virginia. However, he had the handicap of being involved in a program that was going nowhere fast.

He was hoping that he would be allowed to remain as head coach, but circumstances would not allow that to happen. Morrison remained in coaching, however, coached at Mercer in Macon, Georgia and was later named head coach at Georgia Tech.

Noe went back to Virginia and had a successful career as a salesman for a company that sold school jewelry. Chuck is gone now and I miss him. He was a very interesting person.

After having the same head coach, Frank Johnson, for 16 years, Carolina was now looking for its fourth head man within the next six years.

THE FRANK MCGUIRE ERA

As if he didn't have enough problems trying to revive the Carolina football program, Marvin Bass now had the additional responsibility of looking for a new basketball coach. He would receive some unexpected help.

Because of a chance meeting with Columbia businessman Jeff Hunt in Asheville, North Carolina, Frank McGuire became an interested prospect for the job. McGuire had left North Carolina to become head coach of the Philadelphia Warriors.

After McGuire had been there one year, losing to the Boston Celtics in the NBA championship playoffs, the Warriors were moved to San Francisco. McGuire was an incurable Easterner and wasn't about to transplant himself to the Golden Gates. So he opted to get out of coaching to ponder his next permanent move.

After McGuire responded positively to Hunt about his interest in coming to Columbia, the Carolina president, Dr. Tom Jones, and board of trustees became involved. The end result was that McGuire met with a committee in Barnwell, South Carolina, home of the chairman of the committee on athletics, Sol Blatt, Jr. There they had a meeting of the minds, and McGuire accepted the job.

When McGuire was leaving the meeting, he was reminded by Blatt that they hadn't discussed salary. McGuire told him, "Just pay me whatever Marvin is getting, build me a 20,000-seat coliseum, and I'll fill it up for you."

It was hard for Carolina fans to believe it. The Gamecocks had been struggling throughout their sports history, and now they had two coaches who had won national championships! Paul Dietzel, in football, at LSU, and Frank McGuire, in basketball, at North Carolina.

It seemed that fate had gone out of its way to steer McGuire toward Carolina. What if the Warriors had not moved to San Francisco? And what if Jeff Hunt hadn't gone to Asheville that day? Think about it.

McGuire's first task in Columbia was to convince Carolina fans that he could accomplish here what he had accomplished at North Carolina. He divided his time between making speeches to any group that wanted him and searching around New York City for his first recruiting class. He had built the program at North Carolina by way of what was described as his "underground railroad." That analogy referred to the smuggling of slaves out of the South during pre-Civil War days, and that was called the "underground railroad."

Among his first recruits were Skip Harlicka, Jack Thompson, Frank Standard and Skip Kickey, all of whom would play prominent roles in future Gamecock teams. Freshmen couldn't play varsity basketball at that time, so it would be another year before McGuire could benefit from this infusion of new talent. That freshman team won 15 of 17 games, scoring over 100 points three times and in the nineties in nine other games.

During McGuire's first season here, 1964-65, I remember going to Due West to broadcast the game against Erskine in their small gym that seated just a few hundred people. The Carolina bench consisted of some folding chairs that were placed against a brick wall.

I thought to myself, "Here's a guy who won a national championship. It really seems out of character for him to be in this tiny gym."

Red Myers was coaching that Erskine team, and they were leading Carolina in the first half. Frank was so mad that he almost broke up the dressing room at halftime. It must have made an impression on the players, because they came back to win the game, 59-57, in overtime.

I doubt that McGuire had ever heard of Erskine, and here he had a team that came within an eyelash of losing to them. He must have been thinking, "What have I gotten myself into?"

McGuire's first game as Carolina coach was at home against Erskine, and it was a comfortable win, but in his second game he faced his former assistant, Dean Smith, who had been promoted to head coach at North Carolina upon McGuire's recommendation.

One of McGuire's great recruits for the Tar Heels, Billy Cunningham, was in his senior year, and he just killed the Gamecocks in that game, which North Carolina won by 11 points. That was the first game of what became a great coaching rivalry, although McGuire and Smith remained close friends when they weren't facing each other on the basketball court. Then it was all-out war!

Carolina didn't have the players to compete with the better teams in the ACC that year, but they did manage a couple of wins over Wake Forest and Virginia. Of all the ACC teams, Wake Forest is the one that McGuire seemed to have the most success in beating. His teams won the final 11 games they played against the Deacons, who have been one of the better teams in the league throughout the years.

In the first game of the ACC tournament, Carolina faced a Duke team that had beaten them by 39 points in the early season at Durham. But the Gamecocks almost pulled the upset of the year over the top-seeded Blue Devils. Near the end of the game, Carolina had a chance to go ahead, but Duke got the ball and scored to win the game, 62-60.

After that game McGuire was terribly upset with the officials, particularly Phil Fox, who made a call against Carolina near the end, when the Gamecocks had a chance to win the game.

So McGuire had to accept a record of six wins and 17 losses in his first year at Carolina, but patient Carolina fans were already looking forward to McGuire's recruiting to click in.

When Frank came here, coaches didn't have all the perks that drive their incomes into the upper brackets. Coaches here didn't even have their own television shows.

Frank wanted to do a show, more to stimulate interest in basketball than to provide extra income. He and I became good friends right from the start, and I wanted to help him in any way that I could. So I got together with WNOK-TV (now WLTX) and made an arrangement with the station for me to host a show with McGuire and allow the station a couple of commercials to sell. I would go out and get sponsors for the other commercial positions, and that money would go to McGuire.

It wasn't big bucks, but it got the job done, until McGuire could become established and make his show a saleable commodity for a television station.

With Harlicka, Standard, Thompson and Al Salvadori, a Chuck Noe recruit, eligible to play varsity ball, McGuire was much better equipped to deal with the opposition. One of the biggest Gamecock victories ever occurred in the third game of that 1965-66 season.

Duke's Blue Devils, coached by Vic Bubas and ranked number one in the nation, came into Carolina Field House, and fans filled every splintery seat, and then some. The Gamecocks shocked the Blue Devils, 73-71, to serve notice to the ACC that "McGuire is back!"

That was not good news, particularly to North Carolina's Big Four, who thought they had seen the last of this adversary when he left North Carolina. It also set heated-up a Duke-South Carolina rivalry that would develop into all-out war away from the court.

Carolina's prize freshman this year was Mike Grosso, a prep All-American from New Jersey that every school in the country, including Duke, wanted in the worst sought of way. When he ended up at South Carolina without benefit of a scholarship, eyebrows were raised, especially by Duke's athletics director, Eddie Cameron.

The eligibility of Grosso was challenged, because he didn't qualify academically for a scholarship, and it was felt that his tuition and board were being paid from an illegal source. That source turned out to be a cocktail lounge owned by Grosso's uncle. The ACC ultimately ruled that this was in violation of NCAA rules and declared the freshman ineligible to play at South Carolina. Mike ended up at the University of Louisville, where he completed his collegiate career.

Relationships between McGuire and Duke became so intense that the conference ruled that the two schools didn't have to play each other in basketball the next season. And they didn't, during the regular season. McGuire considered the loss of Grosso to his program was such a blow that I don't think he ever got over it, and I think it was always in the back of his mind when his team played Duke.

McGuire's record improved to 11-13 overall in his second season, and I believe he thought that his program was headed in the right direction, despite the loss of Grosso. He was still on the recruiting trail, which usually led to New York.

His major recruit of that year was Bobby Cremins, although Bobby was not a highly sought-after player. I happened to be with Frank the first time he saw Bobby.

I had gone with McGuire and John Terry, who worked with me on the broadcasts, because his son, Tommy, was playing for Bullis Prep School in Maryland. Corky Carnevale, the son of Frank's friend, Ben Carnevale, was on the same team with Tommy.

They were playing another prep school, and a player on that team seemed to be all over the floor, diving after balls and showing that he was an intense competitor. After the game we talked about it and agreed that we liked what we saw in this young man. McGuire offered him a scholarship, and any Carolina fan knows the rest of that story.

66

The big thing that was happening to the Carolina basketball program that year was a plan to build the long-awaited coliseum. This is what McGuire needed to attract the blue chip players and to bring in more fans and the resulting revenue to support the program.

McGuire was helping Clemson, too, because when the General Assembly appropriated four million dollars to help support construction of the coliseum at Carolina, they also had to appropriate an equal amount for Clemson to build a new arena. It's hard to believe, but Clemson's field house was worse than Carolina's. Frank Howard, the athletics director, and other school officials actually sat on a stage at one end of the basketball court.

Although he didn't have Grosso, McGuire's squad did get a boost for the 1966-67 season, because Gary Gregor, a 6-7 forward who was a Chuck Noe recruit, had regained the eligibility he had lost at mid-semester of the previous year. He would be a force for the Gamecocks the next two seasons and go on to a successful career in the NBA, playing for five different teams.

Of course, Carolina wasn't playing Duke this year, so they had only a 12-game conference schedule. Two games from that season bring back special memories for me.

The first one took place early in the season, when we were playing in the Milwaukee Classic, one of the many holiday tournaments. This matched Frank with one of his former players, Al McGuire, for the first time. The game was a battle, not only of players but of opposing coaches, because both were well schooled in working the officials.

Before the game Frank told me, "I'm going to get some technicals tonight, because we have Big Ten officials, and they aren't going to help us."

Sure enough, as the game rocked along - and it was close all the way - Frank protested a call enough to get a technical called. Then later in the game he drew another, and then another.

At that, Al McGuire got into the act, screaming at one official, "Stop calling technicals on him. Can't you see what he's doing? He's trying to turn this game around." Frank just frowned in the direction of Al and straightened his tie in the customary manner.

As time was running out, Carolina took a two-point lead, but Marquette had the ball and a chance to send the game into overtime with a basket. The first shot at the goal missed, but the Marquette center leaped over everybody and tipped it in, as the crowd roared. The roar didn't last long, because an official ran toward the scorer's table, as he gave the signal that the basket didn't count. Offensive goal tending was the call, and the Gamecocks won the game, 63-61.

It was a correct call, but I seriously doubt that it would have gone that way, had it not been for McGuire getting those technicals called. Frank was one of the best I've ever seen in working the officials, and sometimes it worked.

Carolina lost the championship game to Wisconsin the next night, but we soon found out how unimportant basketball games really are. I got a call from my wife, Dody, and she told me that Frank's wife, Pat, had been diagnosed with cancer.

The Carolina players were heading to their homes for Christmas, mostly to New York, so Frank and I were traveling separately. We rented a car and drove from Milwaukee to Midway Airport at Chicago, about 80 miles away, in the snow. We had to wait about four hours to catch a flight to Atlanta, where we took the plane to Columbia. Pat met us at the Columbia Airport and told us that she had learned about her cancer by overhearing doctors and nurses talking in the next room to hers at the hospital.

Pat was a great lady and a real strength behind Frank. She was, for all practical purposes, his manager, because she handled all of the family's personal business. That's the way Frank wanted it, because he didn't care about money matters and such things. All he wanted to do was coach basketball.

Pat lost her battle with cancer in September of 1967, so that left Frank with two daughters and a son, along with his second love, outside of his family, basketball. For a long time after that, Frank had a lot of trouble sleeping when we were on road trips, and that was out of character for him.

Quite often Frank and I would stay in the same room, and I remember waking up one night, and he scared me to death, because he was just sitting there in a chair right beside my bed. He eventually reached a point where he could sleep normally.

A late season victory over North Carolina has to rank as the most satisfying victory of 1966-67, because it was his first in his fledgling coaching rivalry with Dean Smith. The Gamecocks defeated the ultimate ACC champions, 70-57, and with a following win over State, finished the ACC season at 8-4, well enough for third place.

The Gamecocks edged Maryland, 57-54, in the first round of the ACC tournament, which had been moved to the Greensboro Coliseum, and that matched them against Duke in the semi-finals. This was a grudge match, if there ever was one, but Duke prevailed in a fiercely contested game, 69-66.

However, with a 16-7 record and a temporary ranking in the polls, McGuire had his program on track. When the ACC sports writers handed out their post-season honors, it might have been indicative of some holdover animosity from McGuire's days at North Carolina. Maybe not, but Frank didn't even figure in the coach of the year voting, which was bestowed on Dean Smith, with Bobby Roberts of Clemson finishing second.

It could have had something to do with the Mike Grosso controversy and the bad blood between McGuire and Duke.

During the spring he would get commitments from several outstanding high school players, including John Roche, Tom Owens, John Ribock and Billy Walsh, who would make-up Carolina's 1967-68 freshman team. Getting Roche and Owens, who attended the same high school in New York, to sign was like a double victory for McGuire. His chief rival for these two stars was Duke.

The varsity still had Harlicka, Thompson, Gregor and Standard, and they were the core of one of my favorite Carolina teams. They played hard-nosed basketball, asked no quarter and were definitely over-achievers in a league that was rapidly being recognized as one of the top basketball conferences in the country. It was also fun traveling with them.

One of our early trips that year was to the Kentucky Invitational at Lexington, and Adolph Rupp was the Kentucky coach at that time. He was one of the most successful coaches in the history of college basketball and, even in his twilight years, was still producing great teams.

When I was just starting out as a young sports announcer, I broadcast a game at Little Rock between Kentucky and Arkansas. Before the game I went to Rupp and asked him for his starting lineup. In the first place, I was sort of nervous about approaching this coaching legend.

He didn't help matters any by growling at me, "Have you got their lineup?"

I said, "No sir." So he barks back, "Well, you go get their lineup and come back here, and I'll give you mine."

I was trembling - just a kid - and he really put me down. Needless to say, after that, I was never a Rupp fan.

McGuire considered himself on the level with Rupp as a coach, and he was. I don't believe the two ever coached against each other while Frank was at North Carolina, but they had been on opposite benches several times when McGuire was at St. John's. This was a rivalry of image, as well as a confrontation between two great coaches.

Before I tell you a story about something that took place at the Kentucky Invitational, let me illustrate how important punctuality was to McGuire. One of the first meetings I had with Frank when he came to Carolina took place at his office in the old field house. He said for me to come at ten o'clock, and I agreed.

Something came up that delayed me a few minutes, but I didn't call Frank, because it wasn't going to hold me up that long - maybe ten minutes. When I drove up the field house, Frank was out waiting for me.

He said, "I thought that you had gotten lost, or something. I said ten o'clock, and here it is ten after ten."

I learned something right there, with this guy, you had better be there when you say you will. He did this, not only to train people to be on time, but I felt that he considered someone being late was a put-down to him. You should consider him more important than to be late. His players learned this in a hurry.

Back to the Kentucky Invitational, Carolina upset a very good Cincinnati team in the first game, and this matched them with Rupp's Kentucky team in the finals. McGuire had called a team meeting in the hotel the afternoon of the finals to discuss strategy for the game with Kentucky.

When the meeting started, there was one player missing, but a few minutes later that player, Frank Standard, slipped through a door in the back of the room and took a seat, as if he had been there all along. That action didn't escape McGuire's attention. He glared at Standard and said, "Where have you been?"

Standard didn't hesitate, replying, "I got held up in the lobby, because I was arguing with a Kentucky fan over who was the greatest coach, you or Adolph Rupp!"

McGuire tried to hide a smile and didn't have a comeback for Standard, so he simply continued the meeting.

Kentucky won the championship game, but Carolina made it close all the way, before losing by nine points.

There were other times that Standard challenged McGuire's more serious moments. The Carolina coach had a policy of never revealing what defense the team would use for a game until it was almost time for the opening tip-off. Sometimes the team would be on the court, ready to be introduced, before Frank would gather them around to announce his defensive strategy.

Once in an afternoon meeting prior to a game, McGuire was discussing the opposition, then suddenly turned to Standard and asked, "Frank, what defense would you use for this game?"

Standard pulled himself up, almost as if to mock his coach's manner, and said, "I'm sorry, but I don't reveal my defense until right before the game!"

This 1967-68 team turned up the temperature on basketball fever at Carolina and set the stage for the excitement that would follow. There were two games that really made the season.

One took place on February 24 at Durham, when Carolina completed a sweep of its games with Duke, which Gamecock fans now considered public enemy number one. To beat the Blue Devils twice in their return to our schedule was especially satisfying.

However, the big one came four nights later at Chapel Hill. The last time the Gamecocks had beaten the Tar Heels at Chapel Hill was back in 1952, when Frank Johnson was South Carolina's head coach, and right before the McGuire era at North Carolina.

Dean Smith had one of his great Tar Heel teams - one that finished the season among the nation's top four teams. But the night of February 28 belonged to the Gamecocks.

In one of the most exciting games I've ever seen, South Carolina won, 87-86, but the real thrill was watching Bobby Cremins, who was just a sophomore, come through under pressure at the end of the game. Bobby was not a good free throw shooter, so the Tar Heels fouled him, as they tried to overcome the Gamecocks' narrow lead.

Cremins made seven out of nine foul shots to hold off the Tar Heels, and the Gamecocks won 87-86. I couldn't help but think back to that night a couple of years before, when McGuire, Terry and I had seen this youngster laid it on the line in a prep game.

On our post-game show, we said how nice it would be for the fans to show their appreciation for the big victory by meeting the team when they arrived back at the Columbia Airport. When we were coming in to land, we could see this huge crowd on the landing field, and they had to move them away from the runway, so that we could land. They estimated the crowd at around 10,000.

Eight days later the Tar Heels gained revenge by edging the Gamecocks, 82-79, in the semi-finals of the ACC tournament, which was played in Charlotte for the first time. Even that didn't take the shine off of the victory at Chapel Hill, because that goes down as one of the most satisfying games I ever had the privilege of broadcasting.

It's worth mentioning that Eddie Fogler was a sophomore on that North Carolina team. I wish I had bet someone a million dollars that he would some day become the head coach at the University of South Carolina. I imagine I would have had a lot of takers.

Carolina's 15-7 record and those big wins in North Carolina began to make believers out of the sports writers, who placed McGuire third in the coach of the year voting.

This season brought another first for Carolina basketball, when Harlicka was the first round pick of the St. Louis Hawks, who would soon become the Atlanta Hawks.

GETTING TECHNICAL(S)

In June of 1996, when I read that Dave Cowens had been named coach of the Charlotte Hornets, it recalled a crazy game that Carolina played at Tallahassee, Florida, in 1969. Cowens played for Florida State, which, at that time, had no conference affiliation and was considered by some as an "outlaw school." That meant that their requirements for athletes to enroll and play varsity sports were below those required at the more closely regulated institutions. They weren't criminals or anything like that.

Why we were playing Florida State, I don't know. I believe that this was the first time the two schools had met in basketball, and the only time, until Carolina became a member of the Metro Conference.

I guess Frank wondered why we were playing there, too, because he told me before the game, "We're gonna get a real jobbing from these officials." The officials made a prophet out of McGuire.

The game was close, because Carolina had a fine team. Roche, Owens and Ribock were in their first varsity year, and the Gamecocks had won eight of ten games before going to Tallahassee. The game resembled a wrestling match at times, and Florida State, particularly Cowens, was very physical.

At one point in the second half, Cremins was just standing there, and Cowens ran over him - just leveled him. The official called blocking on Cremins. Moments later Ribock got stood on his head, and the foul was called on Ribock. That was all McGuire could stand.

Frank started telling one of the officials, in language that wasn't suitable for broadcasting, what he thought of the calls. The official started calling technical fouls, but that didn't slow Frank down one bit. When the official called a seventh technical, Frank decided that this was enough, so he gathered his squad and left for the locker room, with several minutes remaining in the game.

The players couldn't believe what was happening, but they weren't about to argue with their coach. You couldn't get away with doing that today, but this was another day - and this was Frank McGuire.

After that game, McGuire told Ribock, "I think you're going to be the kind of player I want, from now on, because you found out tonight that this is a game of contact. You've got to get rough. Up until then Ribock hadn't used his strength, but he did from that moment on and became Carolina's "enforcer."

This was the year that Carolina Coliseum was finished, and every Carolina fan remembers John Roche's last-second shot that won the first game over Auburn, 51-49. That field goal and the one Owens scored to beat North Carolina in the ACC championship two years later are probably the two most famous baskets in Carolina's basketball history.

However, if I had to pick Roche's two best performances - and there were many - they would be two games from his sophomore season.

One took place early in the season in the Quaker City Classic in Philadelphia. The Gamecocks defeated Rhode Island and St. Joseph's of Pennsylvania to reach the championship game against the host team, LaSalle. LaSalle doesn't sound like much in 1996, but in 1969 they finished the season ranked number two in the nation with a 23-1 record.

That one loss was to Carolina in that game, which Roche controlled. He scored 26 points, but his floor game was outstanding, offensively and defensively. This was the game that convinced me that he was something special. John was the easy choice as MVP of that prestigious tournament.

The other game that confirmed Roche's greatness as a player came in the North-South doubleheader in the Charlotte Coliseum. McGuire renewed his coaching rivalry with Dean Smith, but the coaches took a back seat. North Carolina had a super star in Charlie Scott, one of the vanguard black players in the ACC. Scott, a junior, led this Tar Heel to a ranking of fourth in the final polls.

Scott had the assignment of guarding Roche, one on one, and that was more than most players in the country could handle. Roche had a habit of dribbling around, catching a defender leaning the wrong way, and driving toward the basket for a short shot or layup, or an over the shoulder pass to a wide open Owens.

John scored 38 points, over half our total, in a 68-66 Gamecock victory, and Scott went to the bench toward the end in total frustration. It was one of those games in which I would like to have stopped broadcasting and just watched.

That game established the Gamecocks in the polls, and they remained there until the final one, in which they were in 13th place. That was another first for Carolina basketball, as was an invitation to play in the National Invitation Tournament in New York's Madison Square Garden. That was in a time when they didn't have 32 teams starting out on courts all over the country and dwindling down to just four that will play in the Garden. It was prestige to play in the NIT then. Now they talk about it like it's the booby prize, compared to the NCAA playoffs.

Apparently the ACC was at peace with the Gamecocks, at least for awhile. The sports writers voted McGuire the conference coach of the year, and Roche, player of the year.

Carolina had arrived on the national scene, with a bunch of skinny players that looked as if they could not have withstood a strong wind. Wilt Chamberlain, the former Kansas All-American who set a scoring average that still stands, while playing for McGuire in his one season as coach of the Philadelphia Warriors, bumped into his former coach. He had seen a Carolina game, prompting him to ask McGuire, "Frank, don't you ever feed these guys?"

Weight programs and special diets were not common in college basketball, which depended more on quickness and finesse than on the physical strength that is so important in the game today. Owens, who led the ACC in rebounding for three straight years, was 6-11 but weighed only 205 pounds. Tom would need about 30 more to pull his weight under the basket today.

The next season, 1969-70, the Gamecocks did add a little bulk, as Tom Riker, a prep All-American, came off a fine year with the Carolina freshman team. He was a natural center at 6-10 and 225 pounds. Riker could mix it up under the basket with the best of them, and he wouldn't have backed off from King Kong.

The addition of Riker and two other high-profile sophomores, Rick Aydlett and Bobby Carver, with the talent already on hand, inspired pre-season magazines. They concluded that Carolina was the best bet to end UCLA's string of three NCAA championships, so, to break the monotony, most of the publications listed the Gamecocks at number one. UCLA's John Wooden would show the futility of that, as the Trojans added another title at the end of the season.

This was one great Carolina team, the best in the school's history, and I felt that doing the play-by-play for this team put me right up there at the top, also. I now had huge audiences tuned into the games, and people would even plan parties around listening to some of the out-of-town broadcasts. It really put me on the spot, because I knew there were thousands of people out there hanging on every word I said. A great problem to have!

At one point in the season this Carolina team had a 17-game winning streak that was ended by Davidson, coached by Lefty Driesell, who would later enter the Gamecocks list of coaches they would most like to beat. Ironically, the only two games Carolina lost were at home.

The Davidson game was played in the Coliseum, as was a 55-54 loss to Tennessee, when a last-second Roche shot bounced off the rim.

After Carolina won all 14 of their regular season conference games, anticipation of a showdown with UCLA heightened. All they had to do is win the ACC tournament and the Eastern Regional, which was to be played in Carolina Coliseum.

As it turned out, Roche injured his ankle in an easy semi-final victory in the ACC tournament, and played, but shouldn't have, in the finals. State won in overtime by stealing a pass for a winning basket. Even if the Gamecocks had won the game - and they should have - they would not have been the same team without Roche. He was on crutches for a couple of weeks.

The Gamecocks felt that State committed a foul on the intercepted pass that won the game, and McGuire was very unhappy over it. After the game, Frank and his friend Jack LaRocca from New York, went from room to room in the hotel, looking for the official who made the call, so they could tell him what they thought about it. They never found him.

The next day we had Frank's Sunday TV show to do, and I really didn't know whether Frank would show up, because he was so upset. About an hour before the show, he and Jack came by the station, and Frank said that he didn't want to do the live show. They were on their way to Florida. I talked Frank into doing it, but I was really scared that he might say something about the official. However, Frank held his temper, kept his composure and didn't say anything that he shouldn't have.

Going through the ACC schedule without a loss and being ranked sixth in the final polls wasn't good enough for the sports writers, who voted State's Norm Sloan coach of the year. Roche did receive player of the year honors for the second straight year over North Carolina's Scott. Scott, a senior, felt that his race might have had something to do with the vote, but I don't think that entered the thinking of anybody who participated.

I think the conference had outgrown any such prejudice. The following year a black player, Charlie Davis of Wake Forest, received the honor over Roche.

One of the oddities of the 1969-70 season was that Carolina defeated Clemson three times, the only time that has happened in that rivalry. It wasn't easy, because Bobby Roberts had his Tiger team holding the ball much of the game, and the Gamecocks were fortunate to escape with a 34-33 win in the ACC tournament.

THE WAITING ENDS

Carolina ended the waiting for an Atlantic Coast Conference championship with the most dramatic play in the school's - and possibly the ACC's - history. Certainly one of the few most dramatic moments I ever faced as a broadcaster.

Here it was the championship of the 1971 ACC tournament in Greensboro, and North Carolina held a one-point lead over the Gamecocks with just six seconds on the clock. Timeout had been called, while both teams contemplated a jump ball between 6-3 Kevin Joyce of the Gamecocks and 6-10 Lee Dedmon of the Tar Heels. That was back when jump balls were really jump balls, rather than the alternating possessions of today. If that rule had been in effect then, with our luck, it might have been the Tar Heels' possession.

If you didn't already know what happened on that jump ball, you wouldn't be interested enough to be reading this book! Joyce out jumped Dedmon and tipped the ball to Owens, who laid it in the basket for a 52-51 victory.

Carolina's championship was a big blow to the rest of the ACC, who couldn't stand the thought of the despised Gamecocks walking away with the trophy. I understand that even the ACC television network, which televised the game, cut away from the game almost as soon as the buzzer sounded. No interviews, no post-game analysis, as they traditionally do. It could have been just a coincidence.

We had stayed in a hotel in Winston-Salem, which is not far from Greensboro, and when we returned there, a porter had hastily decorated our room. In the room were Frank, John Terry, Homer Fesperman, and I. Frank said, "I don't want anybody else in here. This is our crew, and we've been through everything together."

While we were having our private celebration, people kept coming and knocking on the door, but Frank would say, "Don't answer it." The players were having their celebration in another location.

The first round of the Eastern Regional was played at Raleigh, and Carolina lost to third-ranked Pennsylvania. Although the game was played in "ACC country," you would have thought that Pennsylvania was the home team, because the fans from other conference schools were pulling against the Gamecocks. That was the end of what has become known as the "Roche-Owens era." Roche was named to the first team All-America, and the Gamecocks again finished sixth in the polls.

This Carolina team had to go through a lot during the season, and it was a poor commentary on the fans around the ACC. The players were cussed, spit on and thrown at, but they seemed to thrive on it most of the time. It bound them together, like it is "us against the world."

In comparison, I think the Carolina fans behaved very well when other conference teams came to play here. The fact that Carolina won all of its home games might have had something to do with it.

One of Frank McGuire's strongest traits was loyalty. If you were his friend, he would go to any lengths for you. If you weren't, stay out of his way.

I was the subject of a demonstration of that loyalty during the 1970-71 season when we went to play Maryland at College Park. An earlier game in Columbia, won easily by Carolina, had included an ugly incident, in which some of the players traded blows, and Lefty Driesell, the Maryland coach, claimed that Ribock had punched him in the mouth. In the heat of the moment, he said something like, "McGuire had better not bring his team to College Park."

When the Gamecocks did play there, a lot of security people followed them around, like they were the President of the United States, and, if I'm not mistaken, McGuire wore a bullet-proof vest. At one time there was talk about canceling the game, but they decided to go ahead with it. Outside of the usual student antics, like this guy beating on a drum, emulating the death knell before the game, there was nothing out of the way.

The rematch at Maryland received a lot of publicity, so WIS-TV, a Columbia station, got permission to televise the game, and then called Paul Dietzel, who was at a meeting in California, and received his okay to use their own announcer. When McGuire heard that they were planning to use one of the WIS-TV announcers, he said he wanted me to do the telecast, as well as the radio.

He was told that the athletics director had already approved their plan to use their own. McGuire then contacted Dietzel and said that if Bob Fulton doesn't telecast the game, his team wasn't going on the floor. McGuire made his point, and that's the way it was. I don't think WIS-TV realized that it would make any difference to McGuire when they planned to use their own announcer. But Frank always tried to do what he thought was best for his friends.

This was the game in which Maryland held the ball much of the game and won it in overtime by a score of 31-30. The halftime score had been 4-3 in favor of the Terps.

This was a bitter loss for McGuire. He usually left a game on the floor, but he took this one with him. Frank sat up all night in the room next to mine, and I could hear him moving around.

A TEAM WITHOUT A CONFERENCE

In the spring, Carolina announced that it was pulling out of the Atlantic Coast Conference and becoming an "independent." McGuire didn't play a role in this decision and never expressed himself publicly about it while it was in the works.

Many people assumed that Frank was all for it, because of the stormy relationship that existed between him and other ACC schools and officials. I don't know what Frank was thinking, but I do know that confrontations didn't bother him, because he was such a fierce competitor. He loved to be, what they now call "in your face!"

Being an independent was a much bigger problem in basketball than it was in football, notably because none of the ACC schools, except Clemson, would play Carolina from that point on. That situation existed until 1990, when North Carolina was matched against South Carolina in the Tournament of Champions at Charlotte. The Gamecocks still aren't on the schedules of the other teams in the conference.

Fortunately, Frank had enough non-ACC friends around the country to put together a respectable schedule. Auburn, California, Boston College, Pittsburgh, Villanova, Marquette, Notre Dame, Virginia Tech, Houston and St. Bonaventure were among prominent basketball schools on the schedule.

We played Pittsburgh two days before Christmas of 1971 and won the game. But the real thrill came on the trip home. The team split-up to go to their homes for Christmas, so there were only a few coming back on the commercial flight to Columbia.

We were cruising along at about 40,000 feet over Charlottesville, Virginia, and Joe Petty, who was in the next seat to me, and I was half asleep. We heard this big noise - the engine blew up, and there was smoke and fire coming out of it.

We looked across the aisle, and there was McGuire, crossing himself! Petty, who was working with me on the broadcasts that year, was white as a sheet.

Joe turned to me and said, "I can just see the headlines now: 'MCGUIRE AND 98 OTHERS GO DOWN IN PLANE CRASH.'"

I said, "This is a helluva time to be thinking about your publicity!"

The airliner managed to make it to Charlotte on one engine, and we changed planes and made it to Columbia without further incident.

Frank's son-in-law met us at the airport, and, of course, he knew nothing about our crisis over Charlottesville. But, what an appropriate Christmas present he gave me. A Christopher Medal, for good luck in travel!

Earlier we had played in the Cable Car Classic, which was played at Santa Clara College, which was near San Francisco. A large group of Carolina fans made the trip out there, and it was a fun time. The tournament was not the big event that the name would indicate, because it was played in a relatively small arena and didn't draw very well.

They actually had a bar set-up behind the stands, and that was the first time I had ever seen that at a college game. I also remember that the public address announcer kept referring to Carolina as Southern California.

The Gamecocks won the tournament by beating Santa Clara and the University of California, and those were two of the seven straight wins for the Gamecocks at the first of the season.

We also had a good trip to Las Vegas that season, as Carolina won over UNLV, but it was an even better trip for Rick Aydlett. Rick walked up to a slot machine at our motel, inserted 50 cents and immediately hit the $500 jackpot. After that you couldn't keep the Carolina players away from the casino.

We also had a big following of fans at Las Vegas, they had a big time, too, and were probably thinking, "Maybe this thing of being an independent isn't so bad after all." Las Vegas was much more exciting than Charlottesville, Raleigh or Durham.

By now what became known as "The Bubbly Group" had been formed. It was a number of avid followers of the basketball team, who would pay their way to distant out of town games, enabling the Gamecocks to charter, rather than take a less convenient commercial route. It's your guess as to why they were called "The Bubbly Group!"

McGuire managed to keep the Carolina players focused on their purpose for the trips, while the followers attended to theirs.

Although Roche, Owens and Ribock were gone, this 1971-72 team had plenty of firepower. Joyce, Riker, Aydlett, Carver and seven-foot Danny Traylor were back from the ACC championship squad, and they were joined by Brian Winters, who had been one of the nation's most sought-after prep stars.

Winters was recruited while the Gamecocks were still members of the ACC, but McGuire would find that his job of attracting topnotch prospects would become much harder, now that the school was in no-man's land.

I thought that Carolina's most impressive performance that year was against Digger Phelps' Notre Dame team in Carolina Coliseum. The Gamecocks hit over 70 percent of their field goal attempts in beating the Fighting Irish, 109-83, for their 20th win of the season. Anytime you can beat Notre Dame by 26 points in anything, you can put that down as an accomplishment of great proportions.

This Gamecock team actually won more games, 24, than the ACC championship team, again receiving a bid to the NCAA playoffs. The NCAA field had been expanded to 32 teams, eight in each of four regionals, but it was still something special to receive a bid. More special than it is in today's 64-team field, which includes champions of conferences that are pretty weak but still have votes at NCAA meetings.

Carolina faced Temple in their first NCAA test at Williamsburg, Virginia, and that was one heck of a ball game. Temple led by as many as ten points in the second half, but Riker and Joyce took over and led a Gamecock rally that had them in the lead with two minutes left. Temple tied the game at 51-all, but the Gamecocks had the ball and a chance at a final game-winning shot.

The ball was in the right hands, because Joyce dribbled around until time was down to just a few seconds, moved to the top of the key and, with two Temple defenders coming at him, lofted a jump shot that hit nothing but net.

Although they lost to North Carolina in the next round, the Gamecocks' 24-5 record was still good enough to earn them a ranking of 5th in the final polls. There used to be a consolation game played prior to the finals of the regionals, and Carolina was able to end its year on a winning note by downing Villanova, 90-78.

One thing that put a damper on the season was what happened when the Gamecocks played at Clemson. A few thoughtless students were very much out of order in what they said and did around the Gamecock bench during the game. They tied a rope around McGuire's seat and would pull it away, when he tried to sit down.

They were unmerciful in the way they treated Casey Manning, Carolina's first black player and who was analyst with me on the broadcasts at the end of my career with the Gamecocks. It got so bad that McGuire told Casey, "If you want to go up into the stands after them, I'll go with you." When we got into the car after the game, Frank said to me, "I will never play Clemson at Clemson again."

That led to a breaking-off of the basketball series between Carolina and Clemson, and it wasn't resumed until the 1977-78 season. Clemson's coach, Tates Locke, was very apologetic about what happened, and I'm sure that he was very upset about the way that his fans had acted. But the damage had been done, and the last of the ACC teams had disappeared from Carolina's schedule.

Fear that attendance at games in Carolina Coliseum might suffer because of the absence of ACC rivals was unfounded. In this first year as an independent, the Gamecocks attracted an average of 12,327 to their home games, not far below the record 12,523 during the final season with Roche and Owens.

On the road, the Gamecocks played before the largest crowd to see them play. They played in Chicago Stadium, and there were 18,462 spectators at the game. The opponent was, of all teams, Northern Illinois, and Carolina won the game, 83-72.

The most important thing that was derived from this season was that the Gamecock basketball program could survive outside the Atlantic Coast Conference.

THE FUTURE PROFESSIONALS

The NCAA voted to allow freshmen to play on varsity teams, beginning with the 1972-73 season, and that had a great impact on the Carolina season. Alex English, Mike Dunleavy, Bob Mathias and Mark Greiner, all freshmen, would become prominent players for McGuire in his efforts to keep his program at a national level. English started his first game as a freshman and was in the lineup for every game for the remainder of his four-year college career. Dunleavy didn't start that first game, but he was a starter through his senior season.

In Joyce and Winters, Carolina had what I consider one of the best - if not THE BEST - guard combination in Gamecock history. Looking at what they did later supports that. Joyce was named to the 1972 Olympics team prior to the season and had a great start in his professional career with Indiana, before a severe knee injury ended his playing career.

Winters was a star for the Milwaukee Bucks for eight of his nine pro years, during which he averaged 16.2 points per game. In 1995 he was named head coach of the Vancouver Grizzlies of the NBA.

Both Joyce and Winters were complete players, scoring, passing and playing defense. They both averaged better than 20 points a game in their senior seasons, although McGuire always emphasized balanced scoring, rather than a one-man show. In this 1972-73 season, for example, all five of Carolina's starters had double-figure scoring averages.

If you had to settle on a marquee game for Joyce, it would have been his performance against an unbeaten Indiana team, coached by Bobby Knight, in Carolina Coliseum. Indiana dominated the first half, leading by ten points at the intermission, and Joyce didn't score his first basket until there was 7:39 remaining in the half. Indiana had a 16-point lead, when something seemed to explode in Joyce. By halftime he had brought his point total to 16, and the Gamecocks were back in the game.

Joyce scored nine field goals in the second half, mostly on outside jump shots, and his basket with less than two minutes to play gave Carolina its first lead of the game. Two free throws by Winters made the final score, Carolina 88, Indiana 85. Joyce's 41 points against a team that emphasized defense was a great achievement. I would have to say that it was not only the most impressive game I saw Joyce play, and there were a lot of them, but it was one of the greatest games by an individual I had the pleasure of describing during my broadcasting career.

You don't want to be corny, but you really are challenged to do justice to a performance like that.

After that game, Bobby Knight, almost as famous for his temper as for his coaching, was still so steamed-up when he arrived at the airport in Indianapolis, he slammed the glass door so hard that he shattered it.

This was Joyce's senior season, and Winters was a junior, and Brian was handicapped by mononucleosis early in the season, but he still made a good contribution to the team. Winters would have his best chance to display his abilities in the season that followed.

If the three-point goal had been in effect when Kevin and Brian played, there is no telling how many points they would have scored. They both had tremendous range, and many of their shots came from the area where the three-point arc is now located.

Dunleavy and English were complete opposites, insofar as backgrounds were concerned. Dunleavy was a white New Yorker, while English was a black Southerner, having grown up in Columbia. On the court they were a perfect fit, Dunleavy handling the ball and directing the team, while English was the inside man. The teams on which they played won 81 games, while losing only 30.

Although English and Dunleavy were good college players, few people saw them as prospects for the NBA. English didn't have the body for it - he was 6-8 and 194 pounds. Dunleavy was a well-rounded guard, but not the shooter that Joyce and Winters were, nor the ball-handler of a John Roche.

English and Dunleavy proved how wrong the experts can be, because English became one of the NBA's all-time top scorers, while Dunleavy was a mainstay in the pros for 11 years and became a head coach of the Los Angeles Lakers and the Milwaukee Bucks.

Now, think of this. How many college teams through this country's basketball history have had four players who enjoyed that type of success in the pro ranks? One perennial all-star, two head coaches and the fourth, Joyce, who undoubtedly would have become a marquee player, had it not been for his career-ending injury.

Only four jersey numbers in Carolina's basketball history have been retired. Joyce's number 43 and English's number 22 are among them. Those two jerseys hang from the Carolina Coliseum rafters, along with those of Grady Wallace, number 42, and John Roche, number 11.

It wasn't until the 1973-74 season that Winters really had a chance to show his ability. He was just fitting in as a sophomore, had the health problem his junior year, and was playing second fiddle to Joyce during both of those seasons

Winters was the best pure shooter that played for Carolina during my broadcast years. He was especially good at playing the ball off the glass - the way you see so many NBA stars do it today - even from outside. He was also one of the best in taking the ball out of bounds after an opponent's goal and throwing a court-length pass to a teammate breaking for the basket.

Winters was the hero of one of the great games played in Carolina Coliseum. It was on a cold January afternoon that Carolina played host to Al McGuire's Marquette team in a televised game. The lead see-sawed throughout the game, and with only 29 seconds remaining, the score was tied, and Marquette was in possession, working for a final shot. Remember, there was no shot clock.

Mark Greiner, one of those rare players who earned his place on the court strictly for his defensive play, saved the day for Carolina by drawing an offensive foul - a charge - and the Gamecocks got their chance.

Winters took over, with seconds ticking off the clock, worked his way to the top of the key, floated into the air and released one of the prettiest shots I ever saw. The clock showed two seconds remaining when Winters' shot went through the basket, and the Gamecocks had won a 60-58 thriller. And this was a Marquette team that would be ranked third in the nation at the end of the season.

As I recall, the only Carolina games that McGuire missed during his 16 seasons were in 1974. He suffered a bleeding ulcer, had to be hospitalized, and he was missing from the Carolina bench for five games. Donnie Walsh took charge of the team for those five games and was a successful substitute for Frank, because the Gamecocks won all five of them.

Walsh guided the team in home victories over Niagara, Canisius and 19th-ranked Dayton, along with road wins at Villanova and Georgia Tech.

McGuire returned for the game between the 16th-ranked Gamecocks and Notre Dame, ranked at number three. It was a deeply saddened coach who entered the Coliseum for this encounter, because his mentor and lifelong friend, Buck Freeman, died on February 14, just two days prior to the game.

Carolina made a run in the game's final minutes, but the Irish held on for a 72-68 victory.

This was also a rather emotional time for me, too. This was my tenth season with Frank, and I had never been involved with a head coach in any sport for that many years. Buck was with him through those years, also, and I grew to love Buck, as would anyone who came to know him.

You stay in the business as long as I did, and you have to see a lot of people you like and respect pass along - coaches and players. The two head coaches when I came to Columbia - Enright and Johnson - are gone. So is McGuire.

It's nice to go back in your memories and relive some of those moments from the past.

Anyhow, McGuire returned to the bench for the remainder of the 1973-74 season, and Carolina scored another victory that year over 14th-ranked Pittsburgh in Columbia. Three of the four defeats they suffered during the season were to teams ranked in the nations' top 20 at the end of the season - Indiana, Alabama and Notre Dame. However,

McGuire accomplished his sixth straight 20-win year at Carolina, a school that had never had a 20-win season before he arrived.

The Gamecocks also received their fourth straight NCAA playoffs bid, being matched with Furman in the old Palestra in Philadelphia. For two schools located 100 miles apart, it seemed to be a long trip to play each other. The trip home was longer for Carolina, as Furman pulled a 75-65 upset.

Before that game with Furman, we were staying in the Cherry Hill Inn over in New Jersey. Everyone was having a big party and acting more like tourists than a basketball team with a mission. Nobody was focusing on the game, because they thought that it would be an easy win for Carolina.

The Palestra was not a good place to play - an old arena with bad lighting. That didn't seem to bother Furman, because they were up for the game and led throughout. I remember the Furman coach, Joe Williams, jumping around in his purple suit. It was a great win for Furman and a disastrous loss for the Gamecocks, who had once again finished among the nation's top 20 teams.

This was the season that Bobby Cremins joined McGuire's staff as a full-time assistant, filling a vacancy left by the retirement of Freeman. Buck remained as a consultant, but he was much too old to withstand the increasing demands on college basketball staff. That reminded me once more of seeing Bobby in that prep school game in Maryland back in the sixties, and now I was wondering if he could be the one to take over when Frank decided to call it quits.

After that prep game, Bobby came over to meet McGuire and was so excited that he committed a cardinal sin. He walked up, shook his hand and said, "Jeez, Frank, I've heard so much about you in New York, and I thought that I'd never get to meet 'cha!" The sin was not calling McGuire "coach." Donnie Walsh took Bobby aside and reminded him of that, and he should never call McGuire by his first name again.

During McGuire's final season, 1979-80, when his retirement had been announced in advance, Bobby used to call me about wanting the job here - said he'd work for practically nothing. I went to see Jim Carlen about it, but he said that they were too far along with Duke's Bill Foster, whom they ended up hiring.

The University also wanted to close out the relationship with McGuire, because of the situation between him and Jim Holderman, so Bobby never had a chance. If it hadn't been Foster, it would have been someone else. Certainly not Cremins. Bobby, after great success as head coach at Georgia Tech, is now the head coach at the College of Charleston, where he really has turned their program around. It is no surprise that all the fans love him.

RECRUITING BECOMES A PROBLEM

By the mid-1970s the character of college basketball had changed, presenting new approaches and new challenges to those in charge.

First, the integration of teams in the Southeast had spread out the recruiting field. You could no longer go into New York City, sign a couple of stars each year and keep the program at a high level. You had to beat the bushes in towns, large and small, in the Carolinas, as well as in the Northeast.

There was also an attraction for playing in high profile conferences that had great basketball reputations, such as the ACC was enjoying. And McGuire had been one of the prime architects of that reputation, but he was now on the outside and unable to reap the benefits.

I'm sure that McGuire was just as good a coach in 1975 as he had been in 1965, but he could no longer attract the numbers of players he had in the past. He would get a blue-chipper here and there, but not in the numbers that were needed to compete with the basketball elites.

I remember that he was right down to the wire in recruiting such great players as David Thompson, who went to North Carolina State, and Mike Gminski, the all-everything for Duke. I believe that South Carolina was in the "final two" in recruiting them, but runner-up accounts for nothing in the game of recruiting.

Mostly because of McGuire, high school basketball was improving in South Carolina, and the proximity to some of them helped McGuire. After Casey Manning became the first black player at Carolina, he was followed by three Columbia products, English, Nate Davis and Golie Augustus. All of them had fine careers under McGuire, but most of the topflight basketball talent was going to the major conferences, with their championships, television networks and inside track to the NCAA playoffs.

A fifth black athlete who played for Carolina was an interesting case. He was Tommy Boswell, who transferred to Carolina from South Carolina State in 1973, the same year that the State coach, Ben Jobe, joined McGuire's staff. Boswell was a 6-9 Alabama who had averaged 24.8 points and 17 rebounds per game during his sophomore year at State. He had to spend a red-shirt season at Carolina before becoming eligible for the varsity.

In 1974-75 Boswell led the Gamecocks in scoring and rebounding, but that isn't where he became a part of Gamecock history. As of 1996 he was the only Carolina player to leave school early to enter the NBA draft. He was an early round pick by Boston and spent six years in the league.

McGuire had spoiled the Carolina fans and administration. Now a school that had never been anywhere in basketball had set new criteria for a successful season - 20 wins and a bid to the NCAA tournament. The Gamecocks suffered two overtime losses by one point each during the season. One was to 11th-ranked Notre Dame at South Bend, and the other was to St. John's in the Ocean State Classic at Providence, Rhode Island. If Carolina had won either of those games, they would have achieved both the 20 wins and the NCAA bid.

The Gamecocks did receive a bid to the NIT in New York and defeated Connecticut in the first round, but lost to Princeton in the second. The Gamecocks were voted to the 19th spot in the final rankings, but they would never be ranked in the final poll again during McGuire's tenure - or anytime since.

Frank was beginning to run out of talent that could compete successfully with the powers of college basketball. He still had English and Dunleavy for one more season, but the pool of talent was growing shallow. Depth was becoming increasingly important, because college teams were using their benches more and more, and you could no longer survive a season with the five-man philosophy that had served McGuire so well in the past.

The Gamecocks of 1975-76 won 18 games against nine losses, which would get a team in to the NCAAs today, but that didn't rate even an NIT bid then. Carolina's home schedule was beginning to suffer, too, and average attendance in Carolina Coliseum dropped below 11,000 for the first time in the building's history. Games against the likes of Hofstra, Toledo, The Citadel, Kent State, Furman and Georgia Southern didn't excite the fans, the way the ACC battles of the past had.

That team had one freshman of note, Jackie Gilloon, a flashy New Jerseyite, who had a good, not great, career with the Gamecocks. Jackie hadn't been a starter for the Gamecocks in the early season, but he was getting some playing time and showing flashes of potential. We played at St. Louis in January, it was a snowy night, and there were few people in the arena. I did something I rarely did with McGuire. I made a suggestion.

I said, "Frank, I've just got a feeling that Gilloon will have a good night. Why don't you start him? You've got nothing to lose." The Gamecocks had just lost five of their six previous games.

When the teams took the floor for the opening tip, much to my surprise, Gilloon was in our lineup, and I was silently praying that my suggestion would turn out to be a good one. It did, because Gilloon just tore them up, and Carolina won the game. That also started an eight-game winning streak that turned the season around.

English and Dunleavy were the two players who made this team tick, game in and game out, and it would be the next year before it would be evident how valuable they were. Both signed professional contracts following their graduation, English with Milwaukee and Dunleavy with Philadelphia. Of course English would make his NBA name at Denver, and Dunleavy at Houston and Milwaukee.

The 1976-77 season doesn't hold too many fond memories, but it did provide a rare treat for me. We played Alabama at Tuscaloosa in the second game of the season, and I had the pleasure of sitting with McGuire and Alabama's football coaching legend, Bear Bryant, while they reminisced. They had been together in the Navy Preflight program at Chapel Hill during World War II.

I regret that I didn't have a tape recorder with me, because here were two coaching giants, both of whom are now gone, talking about their days at Chapel Hill and about sports in general.

When Bryant was coaching at Kentucky, there was a much publicized conflict between him and basketball coach Adolph Rupp, involving budgets and public attention. When Bear went back to his alma mater, Alabama, he was also given the title of athletics director.

He had hired the Tide's basketball coach, C.M. Newton, and later that day Frank asked Newton what kind of budget he had been given when he came there.

Newton said that he asked Bryant what the budget would be and that Bear had replied, "You can spend all the money you want to, but at the end of four years, if you aren't winning, you're gone!"

The game itself wasn't that exciting, from a Carolina standpoint, because Alabama dominated from start to finish. After the game, I remember McGuire saying to the press, "Off the record, I want to thank Coach Newton for putting his two white players in the game near the end, and that enabled us to come out with a respectable loss." It wasn't really that respectable - 90-66.

Frank attracted his last Blue Chip recruit that year. He was Jim Graziano, a highly-recruited 6-9 prep All-American from Farmingdale, New York. Jim never lived up to the greatness that Frank had hoped he would achieve, and Carolina began to slip in the win column.

The loss that was hardest for Frank to take was to Georgia Tech in Carolina Coliseum. Tech was coached by former Gamecock player and assistant coach Dwane Morrison. Tech slowed the pace of the game to a crawl, as the Gamecocks were in their usual zone defense and not contesting the ball on the outside.

At halftime an assistant coach talked Frank into going man-to-man, and he did. The Yellow Jackets "back-doored" us to death and won the game by a score of 47-45. The Carolina dressing room, following that game, was no place to be, and that assistant coach didn't want to get too close to Frank McGuire.

Attendance at home games continued to decline, as the home schedule became less attractive. Schools with conference affiliations were not eager to supplement their conference schedules with strong non-conference opponents, and the Gamecocks had to settle for a number of lesser basketball schools.

The bright spot of that home season was McGuire's 500th college coaching victory, which was achieved on February 9 against The Citadel. But a very interesting drama preceded that game by several days.

We played Temple in Philadelphia on February 5 and had a very thrilling one-point win in a slowdown game. We were then scheduled to go to Olean, New York, to play against a very good St. Bonaventure team. The win over Temple was the 499th of McGuire's coaching career, so his next win, obviously, would be a landmark.

There was a lot of snow in the Philadelphia area and also around Olean, which is just south of Buffalo. None of our broadcast crew really wanted to go there. I thought, "If Carolina should win this game, what an awful place it would be for Frank to win his 500th."

Honestly, we didn't stand much of a chance of beating St. Bonaventure. So, I talked to Frank and told him, "You don't want to win your 500th game at St. Bonaventure, if that should happen. You want to win it at home, and you should do that against The Citadel."

Frank didn't want to travel through that snow and wasn't that eager to play up there, anyhow. So we talked him out of going.

McGuire had Tom Price, the sports information director, calls the athletics' director at St. Bonaventure and tells him we weren't coming, because of the snow. The people up there were really upset, because the game had been sold out. Then, too, Carolina had beaten the Bonnies up there several years before, and they wanted to avenge that loss.

They tried a number of times to get Frank on the telephone, but he would never take their calls - Tom Price took them. Frank knew several of the priests at St. Bonaventure, and they couldn't understand why he didn't want to come there. They even offered to send a bus with state troopers to bring us to Olean, but nothing made us change our minds.

Really, we shouldn't have gone up there. We could have been snowed in, and then we would have had to cancel the game with The Citadel.

I believe that the University had to pay St. Bonaventure some money, because of that cancellation, but things worked out in the end, and Frank had his 500th win and an appropriate ceremony to honor him in the Coliseum.

Carolina had to win nine of their final games to claim a winning record of 14-12, and not even the NIT looked our way. It was Frank's worst record since his second season with the Gamecocks, and, all of a sudden, people were beginning to discuss the possibility that he had become too old to coach.

Things picked up the next year, and the Gamecocks even scored a home victory over sixth-ranked Notre Dame. Clemson and Carolina also agreed to start playing each other again, with Carolina winning in Columbia and Clemson taking the game up there.

Probably the best game Carolina played that year was a home loss in double overtime to a Marquette team that finished the season ranked among the nation's top three teams.

We did go back to the West Coast that year to the Cable Car Classic, which had degenerated into sort of a nothing tournament played in a high school gym. Carolina lost to Portland by a point, but beat San Jose State in the consolation game.

Carolina had more people there than the other teams, because several chartered airliners took the Gamecock fans out there.

I could hardly keep a straight face, when they presented the teams their souvenirs of the tournament - boxes of peanut brittle! That was fine with McGuire, however, because peanut brittle had always been one of his favorite things to eat! He had friends back in Columbia who used to make it for him.

By winning their final five games of the 1977-78 season, the Gamecocks earned another bid to the NIT in New York. One of the pluses of the NIT for McGuire was, although he loved South Carolina, he was an incurable New Yorker. He knew the town like the back of his hands, and he had legions of friends there - from bus boys to governors.

The Gamecocks drew North Carolina State in the first round and lost, 82-70. That was Frank's final team in a post-season tournament. It was also his 12th straight winning season at Carolina.

THE END OF A CAREER FOR MCGUIRE

Serious off-the-court distractions at the beginning of the 1977-78 school year might have had some impact on the basketball team and its coach. Dr. James Holderman had assumed the presidency of the University in September and immediately brought into discussion McGuire's status as basketball coach. This really upset Frank, and from then on, he and Holderman had a strained relationship.

Holderman had even suggested that Frank take the position of athletics director of Carolina's regional campuses, but that had no appeal to McGuire. He was a basketball coach, not an administrator.

This issue quieted down, as far as the media were concerned, but there was still this undercurrent and behind-the-scenes strategy that sought to place Frank in retirement. The combination of that and an unattractive schedule made home attendance continue to decrease.

Teams such as Wheeling, East Tennessee, Georgia Southern, William and Mary, Baptist and Western Carolina dotted the home schedule. The 2,236 who showed up for the Western Carolina game was the smallest crowd I can ever remember in the Coliseum, even until this day.

Carolina's final record that year, 15-12, not only didn't impress those who selected post-season tournament teams, but it didn't excite those in authority at the University, including the board of trustees.

When the 1979-80 campaign started, the issue had already been settled. McGuire agreed that this would be his final season. That gave groups and schools on the schedule, even Clemson, a chance to recognize Frank for his contributions to college basketball. I

84

don't know why I should say EVEN Clemson, because that institution owed him a lot. McGuire was responsible for Clemson getting the money to build Littlejohn Coliseum.

It was a bittersweet year for me. On the one hand, it was nice to see Frank receive so many well-deserved accolades along the way. It was also sad to ride out this final basketball journey with him.

Frank normally didn't show his emotions, but it was early in the season at Lexington, Kentucky that he melted a little bit. We were sitting in the locker room prior to the game with the Wildcats, and he became rather sentimental.

He said, "You know, I'm really going to miss this." I could see a tear rolling down his cheek. This probably reminded him of his days as a rookie coach at St. John's and his first trip into Lexington to play Adolph Rupp's team.

The only other time I had seen Frank shed tears was after the 1967 ACC tournament at Greensboro. That was when Frank's wife, Pat, was so ill. We were walking out to the parking lot, and Frank said, "Damn, I wanted to win this one for Pat, because I don't think she'll see another game."

Pat died later that year, and that was a devastating blow to McGuire, because he depended on her in so many ways.

I believe that the players put out extra effort for McGuire in 1979-80, because they knew that they were his final team. They didn't have the talent to be a great team, but it was a winning year at 16-11.

The only game of historic proportions was the first meeting ever between the Gamecocks and South Carolina State, the predominantly black institution in Orangeburg. And that was a heart-stopper.

With only four seconds remaining in the game, a State player scored a field goal to give the Bulldogs a one point lead. The Gamecocks managed to stop the clock with two seconds left by calling timeout.

In one of the most dramatic shots I ever saw in Carolina Coliseum, Cedric Hordges took a long pass to the left of the key, pivoted and launched a desperation shot that hit nothing but net. Carolina had won, 79-78.

There were no notable victories, as the season wound down to what would be the final game of McGuire's career. Chances of his winning his swan song didn't look too good, because the Western Kentucky team the Gamecocks faced were good enough to win 20 games and make the NCAA tournament that year.

On the night of February 23 a crowd of 11,000 turned out to see McGuire's final game, and it was preceded by the appropriate ceremony. Earlier in the day Frank had been honored in ceremonies at the Duke- North Carolina game at Chapel Hill, where McGuire still had a lot of fans. They gave him a great ovation, and this really bolstered his spirits for the evening in Columbia.

The regulation game with Western Kentucky ended in a 54-54 deadlock, so Frank's career was extended five minutes. When neither team scored in that overtime, another extra period was needed. Carolina arose to the occasion in the second overtime, and McGuire owned a 73-65 victory in his finale.

With his final record of 16 wins and 11 defeats and his connections in New York, I don't doubt that Frank could have played in the NIT, if he had wanted to. He never discussed it with me, but I sensed that he was just tired of all the hassle and wanted to get it over with.

I don't read minds very well, but he could have been thinking that he had finished his career with a victory, and to go into post-season would jeopardize that. In other words, go into the NIT, and you have to win the tournament, in order to win your final game. That's all speculation, and doesn't really make any difference.

What is certain is that the career of the most successful and most popular coach in the history of the University of South Carolina was now history, as far as coaching was concerned. The University made moves toward placating Frank by subsequently naming him "Coach Emeritus" and naming the playing area in Carolina Coliseum, "Frank McGuire Arena." Frank took great pride in both of those, and the license tag on his car bore the words, "Coach Emeritus."

More about my personal relationship with Frank is discussed later in this book in the chapter about coaches with whom I have worked.

BILL FOSTER COMES SOUTH

Eight days after McGuire's final game, the University announced that Bill Foster, the head coach at Duke University, would succeed McGuire here. Foster's team had just won the ACC tournament and was ranked in the nation's top 20 for the third year in a row.

During several months of speculation that followed the pre-season announcement of McGuire's retirement, many Carolina fans expressed hope that Bobby Cremins would get the job. Bobby was having great success at Appalachian State, and he had been and unusually popular player for the Gamecocks.

But how could you miss with a coach with Foster's credentials. He had already had 20-plus seasons at three difference schools, Rutgers, Utah and Duke. So he seemed like a sure bet to do the same at South Carolina. He did achieve the 20-win plateau (22) at Carolina in the 1982-83 season, but he didn't reach that number of wins in any of the other five seasons he coached the Gamecocks.

The bulk of McGuire's final Carolina team was seniors, but there was one notable carryover to the beginning of the Foster era. That was Zam Fredrick, a guard from Calhoun County, a consolidated school close to St. Matthews, who had racked up astronomical scoring totals as a high school player. He never seemed to quite gel in his three seasons under Frank, but he showed flashes of brilliance.

Zam was a big reason for Foster's good start with the Gamecocks, leading them to a record of 17 victories against 10 defeats, with an individual scoring average of 28.9 points per game. He won the national scoring title by hitting 43 points in his final game of the season against Georgia Southern.

Fredrick was a great perimeter shooter, and if the three-point goal had been in effect, there's no telling how many points he would have scored. He didn't get a good chance at an NBA contract, but he played in Europe for several years and did very well.

Zam is now back in South Carolina and head coach of his high school team at Calhoun County. In fact, his team has won several state AA championships in Carolina Coliseum, the scene of so many of his collegiate exploits. Zam's son, after playing a year at Georgia Tech, has transferred to Carolina and has become a member of Carolina's basketball team.

Foster hastily put together his first recruiting class at Carolina, but it included no players of the stature that he was able to attract at Duke. No Mike Gminski or Gene Banks. His most interesting freshman was Jimmy Foster, a 6'9" from Greenville, South Carolina,

86

who hadn't played basketball during his senior year at Wade Hampton High School, "for personal reasons." He did offer his services to the Atlanta Hawks of the NBA, but they politely declined.

Foster was an unusual player and personality. His confidence level ran out of the top of the scale, and he figured that he was the only player with the right to be under the basket. He led the Gamecocks in scoring in his final three seasons, and if he could have hit half his free throws, who knows what his average could have been?

Jimmy had a shooting range of about three feet, and at that time was the University's third leading career scorer, behind Alex English and John Roche, and had the fifth best rebound total. Most of the time he got the ball under his basket, he ended up with either a field goal or a foul. The best bet for an opponent was to foul him, because that was almost like getting the ball out of bounds.

After his final season Foster left to play basketball in Australia, and I understand that he is now back in the United States and living in North Carolina. I'm not sure.

Marquette was not a national power in 1980-81, but Foster's Gamecocks defeated the Warriors in Milwaukee, 91-89, for the most impressive win of his initial season.

Carolina received an unexpected bonus Florida vacation during the Christmas holidays, thanks to a coincidence of scheduling by the Gamecocks, who were scheduled to play Florida State in Tallahassee on December 30.

Because Florida State's football team was to face Oklahoma in the Orange Bowl on New Year's Day, FSU officials reasoned that they wouldn't have any fans in Tallahassee, so they told the Gamecocks, "Meet us in Miami on New Year's Eve, and we'll get you tickets to the Orange Bowl game!" That was an offer Foster couldn't refuse.

The two teams played in the Dade South Junior College gym, and the Gamecocks came out with a close win, 80-78. They probably couldn't have done that in Tallahassee.

The next day the Gamecocks saw the Seminoles and Sooners in the bowl game, and Oklahoma scored in the final minute to win, completing a disappointing experience for Florida State.

Carolina's travel wasn't over, however, as they had to go from Miami to Johnson City, Tennessee, for a game with East Tennessee State on January 3. Carolina won that, also, completing a fun trip for the team.

In contrast to the South Florida vacation was a trip we made to Boston in February to play Boston University. The arena there was also used for ice hockey games, and the basketball floor was actually sitting on the ice. Before the game was over, I thought my feet were suffering from frost bite! It must not have bothered the Gamecocks, because they had hot hands in winning the game by a score of 93-86. Zam Frederick had 39 points.

I never really knew Foster, or any of the Carolina coaches, like I knew Frank McGuire, so it was an adjustment for me to make. With Frank, I was family, while it was just a job with most of the others. That's not saying that I didn't like the others, it was that my relationship with McGuire had been unusual.

Carolina's 17-12 record in 1980-81 was achieved with a 9-4 run at the end of the season. During those 13 games, Fredrick averaged 36 points per game, scoring under 30 only once.

The Gamecocks appeared to be a lock for a bid to the NIT - 17 wins and the nation's top scorer - but, for some reason, they were left out.

Carolina didn't realize how valuable Zam Fredrick was, until they had to play without him. The 1981-82 season was a loser, 14-15, for Foster. I know that was hard for him to take, because he hated to lose as much as anyone I've ever known. He would become accustomed to it at Carolina, however, because he had three losing seasons in his six at the University.

The only time I saw Foster relaxed after a loss was in early December of that year, when we went to Hawaii to play Chaminade and Hawaii. We lost both of those games, but when you play out there, it's tough to win. The visiting team is on vacation, and the home teams are dead serious.

After one of those games we were taping Coach Foster's Sunday television show, and they were in there taking down the basketball floor. We had to stop taping, because we started laughing at the circumstances and couldn't restrain ourselves.

The worst trip we took that year was to Chicago for a game with DePaul. First, we got the hell beat out of us, 92-59. After the game, Tom Price, Carolina's longtime sports information director, told us that he wasn't feeling too well. At first we thought it was a reaction to the game, because there has never been a more avid Gamecock than Tom, and he lived or died with the sports teams.

This was for real, however, and when he arrived back in Columbia, via the usual changeover in Atlanta, he was really in bad shape. He was rushed to the hospital and had to undergo multiple by-pass surgery.

For Bill Foster, this was a preview of things to come, because he underwent the same type of surgery during the next basketball season.

Getting back to Tom Price, I truly believe that when they operated on him, they found that his blood was garnet, instead of red. As I said, if ever there was a loyal Carolina supporter, Tom was one.

He was also the beneficiary of Frank McGuire's sense of loyalty and fair play. When Jim Carlen was appointed head football coach, following Paul Dietzel's final (1974) season, he came here with his own ideas about the organization.

That has been a problem through the years with Carolina's frequent changes in coaches and athletics directors. The "generic" support staffs get caught in the middle. Sometimes they fit - sometimes they didn't.

Among Carlen's new ideas was that he wanted to bring in "his own" sports information director, even though Price had been there for years and was doing a good job. Sometimes people want change for the sake of change.

I called McGuire about this, and he didn't like Carlen's rejection of someone he didn't know and hadn't worked with, and went to bat for Tom. McGuire and Price weren't that close to each other, but Frank knew fairness when he saw it, and Tom had been a loyal staff member.

So, go back and check the media guides. In the 1975 football book, Julian Gibbons is listed as "sports information director for football," while in the basketball counterpart, Price is listed as "sports information director." The plot would thicken in 1982.

Back to basketball, nothing particularly exciting happened on the court that year, outside of a brief skirmish that followed an overtime loss to San Francisco in a game that was televised from Columbia. The Gamecocks were playing a lackluster schedule that should have been made to order for a winning season.

The major wins were over Clemson and Nevada-Las Vegas (UNLV) in the Coliseum and Florida State at Tallahassee.

Toward the end of the season, I got another look at the Foster temper and aversion to losing. We lost a game at Penn State, 62-60, in the closing seconds - a game we should have won. Bill was fit to be tied.

In the field house at Penn State there's a balcony, and that's where our broadcast booth was located. Bill had to come all the way up there to do the post-game show, and while he was waiting to go on the air, our engineer was talking to somebody back at the station in Columbia. Whomever he was talking with said something funny, so the engineer laughed. Foster didn't like that, so he took a folding chair and threw it the length of the balcony.

We had to take a bus to Harrisburg to get our charter. It was snowing, bitter cold, and I was hungry. I hadn't eaten since the pre-game meal at about three o'clock that afternoon.

Later when the bus stopped at a fast food place, and I was ready for it, but Foster had other ideas. He said, "Nobody outside of the basketball team gets out of this bus to eat!"

I thought to myself, "What did I do to lose that game?"

Steve Steinwedel got off the bus, then came back and asked me what I would like. He would bring it to me. I said, "No, thanks."

Several days later, Foster wrote me a note and apologized.

Another change took place in the Roundhouse in the middle of the 1981-82 basketball season, as Bob Marcum replaced Jim Carlen as athletics director. This didn't impact basketball very much at the time, because Marcum was busy hiring a football coach.

Marcum did make a change in the Coliseum, purchasing a wooden basketball court to be placed over the old Tartan surface. This would give Carolina teams the opportunity to practice on the type of court they played on in most of the time in other arenas, and that made sense. Give Marcum a plus for that.

Meanwhile, Tom Price's heart was back on track, and he was THE sports information director. Marcum brought in "his own man" – Sid Wilson - from his previous staff at Kansas, and appointed him assistant athletics director/media relations. I had always thought that this is what the sports information director was - anyway, to each his own.

A big boost for the Carolina basketball squad came in the summer of 1983, when they made a trip to the Orient to play a series of games with teams in China, Japan and Hong Kong. This trip was sponsored by the State Department and sanctioned by the NCAA.

I didn't make the trip, but it was not only a great experience for the players, but it also must have helped their basketball. In the season that followed, 1982-83, the Gamecocks won 22 and lost only nine.

It was following one of the better wins of the year, over Purdue on December 11 in Carolina Coliseum, when Bill Foster suffered what was described as a "mild heart attack." It was not all that mild, because four days later Bill underwent quadruple coronary by-pass surgery. This would keep him off the Carolina sideline for the next 17 games, while his assistants ran the team, with Steve Steinwedel in charge.

The substitute staff did a fine job, and the Gamecocks won 12 of the 17 games they were without the head coach. The last of those 17 brought Bobby Cremins back to the Coliseum for the first time has head coach at Georgia Tech.

At least some of the fans probably looked at this game with mixed emotions - wanting Bobby to do well, but wanting Carolina to win. I think it came out that way, as it was a close game all the way, with the Gamecocks prevailing, 61-53.

Foster returned for a home game with Holy Cross, and the Gamecocks presented him a victory. They finished with three wins in their final four games to run their record to 20-8, giving Foster the distinction of being the only coach to win 20 or more games in a season at four different colleges - Rutgers, Utah, Duke and Carolina. Of course, few coaches serve as head coach at that many schools.

Carolina didn't receive a bid to the NCAA playoffs, because an independent, particularly with Carolina's non-impressive schedule, didn't stand a chance against teams from the prestige conferences. However, the Gamecocks did receive a bid to the NIT, which had changed its format, featuring early round games at home arenas of participants, with only the final four reaching Madison Square Garden.

Carolina missed the Big Apple by one game, beating Old Dominion and Virginia Tech at home but losing to Wake Forest at Greensboro.

THE METRO – ANY PORT IN A STORM

The problem of being an independent disappeared after this season, because the Gamecocks became a member of the Metro Conference in the spring of 1983. The league included Cincinnati, Louisville, Tulane, Memphis State, Southern Mississippi, Virginia Tech and Florida State. This was no ACC or SEC, but it was the best the Gamecocks could do.

It did nothing for the Gamecocks' post-season chances, because the season produced records of 12-16 overall and 5-9 in the Metro. Despite their record, they could have received a NCAA bid by winning the Metro tournament, but they were eliminated in the first round by Florida State.

For two straight seasons, Carolina had rather odd experiences with FSU, as the teams won the road games and lost at home. In fact, during the 1983-84 season, the game with Florida State at Tallahassee was the only road game won by the Gamecocks, who lost the other ten.

Another oddity of that season was that Carolina's home date with Clemson was a "designated" Metro Conference game. Carolina didn't have time to arrange a complete home-and-home schedule of Metro opponents, so games with Clemson and DePaul were counted against their Metro record. They lost both of the games, but it really didn't hurt that much, because they were substitutes for Louisville, which was the strongest team in the Metro and one of the best in the country.

Carolina played a third "designated Metro game," and the opponent was Notre Dame. This proved to be the Gamecocks' best win of the year, as they upset the Irish in a slowdown game, 52-42.

Bobby Cremins claimed his first victory over his alma mater, when Mark Price led Georgia Tech to a 68-50 win in Atlanta.

Membership in the Metro Conference didn't excite the Carolina fans. They found it hard to relate to these teams, as the schools had little in common with the University, and the closest one, Florida State, was over 300 miles from Columbia. This was reflected in the attendance, which averaged around 7,500 for games in Carolina Coliseum. That wasn't good for the budget or recruiting.

The 1984-85 season showed slight improvement in the overall (15-13) and Metro Conference (6-8) records, but it did nothing for the road trips. Carolina lost all ten games they played on the home courts of their opponents, and the only game they won outside of Carolina Coliseum was over Wofford, 73-65, in Charleston. The Wofford game was part of an illogical doubleheader that also matched The Citadel against Erskine.

The Gamecocks did defeat six of their seven Metro opponents played in Columbia, including conference champion Memphis State and tournament finalist Louisville.

Carolina's home attendance continued to fall during this season, averaging a little over 6,000 per game. When only 2,589 showed up for the final home game of the season against Florida State, it was obvious that the fans were not excited over the progress of the basketball program under Foster.

Bill's recruiting was suffering, and, for whatever reasons, several outstanding players from the Columbia area went to other schools, where they were had excellent careers. Right or wrong, the rumor mill had it that Foster didn't try to attract such local players as Xavier McDaniel and Tyrone Corbin, who later became NBA stars. I really don't know.

The 1985-86 season was not one to remember. The Gamecocks won 12 and lost 16, including a Metro Conference record of 2-10. They won only one game on an opponent's court, and that was at The Citadel, 80-70.

The radio talk shows in Columbia were not being kind to Bill Foster, and Carolina fans were avoiding home games like the plague. There were eight home crowds of under 8,000 and only two that exceeded 8,000.

As the clock ticked off the final seconds of Carolina's 100-59 loss to Memphis State in the Metro tournament at Louisville, Bob Marcum was present and sitting at courtside in that big coliseum, filled with 19,000 spectators.

I watched Marcum to see if he would follow the team to the dressing room, as athletics directors usually do, especially at conference tournament games. Marcum didn't make the move, and that made it obvious to me that it was over for Foster, as far as Marcum was concerned.

Marcum confirmed this by making the announcement that Foster would be terminated as the Gamecock head basketball coach. This would again open the search process for a new coach, amid the usual speculation that takes place.

Foster landed on his feet, took a sizeable chunk of cash from a contract settlement with the University, and headed for Chicago, where he was head coach at Northwestern for a number of years.

GEORGE FELTON – A NEW BREED
Bobby Cremins was, of course, the first name to surface. He was enjoying great success at Georgia Tech, but he was still loved in Columbia. However, his time hadn't come.

Marcum's choice was a Cremins assistant, George Felton, who had been on McGuire's Carolina squads in the mid 1970s but saw very little playing time. He had been on Cremins' staff at Tech for five years and was receiving a lot of credit for the fine basketball talent that was being attracted to that institution.

After Felton's arrival in Columbia, he related the story of his hiring to a small luncheon group. This is the essence of it.

It seemed that Marcum was in Atlanta and received a telephone call from Cremins. Bobby wasn't applying for the job at Carolina. Instead, he asked Marcum if he would talk to Felton about it. Marcum resisted, but Cremins insisted. Marcum finally said, reluctantly, that he would give Felton twenty minutes.

The two met, and that "twenty minutes" grew into about an hour and a half conversation. Marcum contacted Carolina President Jim Holderman back in Columbia and made arrangements for Felton to come meet with him. Felton must have done a good job in that meeting, also.

Late in the day Felton was in his backyard shooting the basketball, when a call from Marcum came. George received the job at a school he knew very well from an athletics director he had scarcely met.

I was now preparing to move forward with his seventh head basketball coach at Carolina.

If the enthusiasm among fans that usually accompanies a change in coaches was present at Carolina for the coming of the "Felton era," it was well concealed. Attendance at the Gamecocks first two home games was a little over 4,000 and only one home game, Louisville, drew in excess of 10,000.

George's first recruiting class consisted of one freshman, and he would drop out of school after two seasons and little action. That season produced a 15-14 won-lost record and 5-7 in the Metro Conference. Thanks to a non-conference schedule that included the likes of Eckerd, East Carolina, The Citadel, Iona, Armstrong State and Mars Hill, a winning season was reachable. The highlight of the season was a double overtime win over Vanderbilt in half-filled Carolina Coliseum.

Felton's first venture into the Metro tournament started well - a one-point win over Florida State - but ended with a loss to Memphis State.

Felton's reputation as a recruiter became more believable, when he landed Brent Price, who had broken a number of Oklahoma prep scoring records while playing for Enid High School. His brother, Mark, had been a superstar at Georgia Tech and became a standout for the Cleveland Cavaliers in the NBA.

Although Brent was a fine passer and excellent shooter, he and Felton never seemed to be "on the same page." I think they had different ideas as to what role Brent should play on the team. Price considered himself a scorer, and Felton felt that he should concentrate on his duties as a point guard.

Felton openly expressed dislike for the three-point goal that had been instituted in the college game and discouraged his players from attempting it. As a freshman, Price followed his own instincts on three-pointers and made 44 percent of his attempts. As a team, the Gamecocks attempted 178 three-point shots, and Price threw up 112 of them.

Compare that to 323 three-point attempts by Carolina opponents.

As a sophomore, Price attempted 139 three-pointers and was good on 49 percent, while averaging 13.4 points per game, second on the team to junior college transfer John Hudson's 13.5.

In the spring Price made up his mind that he wasn't made for the Carolina offense and transferred to the University of Oklahoma, where he starred for two seasons and set a Sooner single-game scoring mark. He later made it in the NBA.

Felton's other "name" recruit for 1987-88 was Barry Manning, a highly-recruited guard for Eau Claire High School in Columbia and considered the best prospect in South Carolina in his senior season.

The crowds began to pick-up at the Coliseum, as the Gamecocks won 19, lost 11 and broke even in their Metro games.

However, the season was marred by one of the worst incidents I've seen in a college basketball game. Before over 10,000 fans in the Coliseum, Carolina held an 11-point lead over Louisville, with less than a minute showing on the clock. How could the Gamecocks lose? This is how.

Carolina's Darryl Martin exchanged punches with a Louisville player, and this brought on a series of exchanges involving players, coaches and one spectator. The result was that 14 technical free throws were awarded, including nine to Louisville and five to Carolina.

The Cardinals made their free throws, while Carolina was good on just two of five, cutting the Gamecock lead to four points. Louisville made up the remaining four-point deficit to send the game into overtime, and the Cardinals outscored the Gamecocks in a second overtime period to win by 98-88.

Carolina had lost control of the team and the game. Things such as that make it extremely hard for a play-by-play announcer, because no one really knows what is going on, and it took the officials an eternity to sort things out. The game was being televised, and I don't know what they did, but at least their audience had something to look at.

This was a Saturday afternoon game, and we were supposed to do Felton's Sunday TV show that night. This is where I made a mistake in judgment.

I decided that George shouldn't do the show, because he was so upset over what had happened, and he should have been. They had just blown a game that should have been a win over an opponent of national stature.

We did cancel the show, but I really gave George some bad advice. As it turned out, people had the impression that he was running away from his responsibility, and, frankly, we would have been better off, if we had taped the show as scheduled. At the time I just didn't think George could do a very good job under the circumstances, and he probably wouldn't have. But he would have gotten credit for showing up.

Later the Gamecocks got another shot at Louisville in the Metro tournament at Memphis. They beat Virginia Tech in the first round, but the Cardinals won an easy 89-57 victory in the second.

Although the schedule included a few "gimmes," it appeared that the basketball program was on the right track. Felton had a solid staff, with Eddie Payne, who later became head coach at East Carolina and Oregon State, and Tubby Smith, who got the head job at Georgia in 1995, followed by a successful stay at Kentucky, and in 2007 moved on to become head coach at Minnesota.

By 1988 recruiting of high school basketball players had become more and more the subject of sports talk shows on Columbia radio stations, and some of the best subjects were coming out of Columbia. It was even better news, because Felton was getting his share for Carolina. Manning was on board, and in 1988 his Eau Claire teammate, Joe Rhett, cast his lot with the Gamecocks. Jo Jo English, who was not as highly recruited as Manning or Rhett, also signed with Carolina and would turn out to be a good college player. He was 6-4 but "jumped" at seven feet.

The player who could have really boosted Felton's stock was Stanley Roberts of Lower Richland. He was about the size of Jacquille O'Neil and was on everybody's recruiting list. He ended up at LSU, as did his high school coach, Jim Childers, who took a job on Dale Brown's staff.

A RETURN TO THE NCAA PLAYOFFS

I don't remember how it happened - could have been "computer error" - but ACC member Maryland was on Carolina's 1988-89 home schedule. That was the first ACC school, except for Clemson, that had been on the Gamecock schedule since 1971. The match-up was greeted with a yawn by Carolina fans, and less than 9,000 turned out to see the Gamecocks down the Terps, 57-51. This was a rivalry that had reached the white hot level at one time.

In contrast, a capacity crowd of 12,400 saw the Gamecocks beat Clemson, 90-70, two nights earlier.

Felton's team won its first eight games of the season, including those against Clemson and Maryland, an overtime road victory at Tennessee, and a win at home over a highly-respected Ohio State team. This was still a young squad, and Carolina fans were seeing a return of some of the excitement of the McGuire era.

One problem faced by Foster, Felton and future basketball coaches at Carolina is comparison to the success of McGuire. Perhaps that comparison will fade, but it was still alive when Eddie Fogler took over in 1993.

The 1989 version of the heartbreak experienced in losing to Louisville the previous season, was a home game against Florida State. The Gamecocks held a one-point lead with just a few seconds left in the game, and the Seminoles had the ball out of bounds at the opposite end of the court from their basket. A half-court pass and a 23-foot jump shot gave the Seminoles a shocking victory, 69-67.

Carolina was still in the NCAA picture late in the season, but that was dimmed by a miserable game against The Citadel in Columbia. The Bulldogs edged the Gamecocks, 88-87, and Felton didn't react with the greatest maturity. He followed the loss with a press conference that was timed at 16 seconds by one of those in attendance. Why it was being timed, I don't know, but that was the report.

The Citadel loss wasn't terminal, however, because the Gamecocks made a great recovery, which began three days later in a televised game with Louisville in the Coliseum. Carolina upset the Cardinals, 77-73, before 12,000 fans who might have been wondering if there would be any carryover from the debacle of the year before.

Road wins over Virginia Tech and Cincinnati and a home victory over Southern Mississippi resulted in a bid to the NCAAs, Carolina's first in 18 years.

Carolina met former ACC rival North Carolina State in the first round at Providence, Rhode Island and was beaten, 81-66, by the Wolfpack.

You would think that back to back 19-win seasons would make Felton solidly entrenched in his position at Carolina, but as in so many cases, the numbers are not all that count in the coaching profession. George was not endearing himself to the Dixon athletic administration.

If ever there was a person who believed in teamwork and chain of command, it was Dixon. That's the way he was as a star football player at Carolina, and that had been drilled into him as a career Marine officer for over 20 years. Discipline and loyalty were as much a part of King as his heart.

Felton was a New Yorker from another generation, and he seemed to feel that what happened with his basketball team was all that mattered. He wasn't a particularly friendly person, and that was sometimes interpreted as rudeness. He reportedly chose not to attend a lot of staff meetings involving coaches of other sports at the University.

He was not what you would call a "loner," but he did have his own group of friends that he associated with. Head coaches of major college sports teams must keep in mind that they are head coach of that team 24 hours a day. Wherever they are and whatever they do, in the eyes of the public, they are representing the institution that is paying them - them a lot.

That's not saying that Felton was doing anything drastically wrong, but he wasn't taking advantage of his opportunities to endear himself with people, in and out of the University.

George's stock dropped during a 14-14 season in 1989-90. Fan reaction is always one of the measuring sticks of coaching success, and Carolina's home attendance during this season averaged 7,500, and only the game with Clemson drew over 10,000.

If you had to pick a highlight for this season, it would be winning the Sun Carnival Classic at El Paso, Texas. The Gamecocks defeated the host team, Texas-El Paso in the first round and won the championship by downing Kansas State, coached by Lon Kruger, who later enjoyed great success at the University of Florida, before assuming the head coaching job at the University of Illinois. Kruger is now the head coach at Los Vegas, where his teams are doing very well.

Jo Jo English displayed rare grace and sportsmanship when awards were handed out after the championship game. He was voted the tournament's most outstanding player, but when he was presented the trophy, he summoned teammate Bojan Popovic to the floor and handed it to him.

Popovic had hit a three-point goal to give the Gamecocks a 67-64 win in the opener, and his shot with seven seconds remaining was the difference in a 62-60 overtime win in the final.
Popvic was one of two Yugoslavian players recruited by Felton in 1988. The other was 6-10 Obrad Ignjatovic, not exactly an announcer's dream.

Carolina avoided a losing season by edging Clemson, 54-53, in the final game of the season in Columbia. The unlikely star of that game was Stefan Eggers, a seldom- used reserve, who scored 18 points and grabbed 12 rebounds against Clemson's "Duo of Doom," Dale Davis and Elden Campbell.

Eggers, a native of Germany, never again reached the level of play that he displayed against the Tigers, but that game was one to remember. Eggers dropped out of school after his junior season.

Carolina still had a chance at a winning record by winning a first round game in the Metro tournament at Biloxi, Mississippi, but that didn't happen. Memphis State eliminated the Gamecocks, 71-56.

The 1990-91 season for George Felton was a perfect example of the saying, "It's not how you start, but how you finish." The Gamecocks started the season with a surge that was reminiscent of the Roche-Owens era.

They won nine of their first ten games, including a monumental upset of North Carolina in the first Tournament of Champions in Charlotte. That 74-72 win was accomplished before 22,680 spectators, most of whom were Tar Heel fans.

When Carolina defeated Houston the following night for the championship, 74-70, you would have thought that Houston was the home team. North Carolina fans still did not hold the Gamecocks close to their hearts.

The Gamecocks had attained a national ranking of 12th, when they traveled to Felton's native New York for the Holiday Festival. They defeated Brigham Young in the first round but lost to Maryland, 78-69.

A victory over Louisville in Louisville added to Carolina's national stature, and they were 18-5 as they entered the final seven games of the regular season. That's when the wheels came off.

The Gamecocks lost six of those seven, beating only Winthrop, and losing at home to Memphis State by 22 points, 80-58. They also lost their first round game in the Metro Tournament to Florida State, giving them a 19-12 record. Because of the late-season collapse, the NCAA tournament committee passed over the Gamecocks, but they were included in the expanded NIT field.

Carolina defeated George Washington in Carolina Coliseum, but the turnout of 4,271 didn't impress the NIT, so the Gamecocks became the visiting team in their second round game against Siena at Albany, New York.

The choice of a site by the NIT proved to be a good one for the tournament, as the Carolina-Siena game drew over 11,000 spectators. It was not a good choice for the Gamecocks, who lost the game, 63-58.

That brought Carolina's final record to 20 wins and 13 losses. There was some speculation that this would be Felton's final season at Carolina.

Since George had come to Carolina, there had been a change in administration, a change in athletics philosophy and an upcoming change in conference affiliation. Dixon had become the athletics director, and he had been charged with strengthening the school's emphasis on and control over things such as academics and drug abuse.

Dr. John Palms took over as president in March of 1991, and he was an educator more than anything, but he was the recipient of one statistic relating to schools in the Southeastern Conference, of which the Gamecocks were new members. The last five presidents of SEC schools who had lost their jobs had lost them over athletics.

The Southeastern Conference is the nation's top conference, and the demands on coaches of all sports are very high. Facing the challenge of this league, Dixon and Palms had to ask this question about every coach. "Can they take us to the top of the Southeastern Conference?"

They obviously concluded that when the question was asked about George Felton, the answer was, "no.

The news that Felton would be terminated as Carolina's basketball coach was broken in a most unfortunate way. Dixon called Felton and made an appointment for the two to meet the next day, at which time the athletics director would inform the coach of the decision.

Someone "close to the administration" leaked the information to THE STATE newspaper that Felton was going to be fired, and a sports reporter called Felton to ask him about it. Felton said that he knew nothing about it, so Dixon was called. He confirmed that he had arranged to meet with Felton the next day for that purpose.

The morning paper broke the news and lamented that Felton "had to receive the news" from a third party. Although, Dixon's intent was to inform George in person, it was not in his plans for the news to be leaked prior to that.

For whatever reasons, THE STATE seemed to "have it in" for Dixon from then on.

Felton returned to New York and served as an assistant at St. John's until 1995, when he joined his former assistant, Eddie Payne, who had been named head coach at Oregon State. George, after many years with Donnie Walsh in Indianapolis of the NBA, is now a member of the basketball staff with the San Antonio Spurs.

To find a successor to Felton, Palms appointed a search committee, headed by Dixon and including a mixture of people from the University and the community at large. This opened up any of their meetings that weren't for the purpose of discussing specific "personnel matters" to the media, under the Freedom of Information Act.

Every name the committee discussed and every move they made was discussed, usually in a negative way, in the newspaper. They did a daily "countdown" on how many days the school had been without a basketball coach, as if it were a matter of utmost urgency.

STEVE NEWTON - COACH WITH A HANDICAP

The circus ended with the hiring of Steve Newton, who had enjoyed great success at Murray State. His teams had won four consecutive Ohio Valley Conference championships and three bids to the NCAA playoffs. In 1988 his Racers had beaten North Carolina State in the first round of the NCAA tournament, and then took national champion Kansas down to the wire, before losing by three points, 61-58.

Newton had played college ball at Indiana State, taking pride in the fact that his jersey number 33 had been retired by the school. He would laughingly add that Indiana State had retired that number, only after it had been worn by Larry Bird.

And, speaking of numbers, Newton was basketball coach number eight in my Carolina broadcasting tenure.

The squad that Newton inherited was not deep in talent. Felton's final recruiting class had consisted of one player, 6-6 Jamie Watson, a talented athlete from Elm City, North Carolina. Jamie's transition to college basketball didn't get off to a sensational start under Felton. He averaged six points per game and had a very low field goal percentage.

Before his college career ended, Jamie would perform under three different head coaches.

In Newton's first season, he was faced with a schedule that included 16 Southeastern Conference games, plus other formidable opponents such as Clemson, Oklahoma and George Washington. Carolina defeated GW and San Diego State to capture the championship of the Texaco Classic in San Diego, California, but that was the peak of the season.

The Gamecocks won eight of their first nine games, but this was before the SEC schedule began. It was down hill from there, as the Gamecocks won only three SEC games, while losing 13. One of the conference wins was over Eddie Fogler's Vanderbilt team, 77-68, in Carolina Coliseum.

Sometimes it seemed that there was a cloud following Newton around. The scariest moment I ever spent during a broadcast took place in the 16th game of this season. South Carolina was playing Mississippi State and seemingly had the game under control when Carolina Coliseum was in shocked silence.

Joe Rhett, the Carolina senior from Eau Claire High School, was having a great season, leading the Gamecocks in scoring and rebounding, as they won 11 of 16 games. Early in the second half, Rhett suddenly went to the floor and was motionless. There had been no contact or collision with another player - he simply collapsed.

As the stunned crowd of over 11,000 watched, Rhett's teammates carefully lifted his limp body and hurried him toward the dressing room. He never returned to the game, and

I had no idea of what the situation was, so that I could tell the listeners. Nobody else knew, either.

I knew that Joe had a pacemaker, which was implanted during his sophomore season, to correct a slow heartbeat. But you don't want to speculate about things, because you might be wrong.

The problem was that arrhythmia, combined with a high level of physical exertion had caused him to pass out. I heard that his blood pressure had gone down to a dangerous level. That ended Joe's playing career, and it was a shame. He is a great individual, a talented player and seemed to have a great future in basketball.

Under those circumstances, what happened in the game seemed to be inconsequential, but here's what happened. With something like three or four seconds remaining in the regulation game, the score was tied at 57-all, and the Bulldogs needed to go the length of the court to score. The inbounds pass was made to Chuck Evans at mid-court, and all he had time to do was throw a desperation shot toward the goal. It split the nets, and Carolina had lost another heartbreaker at the buzzer.

The Gamecocks weren't the same team without Rhett, who had been not only the team's top performer, but its spiritual leader. The latter is much more important than most people realize.

The 1992-93 season, Newton's last, was very depressing. Watson was the only returning player of consequence, and he still hadn't reached the level of play that was predicted for him when he signed with the Gamecocks. He had upped his scoring average to 7.5 in his sophomore season, but the Gamecocks desperately needed players who could put points on the board in big numbers. Newton brought in a junior college transfer, Emmett Hall, who would be a big help, but Newton needed more help.

Alleged recruiting violations had put a damper on the team's morale, and the compliance coordinator made many of the road trips to see what the Gamecocks were doing. He would interview the players on these trips, and this made everyone sort of uptight. It just wasn't a good climate for basketball, and I think everyone was glad when it was over.

During this 1992-93 season, the Gamecocks won only nine games but improved their SEC record to 5-11. They even beat Tennessee and Florida on the road and ran up one of the highest scores ever in the Coliseum when they beat Tennessee in Columbia, 111-107.

Going into this season, Palms had announced that King Dixon would be moved into an administrative position in the president's office. He was later succeeded by Mike McGee, who assumed the position on January 1, 1993.

Newton plodded on, fending off barbs from the media, trying to lure players to his program and trying to satisfy the watchful eye of David Didion, who had joined the athletic department as NCAA compliance coordinator midway through Newton's first season.

McGee decided that the basketball program needed a fresh start and re-assigned Newton to the position of assistant athletics director/special projects. Steve did a good job in this position, adjusted to an administrative role and, in 1995 accepted the job of athletics director at Southern Indiana University at Evansville. Later Newton retired, and he and his wife are living in Florida.

McGee thus accepted the major challenge of attracting an outstanding basketball coach to a school he was still learning about. Several well known coaches were mentioned and some interviewed, but Mike surprised everyone by announcing that Bobby Cremins would become Carolina's coach.

Carolina fans and the media went berserk. Live television of the press conference, a TV special on WIS, bumper stickers and instant billboards welcomed Bobby "home." Bobby seemed a little nervous about the whole thing, while the Atlanta media pronounced him temporarily insane for leaving a great place like that to come to Columbia.

Bobby must have agreed with the Atlanta diagnosis, because he called McGee three days later and said that he had changed his mind. Glee turned to consternation in Columbia, and Carolina fans cancelled their plans for immediate ascension into the basketball promised land. McGee wasn't all that happy, either.

EDDIE FOGLER BEGINS REBUILDING

On April 3 McGee introduced another new Carolina basketball coach - Eddie Fogler, who had recently been acclaimed NCAA Division I coach-of-the-year for the great job he had done at Vanderbilt. Eddie's team won 28 and lost only six in 1992-93, winning the SEC-East championship and advancing to the "sweet sixteen" of the NCAA playoffs.

In his seven seasons as a head coach, including three at Wichita State and four at Vanderbilt, he had never failed to take his teams into post-season play. His 1989-90 Vandy team won the NIT championship. What better credentials could you have?

Eddie had played and coached under Dean Smith at North Carolina, and he had learned well. His teams played smart and were well disciplined, usually over-achieving.

However, Eddie had never faced a rebuilding job like the one he would have at South Carolina. That didn't bother Fogler, because he is a competitor and had the confidence that was accumulated through participating in post-season tournaments for 25 consecutive years, as a player, assistant coach or head coach. I doubt that anyone this side of Dean Smith could match that record.

Why would Fogler leave a fine institution like Vanderbilt, where he had already established a winning program, and accept a rebuilding job at a school whose program was in disarray? As openers, Carolina offered much better income opportunities, and anyone who says that money isn't one of the most important factors is lying.

In a recent listing of coach's incomes in THE STATE newspaper, Eddie was at the top of the list in South Carolina, with a sizeable salary, along with television, radio, camps and endorsements.

Fogler was making ends meet in Columbia, and McGee had come through with a second big promise that lured Fogler. Midway of Eddie's second season, in early 1996, the University unveiled a handsome, $4 million practice facility adjacent to the Coliseum. This would allow Fogler's players to practice on their own during off-seasons, and the team wouldn't have to relocate to the physical education center every time one of many non-basketball events was scheduled in the arena.

Carolina Coliseum was not one of the larger arenas in the SEC - there were six with greater seating capacities - but it was adequate, and Fogler felt that it was conducive to a home floor advantage. Of course, at Vanderbilt he had been accustomed to playing on a floor that was far removed from the spectators and not quite as "personal" as the Gamecock facility.

The Gamecocks won 16 of 18 the games they played in Carolina Coliseum during the 1995-96 season, the only losses coming against Kentucky during the regular season and Alabama in the third round of the NIT.

I was fortunate enough to be the radio broadcaster for Eddie's first two seasons, and I found him to be a delight to work with - a breath of fresh air. Ask Eddie questions, and you got answers - not lectures. He was "up front" with his players, the media and the public.

He didn't have a lot of talent during his first two seasons, but he managed well with what he had. I think he had a lot to do with Jamie Watson becoming a complete basketball player. Under two previous coaches, Jamie didn't seem to get it all together, but he had an excellent senior year under Fogler.

Watson averaged 18.1 points per game that season, made the All-SEC second team and was the second round pick by Utah in the NBA draft.

Fogler's first team at Carolina won only nine games, but it made him feel better when I told him that Frank McGuire's first Gamecock team won only six. He told me, "If that's good enough for Coach McGuire, it's good enough for me!"

It really wasn't good enough for Eddie, because he had never been associated with a losing team before. He also knew that it wasn't good enough for McGuire, and he could empathize with Frank in the major rebuilding job he faced here.

The first season did produce two great boosts to Eddie's morale. One was beating Clemson at Clemson. It was the first time the Gamecocks had beaten the Tigers up there since Frank McGuire's team did it in 1972.

The other was a great victory over Kentucky in the final home game. Emmett Hall's last-second basket won it for Carolina, 75-74, and the reaction among Carolina fans was reminiscent of the glory days.

Fogler also guided the Gamecocks to their first-ever victory in the SEC tournament, played at Memphis. They blew out Mississippi, 80-57, but lost the following night to Florida.

The 1994-95 season was my final one, and it wasn't a winning one, but it was enjoyable. The Gamecocks improved to 10-17 overall and won five SEC games.

It also produced the first coaching confrontation between Fogler and his former boss, Dean Smith. To Eddie it was still "Coach." The two faced each other in the first round of the Tournament of Champions in Charlotte, and it was an easy win for North Carolina.

As I discussed earlier, my final broadcast from Carolina Coliseum was a 66-50 win for Carolina over Tennessee, and I was ready to pack it in. However, the Gamecocks had to face Auburn in the SEC tournament in Atlanta, and that, of course, was a loss.

But I was saying a reluctant goodbye to a program that I knew was on the way back, and that was confirmed by the 19-win record the following year, when the Gamecocks returned to post-season play in the NIT.

During that season there were no greater supporters of Eddie Fogler and the Gamecocks than two fans sitting in section M, behind the Carolina bench. They were Carol and Bob Fulton.

Bob Fulton "My Career My Life"

~VOICE OF THE GAMECOCKS~
(BASEBALL)

You really couldn't consider baseball a spectator sport when I arrived on the scene at Carolina in the early fifties. I don't recall seeing many, if any, games during my early years here.

Ted Petoskey, an assistant football coach under Red Enright, doubled as baseball coach, and his players were the students who "came out" for the team and made it. He had a few football players who could play both sports well, but baseball had a small budget and couldn't provide much in the way of incentives to lure talent. The same was true with other colleges, also, so it was what they call "a level playing field."

In the mid-1950s Petoskey left to join the South Carolina Department of Corrections, to supervise athletic activities. He was succeeded by Joe Grugan, a physical education instructor and former Gamecock athlete.

One of the interesting sidelights of Grugan's tenure was that Kirby Higbe, the former Brooklyn Dodger pitching great, was a volunteer assistant. "Hig" was a delightful personality and the consummate old-timer in baseball terminology.

A native Columbian, Higbe spent 12 years in the majors, his last being 1950, four years before I did the Mutual Game of the Day. His best season was 1941, when he won 22 games and led the Dodgers to the National League pennant. He loved the game of baseball and recorded that in a book entitled, "The High Hard One," in memory of his favorite pitch.

In 1964 Bob Reising, a Michigan State graduate who was on the University faculty, became the baseball coach, upon Grugan's retirement.

Carolina had not been faring well, even on the level playing field, going 7 and 14 in 1963. That adds up to 21 games, so compare that to the 60-game schedules colleges play today, and you get a good idea of how far the college game has progressed in three decades. The season started in mid-March and ended in mid-May. Now, colleges are well into their schedules in late February.

One of the recognizable names on the rosters of 1961 through 1964 was outfielder Dan Reeves, the Gamecock football quarterback who is now retired after many successful years coaching in the NFL. His last stop was with the Atlanta Falcons.

Reising coached the Gamecocks for two years and had winning seasons, but he left after the 1966 season, and Dick Weldon, a member of Paul Dietzel's football staff, coached the team in 1966, posting a 15-8 record.

Weldon was followed by Jackie Powers, who had a three-season record of 47 wins against 40 losses.

In 1970 Paul Dietzel was still busy building his football program, but he was also director of athletics and responsible for making the Gamecocks competitive in all sports. He knew Bobby Richardson and liked him for the kind of person he was, as well as knowing him as an outstanding baseball player.

Bobby had grown up in Sumter and played American Legion baseball, attracting the attention of major league talent scouts. At the age of 17 he signed a contract with the New

York Yankees organization. He worked his way up the ladder and by 1955 had made it to Yankee Stadium.

Bobby was a fixture at second base for the Yankees from 1955 until 1966. He played in seven World Series and received the Most Valuable Player award in 1961, when the Yankees won four of five games from Cincinnati. That was the year that Roger Maris set the home run record at 61, and Whitey Ford won the Cy Young award for pitchers. Mickey Mantle was also on that Yankee team, but Bobby outperformed them all in that series.

So Dietzel brought Richardson to Carolina to raise the baseball program to new heights. That wasn't an insurmountable task. Paul told Bobby to spend whatever it took but not to violate any rules. That last stipulation was absolutely unnecessary with Bobby, who probably felt the pain of guilt for even stealing second base.

Richardson was able to improve the program rapidly, because there were few limits on baseball scholarships, nor did they really need any. A few colleges had begun to increase their baseball budgets, but they were in the vast minority.

I had never broadcast a Carolina baseball game before 1974, and I don't believe Clemson had their games on the radio at that time, even with the fine ball clubs they had under Bill Wilhelm. That says something about the interest, or lack of, in baseball at the two schools.

Speaking of Clemson, I did broadcast their games from the College World Series back in the early fifties. Nobody was going to broadcast the game, so I decided that it should be done, and a statewide network was arranged, with the help of Bob Bradley, the Clemson sports information director. We arranged to do a re-creation by way of Western Union reports from Omaha.

Before one of the games, I had to take my wife to catch a train at five o'clock in the morning and spent the rest of the day getting ready for the broadcast. I had to learn something about the Clemson team, because I had not followed them during the season - or any other college team.

The Clemson game was delayed and didn't start until about midnight, Columbia time, and that's the only time I ever almost fell asleep on the air. Between each pitch, I would put my head down on the table, and I actually dozed at one point. The next thing I knew, the engineer was shaking me. From then on I kept splashing water in my face!

During a game on Sunday afternoon, the Western Union wire went out, so we had no information to go on. We made up some excuse why the game was being delayed, until someone could call Bradley in the press box. By this time, the game was almost over, but Bob had everything in his scorebook, so he just gave us the information over the phone.

Bob filled us in "live" on the few remaining outs, so we finished the game by that makeshift arrangement, and we never told anyone what had happened.

Think of this. When I did my last season of Carolina baseball broadcasts, I was fourth in the nation in terms of longevity among college baseball announcers.

In 1974 Carolina received a bid to play in the NCAA regional tournament at Starksville, Mississippi, so I decided that it was worth broadcasting. When I mentioned carrying the games to radio station managers, they looked at me as if to say, "Are you out of your mind?" They looked at baseball as something that was barely above the intramural level.

I finally talked WIS into carrying the games, and it worked out very well. The Gamecocks advanced to the championship game by defeating North Carolina State, Georgia Southern, while losing to Miami. Miami was undefeated, so the Gamecocks met them in a game to stay alive and won. However, the Hurricanes won the championship game an advanced to the College World Series, played every year in Omaha, Nebraska.

Interest in Carolina baseball picked up in 1975, when the Gamecocks won 51 games and lost only six. They made it to the College World Series by beating North Carolina State in the final game of the Eastern Regional in Columbia. I broadcast that tournament and distinctly remember how hot it was for the championship game, which the Gamecocks won by a score of 4-3.

Earl Bass, the Columbian who had made a name for himself in Pony League and American Legion ball, was Carolina's top pitcher. He was named to the All-America team in 1974 and had a great year in 1975. His career record at Carolina was 34-3, including a NCAA record of 23 consecutive wins.

Earl was a starter, but he came out of the bullpen to save the regional championship against State. Bass was also a fine hitter, and Richardson liked to have him in the lineup any time that wouldn't jeopardize his role as a starting pitcher.

At Omaha the Gamecocks defeated Eastern Michigan and Arizona State, lost to Texas, and then downed Arizona State a second time to advance to the championship game against Texas. Bass had already pitched two days earlier, but he started the game against the Longhorns and was effective until he began to tire in the latter innings. Texas won the game, 5-1, and that is the only ball game I ever saw Earl Bass lose.

I had covered Earl's play even when he was in the Dixie Youth, Colt and Pony leagues, and I covered his Legion games in the Little World Series at Tuscon, Arizona. He is, without a doubt, the best pitcher I ever saw in my years at Carolina.

Richardson had gathered some fine baseball talent, including one of the finest hitters I ever saw in college baseball. He was Hank Small, an outfielder who was named to the All-America teams in 1974 and 1975. He set a number of batting records for the Gamecocks, including most home runs in a season and a career. He was signed by the Atlanta Braves and was named the most valuable player in the AAA International League in 1978, when he played for the Braves' farm club at Richmond, Virginia.

It seemed as if I was doing a lot of station hopping, in order to get Carolina baseball on the air. WIS carried the 1974 regionals, then WNOK was the station for the 1975 College World Series, and WSCQ agreed to broadcast a limited number of games in 1976. I was enjoying doing the games, and it was keeping me busy between basketball and football seasons. By busy, I mean I had to sell the stations on the idea of doing the broadcasts, help get sponsors, and then do the broadcasts.

Carolina made it to the NCAA regional tournament in 1976 but didn't win it, so they did not return to the College World Series. That was Bobby Richardson's final year as coach. Bobby ran for Congress as a republican but was defeated in a close election. He later became baseball coach at Coastal Carolina, a branch of the University, and then took the position of athletics director at Liberty University, an institution founded by evangelist Jerry Falwell. Bobby is now retired and living in his home town of Sumter.

With Richardson's departure, the head coaching job went to June Raines, who had been an assistant to Jackie Powers for one year and to Richardson for three, while completing work on his bachelor and masters degrees at the University. Raines had enrolled at Furman in 1957 but went into professional baseball following his freshman year and spent ten years in the Cleveland and Washington organizations.

It was a sensational start for Raines, as his first Carolina team won the Eastern Regional and advanced to the College World Series.

Carolina's first game, against Baylor, in that 1977 tournament produced one of the most exciting plays I've ever seen in baseball. With a runner on base, the Gamecocks' Chuck McClain hit a towering drive to right centerfield, and he used his better-than-average speed to make it around second base before the ball was retrieved. Raines' assistant coach, Johnny Hunton, was the third base coach, and he kept his arm in a windmill motion, as McClain neared third. McClain didn't slow down, beating the throw to the plate for an inside-the-park home run. That was the winning run.

The Gamecocks had two great pitchers that season, and both of them were gifts to the baseball team. They were Randy Martz and Ed Lynch.

Martz was a Pennsylvanian who had been recruited for the football team by Paul Dietzel. He was a sophomore when Jim Carlen became head football coach, and he was getting little playing time as a quarterback. Prior to the 1977 baseball season, Raines asked Carlen if he could have Martz for the baseball team. Carlen said, in effect, that Raines could have him and that he didn't see that he was much of an athlete.

Martz won 14 games that year, including two in the College World Series, and received the Lefty Gomez Award as the top college pitcher in America. He pitched three seasons in the majors and had a record of 11 wins and 10 losses for the Chicago Cubs in 1982.

Lynch was recruited by Frank McGuire for basketball in 1973 but didn't receive enough playing time to earn a letter, eventually dropping off that squad to devote his time to baseball. A native of Miami, Ed was on the Gamecock squad for three years, during which he had a 15-2 won-lost record.

He also made it to the major leagues, playing for the New York Mets, for whom he was a ten-game winner in 1983 and 1985. He later became general manager of the Chicago White Sox.

Martz and Lynch led the Gamecocks to the championship game at Omaha. They met Arizona State, which had beaten them earlier in the week, and were again edged by the Sun Devils, 2-1.

In spite of a 31-14 record in 1978 and 31-16 in 1979, Raines' Gamecocks didn't get invited to the NCAA regional playoffs. However, the Gamecocks were in the regionals for the next seven years in a row, 1980 through 1986. Few schools have made the NCAAs that many consecutive years.

By this time baseball had become easier to sell to radio sponsors, and I was doing a good percentage of Carolina home games and an increasing number away from home.

We made it back to Omaha in 1981, when the Gamecocks won 46 games, including those in the NCAA playoffs and in the College World Series. Dennis Lubert (12-2) was Carolina's leading pitcher, and Jim Curl was the top hitter, with 17 home runs and 45 runs batted in. In the World Series the Gamecocks beat Maine and Mississippi State but lost to Oklahoma State and Arizona State.

This was my third trip to the College World Series, and, as always, I was greatly impressed by the great job they do there. The whole city gets involved, and they go out of their way to make sure that the teams and everyone else enjoy their trip there.

That event fully deserves the national coverage it now receives, with ESPN and ESPN2 televising all the games including the championship series. It has gone a long way toward elevating college baseball in the minds of the media and the public in general.

Both Carolina and Clemson participated in the 1977 event, and we pooled our resources to bring games involving the Gamecocks and the Tigers back to South Carolina. We combined the two networks, so that we needed to order only one telephone line to Omaha for the broadcasts. Jim Phillips, the Clemson broadcaster, and I split the play-by-play duties, and the two sports information directors, Bob Bradley of Clemson and Tom Price of Carolina, divided the duty as analysts.

Both Price and Bradley are baseball nuts, but Bradley took it a step further, as he was also an avid tobacco chewer. He might have picked up that habit from his longtime football coach, Frank Howard.

At one point in the broadcast, Bradley was sitting next to me, and we were both drinking soft drinks. When Bradley finished his, he found the cup to be a convenient place to deposit tobacco juice - a makeshift spittoon.

With my eyes on the game, I reached over for my drink and brought it to my mouth for a much-needed sip. It was Bradley's cup, and I had taken a big swig of tobacco juice. I got sick and threw-up in the corner of the broadcast booth. It didn't take long, so I didn't have to call in a pinch-hitter to the microphone.

Everybody died laughing - they thought it was a riot. As I write this, it is funny, but I couldn't find a thing amusing about it at the time.

When the Gamecocks returned to the College World Series in 1982, I was not with them. Bob Marcum had become athletics director in January, while I was busy broadcasting basketball games. Late in the season we had a game at Penn State and had to take a bus to Harrisburg to catch our plane to Columbia. It was the wee hours when we got home.

Early the next morning, I got a call from John Moore, associate athletics director, and he told me that WSCQ had decided not to carry baseball that season. The station had hired a consultant, who told them that they didn't need to be doing college baseball. I don't know what his reason was. I guess he felt that he needed to make changes.

WIS heard about the decision by WSCQ, and sports director Len Hathaway went immediately to Marcum, who said that WIS could have the baseball games.

I hardly even knew Marcum, because he had been there only a short while, and we were both busy with the jobs at hand. He was almost a stranger to me. I called him, and it wasn't a very good conversation.

He told me that he had given WIS the rights, and Len Hathaway was going to do the games. I told him that I was pretty sure that I could get WNOK to carry all of the games, which WIS was not going to do.

Marcum said, "Do you want me to take you before the baseball team and explain that, if this doesn't work out, that they may not be on radio, and that you would be hurting the baseball program?"

This was difficult for me to swallow, because if it had not been for my work in the past, the games would never have been on radio to start with. I got it started and had worked hard at it, but now that counted for nothing. But Bob Marcum knew nothing about that, and obviously didn't check with Tom Price or anybody.

Marcum did say that he would give me until the next day to see if I could get WNOK to carry all of the games. I went to WNOK and they agreed to do all of the baseball games on their AM signal, and that made me feel better about the situation. That is until I called Marcum again.

I told him that WNOK agreed to do the games, as we had discussed, but he said, "It's too late. WIS is already selling the games."

That was it, and I was out of the baseball broadcasts for two years.

This is one thing that frustrated me, as the University made its frequent changes in members of the athletic department staff. Throughout most of my 43 years of working for the school, doing my best and showing unbending loyalty, I still found myself on so many occasions "applying for a job." It was almost like I had just come to town.

In 1984 I "got my job back" as baseball broadcaster. Their play-by-play man had left for greener pastures and WIS did not have anyone left on their staff with play-by-play experience. Mick Mixon who was handing sports at WIS was anxious to take over but, of course, he would need help. WIS wrote me a letter asking me to do most of the play-by-play work, with Mixon working only two innings during the game. They said they could pay me only $35 a game. I always spent around two hours of preparation for a game – drive to the ballpark and after about four hours - drive home. The very least time I would be involved in the broadcast was six hours, thus I was working for less than $6 per hour. Yes, I was upset and embarrassed. I had left the most prestigious job in major league baseball, which would have paid me a yearly salary in six figures to return to Columbia and USC.

Believe it or not there was a trip we made for a series in New Orleans. We traveled in one of those buses that carry rock bands from town to town. The sleeper was like a tomb. We spent four days in New Orleans and three of our four scheduled games were rained out. I broadcast only one game and was paid a whopping $35 for it, plus expenses for the entire trip.

Why did I put up with all of this? I enjoyed broadcasting baseball. The Gamecocks continued their string of NCAA regional appearances. This was the first year in the Metro Conference, and the Gamecocks won their first three games in the conference tournament, only to miss the championship by losing two in a row to Virginia Tech and Florida State.

Carolina was also knocked out of the South Regional by losing two straight games.

I finally made the trip back to Omaha in 1985, after the Gamecocks won the regional tournament in Columbia by beating St. John's, Western Carolina and LaSalle (twice).

We made a quick exit from Omaha by losing to Arkansas and Oklahoma State, but that first game was one of the best baseball games I ever broadcast. The game was scoreless for 13 innings, but Arkansas squeezed across a run in the 14th to win the game, 1-0.

Prior to the Oklahoma State game, I had lunch with Larry Price, one of our pitchers and a great young man, who grew up in Cherry Hill, New Jersey. The Cowboys had a great hitter - his name was Pete Incaviglia - and he set the NCAA home record of 48 that season. Larry said that, outside of playing in the College World Series, his one wish was to face Incaviglia.

Price got his wish, because he started against Oklahoma State. He got the Cowboy slugger out on strikes twice, but his luck ran out. Incaviglia came to bat with two men on base, took one of Larry's pitches and delivered it to a road that was at least 100 feet beyond the outfield fence. Larry got his wish, but it didn't end up exactly the way he wanted it to.

That home run was not the difference in the game, which Oklahoma State won by a score of 16-11.

That was Carolina's last trip to Omaha while I was the broadcaster.

One unusual thing that happened in 1985 was that Carolina defeated Clemson six times, three in Columbia and three at Clemson. As far as I know, that's the only time that ever happened.

Raines continued to have excellent teams for the next three years, although they weren't able to win a Metro Conference championship, mainly because of the presence of Florida State in the league.

Returning to the regionals in 1986, Carolina beat Alabama in the first game but lost to Miami and Alabama to be eliminated.

The Gamecocks not only didn't make it to the regional tournament in 1987, but they made a quick exit from the Metro tournament, which was played at Sarge Frye Field. Carolina started fine, beating Memphis State, but the home field advantage disappeared after that. Florida State beat them, and then came one of the stranger turnarounds I've witnessed.

During the regular season Carolina had beaten Cincinnati five times, twice on the road and three times in Columbia. In their three home games against the Bearcats, the Gamecocks scored 26 runs. In the Metro tournament Cincinnati got most of them back, pounding the Gamecocks, 19-4, to the embarrassment of the home crowd, and this eliminated them from the tournament. Although Carolina again missed the regionals in 1987; they were back in the Atlantic Region playoff in 1988. The Gamecocks won three games in that tournament, played at Miami, Florida, but they were eliminated by losing to Georgia Tech and Miami.

Carolina made two more visits to the NCAA regionals while I was broadcasting, to the Atlantic Region in 1992 at Coral Gables, Florida, and at Atlanta in 1993. We beat Notre Dame and North Carolina State to open the 1992 tournament, but our pitching disappeared, and we lost to Miami, 17-2, and Notre Dame, 11-2. I guess our hitting must have disappeared, also.

In 1993 we downed East Carolina but lost to Wichita State and Georgia Tech.

Carolina had a lot of good ball players during the years that I broadcast their games, and I wouldn't attempt to name all of them, because my memory isn't that good, and I also wouldn't know where to stop.

THE BEST OF THE BEST WHO MADE IT TO THE PROS

Mookie Wilson, an outfielder who played for the Gamecocks in 1977, spent nine and a half seasons in the National League with the New York Mets, and two and a half with Toronto in the American League.

Dave Hollins went up to the Philadelphia Phillies in 1990.

Bill Landrum, a right-handed pitcher, went to Cincinnati in 1986 and has played with the Reds, Chicago Cubs, Pittsburgh Pirates and Montreal Alouettes. Landrum has now retired from baseball.

Brian Williams, also a right-handed pitcher, was called up by Houston at the end of 1991 and later pitched for the Detroit Tigers.

Ed Lynch's career saw him not only as a player but also as a general manager of several major league teams.

Garry Hancock, and outfielder, had a six-year major league career with Boston and Oakland, both of the American League.

Randy Martz, the 1977 Lefty Gomez Award recipient, pitched for the Chicago Cubs three years and for the Chicago White Sox one year.

Several others moved up for brief periods but not long enough to be considered established major leaguers.

As for the coaches, I was only associated as a play-by-play broadcaster with two Carolina coaches, Bobby Richardson and June Raines. They were both winners and great people to work with, and they are both discussed in a chapter on coaches later in this book.

Doing college baseball was a far cry from my experience with the Mutual Major League Game of the Day. Not many of the schools had baseball fields that were equipped for broadcasting, so you might find yourself using a makeshift booth - anywhere from a card table on the foul line to roping off a few seats in the bleachers.

When Sarge Frye Field was upgraded, the broadcast facilities there were some of the best we worked in. Now a lot of colleges have better baseball parks than Carolina, particularly those in the Southeastern Conference. However, Carolina is in the process of building a beautiful new, riverfront coliseum, which is scheduled to be completed by the 2008 baseball season.

Another thing I enjoyed about college baseball was getting to know some of the coaches and players. They were a great group.

One of the better baseball programs in the South was at Georgia Southern at Statesboro, Georgia. For years they didn't have a football team there, and basketball didn't draw much support, so baseball was the big sport. Statesboro is just a three-hour drive from Columbia, so Carolina and Georgia Southern developed a very healthy baseball rivalry.

The Eagles' coach, Ron Polk, did a great job for the school. He was very friendly and cooperative, and we became casual friends - as much as you can under those circumstances. We were playing at Statesboro, and it was an important series to both schools, as they were battling for NCAA playoff bids. I had lunch with Ron on one of the game days, and I asked him how he liked his job.

He replied that he liked his baseball job but that he had to teach some classes and that was taking away from the time he could spend working on things that a baseball coach has to do. "When I'm on the road, for instance, I'm having to grade papers to keep up with my job as a teacher," Ron explained.

When I asked him if he planned to stay at Georgia Southern, he said, "Yes. It's great here. I love the town and the people, and I'm planning to stay here."

Carolina won the games on Saturday and Sunday, and following that final game of the series, Tom Price and I were sort of wrapping things up. Our booth was situated right next to the Georgia Southern booth, and we could here what was being said by the announcer.

What we heard was Ron Polk talking to the Georgia Southern broadcaster, Nate Hirsch, and saying that he was resigning! He said that he had done about all he could do there, and he would move on to something else. So, at the end of our broadcast we reported what we had heard. Ron is now the head baseball coach at Mississippi State in Starksville, Mississippi, where he has had great success over the years, not only as a coach but as an outstanding promoter – as evidenced by the big crowds the Bulldogs draw for every game. Polk has indicated that he feels it is time to resign. We'll see!

That was one of two times that I've had a coach resign "on the air." The other was, of course, when Paul Dietzel resigned after the Duke football game in 1974.

College baseball was fun to do, even with the lack of interest and excitement that surrounds basketball and football. There was also the lack of pressure that is involved in the two leading college sports.

However, the sport grew in leaps and bounds during my 20 years of doing games for Carolina, and the emphasis and support has increased to a level I never thought attainable when I did that first College World Series in 1974.

~MUTUAL'S GAME OF THE DAY~

As a sports announcer you really can't plan your future insofar as where you want to be at this point in time or how height you might climb on your concept of the ladder. What you can do is prepare yourself to do the best possible job of whatever sport you are broadcasting, so that when opportunities present themselves you are in a position to take advantage of them.

I was in Columbia, not because I set that as one of my career goals, but because I considered it a step up from where I was, and I was fortunate enough to be chosen. After two years in Columbia I was feeling more at home than at any place I had ever worked. I wasn't searching the ads in BROADCASTING, as had been my inclination in previous situations.

Most play-by-play announcers who take their work seriously would jump at the chance to join a major network. That means you've reached the top of the ladder, although you shouldn't consider yourself a failure if you never attain that status.

As I said earlier, my high school yearbook prophesied that I would be a major league baseball announcer, rather than predicting that my violin would take me to the heights of Jascha Heifetz! I'll readily admit that broadcasting major league baseball is something to which I passively aspired.

My experience with the Columbia Reds was most valuable to me, both from working and contact standpoints. I had a chance to follow a championship club, managed by a former major league pitcher, in a league that featured a number of marquee-players-to-be. Aaron and Robinson were at the top of that list.

The contact that helped was Sally League president Dick Butler, who later became president of the Texas League and ultimately in charge of umpires for the American League, with offices in Boston. Butler lived in Columbia and became a good friend and associate. He liked my work and told me that if he could ever help me move up, he would.

It so happened that in 1954 a spot came open on the Mutual Game of the Day broadcasting crew. Mutual had a network of 450 stations across America, reaching audiences varying from 35 to 50 million. It was THE baseball network, doing games each day from selected parks in both the American and National leagues. When I first heard about it I wanted a shot at it, but I reminded myself that small Southern cities are not considered the most prolific launching pads for major league announcing jobs. However, a plus for me was that Dick Butler was a good friend of Paul Jonas, who was director of sports for the Mutual Broadcasting System.

Dick called Jonas and told him about me, and Jonas told him to have me send them a tape. Mutual was getting tapes by the truckload from all over the country, so I had convinced myself not to get my hopes too high, although Butler's influence had more or less assured me that they would at least listen to my tape.

I got the job, or I wouldn't be including this part of my book. I later learned of the unique way in which Mutual made the final selection. They narrowed the tapes down to the five that they considered the best, and then they brought in 75 people and put them in a large studio. They told them, "We're going to play five tapes of play-by-play announcers for you, and we want each of you to tell us which one you like the best."

I happened to win out, and when Mutual called me it was one of the best days of my life. With my limited experience I never thought I'd get to the major leagues - at least not that soon.

110

Mutual stationed me in Chicago and rented an apartment for Dody and me. It was an upscale apartment one block from Lake Michigan and occupied by well-to-do people, including Frank Lane, general manager of the Chicago White Sox.

Mutual was very good to us on expense accounts - never questioned them - and it was nice to always travel first class - by air - and stay in the best hotels. That's a giant step from the accommodations you have following minor league clubs.

The Mutual Game of the Day crew consisted of Al Helfer, who was the number one man, Art Gleason, me and sometimes Buddy Blattner, Gene Kirby or Dizzy Dean. Dean and Blattner were doing television games for CBS on weekends.

For the young and those who didn't follow baseball prior to World War II, Dizzy Dean, Christened Jay Hanna but self-renamed Jerome Herman, was an all-star pitcher for the St. Louis Cardinals in the 1930's. He won a near record 30 games in 1934.

He and his brother, Paul, who also pitched for the Cardinals, grew up in Chickalah, Arkansas, where Dizzy concluded his formal education in the second grade. Although he was a great pitcher, Dizzy became just as famous as one of baseball's all-time characters and a nightmare to grammar teachers from coast to coast, because of his classic grammatical errors.

Dean and Blattner worked only Wednesday games because of their weekend commitments, but they definitely provided a change of pace to the broadcasts.

Typically, Helfer was the swing man in the East and would be joined by Paul Jonas and Art Gleason and sometimes Gene Kirby, with Jonas serving as producer. In the West I would be the announcer with Dean and Blattner when they were on the broadcast, or Helfer would fly out and work games in the West with me.

We always had back-up games scheduled in the other section of the country in case a game should be rained out. For instance, if a game in the East should be rained out, I would be assigned a back-up, such as Chicago, Milwaukee, Detroit, Cleveland or Cincinnati. Major League baseball didn't have a club on the West Coast then.

Before the season was over I had a chance to work some games in the East. In fact the final game I did for Mutual was at Ebbets Field, home of the old Brooklyn Dodgers, on the same afternoon that South Carolina upset a great Army football team at West Point.

As a public relations move, Mutual would broadcast minor league games on days when the majors weren't playing, and I did games in Columbia, Charlotte, Jacksonville, Savannah, Tulsa, Des Moines, Wichita and Oklahoma City. This was done as a good will gesture to minor league baseball, which feared that our broadcasts of major league teams might draw fans away from their games. Mutual felt that whatever increased interest in baseball on any level was good for baseball on all levels.

Doing minor league baseball did set the stage for the hottest game I ever did. I was at Oklahoma City with Buddy Blattner, and it was blazing hot, even for Oklahoma. We were high on the roof, and someone told us that the temperature was 127 degrees up there, and I believed it. It was so hot that a batter would hit a ground ball and not even bother to run it out. As Johnny Carson once said, "It was so hot that he saw a dog chasing a cat, and they were both walking!"

Umpires wore black coats back then, even on hot summer days, and one of them collapsed from the heat in the first inning. Dick Butler, who was then president of the Texas League, decided that Texas League umpires would never wear coats again, because of what happened in that game. By the seventh inning I was so hot that I didn't know where I was, and Blattner had to finish the game.

I must say that doing minor league baseball was generally a pleasant experience, because all of the towns gave us the VIP treatment and really entertained us. They really entertained us too much, because they kept us up very late, meaning that we had to catch a plane the next morning without getting much sleep.

Al Helfer was a big, big man - weighed about 300 pounds, which was to my disadvantage on one trip we made to do a game in Wichita, Kansas. It was the championship game of the National Professional League, and I don't know how it got that name, because it was made up of Amateur teams. It was a hot day, and when we were getting on the plane to leave Wichita, Al was climbing the stairs in front of me.

All of a sudden he fell backwards, right on top of me, and took me down with him, pinning me on the ground. Luckily, we didn't have far to fall, and I escaped injury. They also found nothing wrong with Al, except a case of wounded pride.

One bit of strategy that I developed early on had to do with my standby assignments. Say there was a game scheduled in Philadelphia, and I would have a standby in Milwaukee. I learned how to cut out a lot of unnecessary travel. I would drive from Chicago toward Milwaukee, and my wife would tune in the game being played in Philly. I would stop at a restaurant halfway to Milwaukee, call her and give her the telephone number there. As soon as they played five innings - an official game - in Philadelphia, she would call me, and I could go back to Chicago. That saved me half the trip.

We did a lot of Chicago Cubs games, because they played nothing but afternoon games at home. The Cubs liked to play doubleheaders, because they drew big crowds. Consequently, if they saw a cloud anywhere in the sky, they would call off a game and schedule it as part of a doubleheader.

I had a good relationship with the weather bureau in Chicago, and United Airlines took good care of me on switching flights. That helped a great deal in the flexibility I had to maintain for last-minute changes in broadcast schedules. During my season with Mutual I flew at least 140,000 miles, but there were no frequent flyer discounts for me to enjoy.

One of the toughest things to handle was a rain delay during a game. Mutual didn't want us to "go back to the studio," for fear that the audience might leave us and not come back. So we had to have something going from the booth for whatever time the rain delay consumed.

One readily available source was the announcers that did play-by-play for the stations of the two teams involved in our game. They liked to be on the network, so they were more than happy to come over and talk with us, and they usually made good interviews.

Making tight travel schedules was a way of life for us, but never any tighter than one I experienced on a minor league broadcast we did in Charlotte. I would be flying back home to Chicago after the game, but I received some disturbing news. They would be working on the elevator in my apartment building, and it would be closed for repairs after midnight. In other words, if I was not on it by then, I would have 14 flights of stairs to climb, not something I cherished after doing a ball game and making a tiring trip.

I got the best flight schedule I could find - Charlotte to Atlanta to Chicago. When I finally found a cab, after arriving at the Chicago airport, it was well after eleven o'clock. I told the cab driver, "If you get me to my apartment house before midnight, I'll give you an extra ten dollars." That inspired one of the more exciting rides I've ever had, but he made it through Chicago and to my apartment with five minutes to spare.

When I got on the elevator I looked at my watch and it read, "11:58." It was the last time the elevator ran that night!

112

The airlines were most accommodating to us and on several occasions held flights long enough for us to make it from one end of the terminal to the other for connections.

An unpleasant aspect of my doing what sports announcers dream about - major league games - was my relationship with Al Helfer. He was impossible under the best of circumstances, but with me it involved an extra negative. When I got the job Helfer had a good friend, Al Wester, who also wanted the job. Wester was in Georgetown, South Carolina, and was a very fine play-by-play man and a fine person.

When I got to spring training Helfer hardly spoke to me at first, and to make matters worse, his friend Wester was down there with a tape recorder doing interviews, and he wouldn't speak to me either.

Finally Helfer said to me, "Let's go out on the beach and talk." I thought it might be an ice-breaking gesture. Well, this was the first time I knew that there was a real feud going on between Al and Dizzy Dean. It started the year before when they got into an argument in a taxi cab and ended up in a fight, which policemen finally broke up. So, Al starts telling me what a lousy person Dizzy is.

I said to myself, "This is a great start. The first time I meet the guy, and this is what I get. I tried my best to keep a good relationship with and with him and Diz.

Al was always correcting me. I was nervous to start with, and he's picking at me on every little thing. Again he would tell me what a lousy person Dizzy is. When I got around Dizzy he would tell me what a lousy person Al was. I got sick and tired of hearing it, although the network managed to keep Al and Diz apart most of the time.

One night we were coming into Cleveland in a cab, and Al started in on Dizzy. So I said, "Al, I don't want to hear any more of this, if you don't mind." He got mad and wouldn't say anything, but the season was almost over anyhow.

At the end of the season we were coming back from Milwaukee, and Al started talking to me very seriously. He was a very emotional person. He said, "Bob, I want to apologize to you. I'm sorry for the way I've been. I didn't give you a chance. I didn't want you to get the job." By now tears were rolling down his cheeks.

"I may not be coming back next year, and I just want to apologize," he added. "You took all this and didn't say a thing. You helped me a lot, and I feel bad about the way I've acted."

It was a very emotional thing. That's the last I ever saw of Al Helfer.

If I had been a longtime veteran of broadcasting, the situation with Helfer wouldn't have been so bad, but here I was only 34 years old and thrust into the situation on short notice. I was nervous when I reported to spring training at St. Petersburg, Florida. We stayed at Treasure Island, a beautiful beach near St. Pete, and that was a pleasant way to start my major league career.

I did my first interview with Walter Alston, who was in his first year as manager of the Brooklyn Dodgers. I took a tape recorder, went to him and admitted, "I'm very nervous about this, because it's the first interview I've done for Mutual."

He laughed and replied, "You're not any more nervous than I am, because this is the first network interview I've done." Alston was a very nice guy, and that interview with him sort of broke the ice for me and made me more relaxed from then on.

Another positive during spring training was that I struck up an acquaintance with Harry Caray, whom everyone now knows as the announcer for the Chicago Cubs and whose son, Skip, does games for the Atlanta Braves. Anyone who has seen Caray on TV knows that he isn't a lightweight, but he was simply amazed at the size of Helfer and his ability to ingest food and drink. Once we were in a bar with Helfer, and when he left, Caray said, "Check me out. He had sixteen stingers, didn't he?" The bartender said he was right.

Harry was broadcasting for the St. Louis Cardinals at that time, and he was married to the daughter of Anheuser Busch, whose brewing company was a major sponsor of the Cardinal games on radio. After a divorce, Caray moved on to Chicago, where he did White Sox games before moving to the Cubs where he closed out a legendary career at Wrigley Field.

Once the season began I worked out of Chicago and had an office at Station WGN. It really surprised me, the amount of mail we received, both to the network and to me personally. I heard from people that I hadn't seen in years and had forgotten about. Also from ball clubs wanting us to mention special nights they were having and from various other people wanting us to plug one thing and another.

Some of the letters were complaining that we were pulling for one team over another, but I can truthfully say that we were neutral. Our main concern was doing a good job of broadcasting and making sure that all of the technical things went right. We were usually worried about making flight connections, particularly if the game was running long, had rain delays or extra innings. I have been under the counter during a game calling the airlines to switch flights.

Most of the ball players and managers I was able to meet in person were very nice. Such as Phil Rizzuto, the New York Yankees shortstop, and Allie Reynolds, who pitched for the Yankees. The most difficult manager to work with was Eddie Stanky, the former Dodger second baseman, who was managing the St. Louis Cardinals. As a player Stanky had the reputation as a no holds-barred competitor, about whom it was said, "He can't run, he can't hit and he can't field, but he's the best second baseman in the National League."

Stanky refused to give us - or anybody else - his starting lineup prior to a game, so we had practically no time to get ready before the first pitch. This wasn't crucial but certainly an annoyance to us and anyone else covering the Cardinal games.

Once I was riding with Jack Brickhouse, who did Cubs games on television, and we got together and decided we'd announce the Cardinal lineup without Stanky's help or approval. So we did this, and when Stanky heard about it he got mad as hell. But it was what he deserved.

It was just a thrill for me to be in the company of some of the immortals of baseball and hear them talk and tell stories. Once I had the experience of riding from a game with Dizzy Dean, Frank Lane, Early Wynn – former major league pitcher - and Bill Veeck, who had become famous as a promoter when he was general manager of the St. Louis Browns.

Lane was one of the most profane people I've ever been around, and he never talked about anything but baseball. If he was in a meeting, and a secretary had to bring a message to him, she would run in and out of the room as fast as possible to avoid hearing his language.

I also became friends with Mel Allen, the Alabaman who reached the top as a network sports announcer. I often traveled to airports with Mel and liked him very much. Mel didn't spend as much time preparing for a game as most of us. His brother would do all of that for him, and Mel would come into the booth just a few minutes before a game and do the play-by-play as though he had been preparing for hours.

The best person to work with at Mutual was Buddy Blattner, who had played with the Phillies. Often the day of a game he would invite me to his room for breakfast, and we'd spend over an hour going over the two teams and planning what we were going to do on the broadcast.

114

When we were in Detroit for a game, we were in a place that had a ping pong table, so Blattner challenged me to a game. He said, "I'll play you left-handed." That sort of got under my skin, because I considered myself a pretty good ping pong player, and I knew that Buddy was a right-hander.

He beat me like a drum, and I was feeling pretty bad, until he admitted that he was a world class ping pong player. I found out that he and a guy named Jim McClure had won the World Doubles Championship in 1936 and 1937.

WORKING WITH DIZZY DEAN

Dizzy Dean was just the opposite from Buddy in preparing for a broadcast. He didn't! Diz never even carried a pencil, and he never knew the standings. But he did know this: If a guy hit a curve ball in the second inning, Diz could tell you that when the same batter came up in the seventh. When it came to pitchers he had a mind like a filing cabinet.

Diz also liked to bet on games, and he'd drive you crazy wanting you to go check on games being played in other places, so that he could keep up with his bets.

As for his incorrect grammar - that was natural, although he hammed it up a bit, because he knew people enjoyed it and expected it. I knew his brother, Paul, because he had a diner right next to my diner in Little Rock, and we became good friends. His vocabulary was a lot like Dizzy's, but he was not the pitcher that his brother was.

Dizzy's wife handled all of his business, and she was very protective of him. She would frequently call Dancer-Fitzgerald, the advertising agency for Falstaff Beer, a major sponsor, and complain that they were taking advantage of her husband - didn't pay him enough money. Diz was just like a big kid, and if he liked you, he would do anything in the world for you. If he didn't like you, he would go out of his way to get you.

Diz always wore a big white Stetson hat, and he had great pride in his ability as a pitcher. I guess the only pitcher that Diz considered in his class was Carl Hubbell, the old New York Giants pitcher who came up with the famous "screwball."

Dean would go into this bar in Cleveland where a lot of the media people gathered. He would walk in the door like he owned the place and would yell, "I want to ask you guys - who was favored when ol' Diz pitched against Hubbell?"

The crowd would yell back in unison, "Podner, you were, Diz!"

Then Diz would say, "Set 'em up," and he would buy drinks for everyone at the bar.

He would carry a money clip full of hundred dollar bills, and I've seen him give a waitress a hundred dollar tip. I would say, "Diz, I don't make a lot of money, and here you are giving away hundred dollar bills."

He would laugh and say, "You want some money?" And, of course, I would say, "No, thank you, Diz."

Diz later got mad with Mutual because of what happened with his friend Gordon McLendon, who had put together the Liberty Network by doing re-creations of major league baseball games. He called himself "The Old Scotsman," and he would have a Western Union operator send him information on the games for his broadcast. There was always about a three minute lag between the actual game and McLendon's version of that game.

We discovered that it was interesting how he was more up to the minute on games we were broadcasting live, and we were convinced that he had someone monitoring our broadcasts. This would give him instant information, which he couldn't have possibly received from Western Union, so Mutual had a plan to trap him. Dizzy was asked to take part in the entrapment, and that didn't set well with him at all. This did nothing for the already tense relationship between Dizzy and Al Helfer.

Our plan was to tape a broadcast by McLendon for which we felt he was using our broadcast as a basis. We would give a false attendance figure or say that a ball was hit to right field, when it was actually hit to left field. Little variances that didn't hurt the accuracy of our broadcasts but provided evidence that the information McLendon used couldn't have come from any other source.

On occasions our booth was situated in the press box within earshot of other people, and when they would hear us say a ball was hit to left field, when it was right field, they looked over at us as if to say, "These guys must be drunk." However, we never did bring suit, because it would have been difficult to prove that he was pirating our broadcast, and it didn't really make that much difference.

Still, Dizzy didn't like the fact that we even thought about doing that to his friend Gordon. What finally killed Liberty was the line charges that they had to pay to connect their far flung network. For instance, they might have a station in Wyoming and the next closest station two states away.

The Liberty Network also did some college football games, including the Carolina-Clemson game in 1951, the year before I came to Columbia. Harry Wismer was the announcer for that game, which was televised internationally on the Armed Forces Network.

Back to Dizzy Dean. He had almost an unlimited expense account in spring training, because he was helping to promote Falstaff Beer, and he was known to buy meals for an entire ball club. I remember that Gene Kirby probably made more money playing gin rummy with Diz than he did working for Mutual.

There was never a dull moment when Diz was present. On a Capital Airlines flight, I was sitting near Diz - it was a prop plane - and he was looking out the window. All of a sudden he saw smoke coming out of one of the engines, so he yells loud enough for every passenger to hear him, "Hey, podner, this plane's on fire!"

The flight attendants came running back and said, "Mister Dean, shhhhhhh." But the damage had already been done, so the airplane had to go back to the airport in Chicago, although it turned out to be nothing serious.

WEATHERING THE WEATHER

Our biggest concerns, as we hopped from town to town to do our broadcasts, were airplane schedules and weather. On one occasion we were doing a game in Chicago, but I had to be at a party in Savannah that evening, because we were doing a game there the next day. The game dragged on, and I had to leave in order to catch the plane for Savannah, figuring the game would be over in a couple of innings.

I had to change planes in Atlanta, naturally, and when I was walking through the terminal, I heard a radio carrying a baseball game, so I stopped to listen. It turned out to be the game that I had left in Chicago a little more than an hour before. I said, "This is funny. I was broadcasting this game in Chicago, and here I am in Atlanta listening to it." The game had gone into extra innings.

When I got to my hotel in Savannah I stretched out on the bed and turned on the radio. A Savannah station had taped the game and was playing it on a delayed basis, so I hear myself on the air in about the third inning of the game I had left earlier in the day.

Weather was often a factor in Milwaukee, and at one game we were preparing to broadcast there were fans from all over Wisconsin. Milwaukee was unbelievable in the way they drew from a wide area, and this was a weekend game, so the stands would be packed.

When I arrived in Milwaukee it was pouring rain, so I just knew they couldn't play baseball that day. But I called Donnie Davidson, the publicity man for Milwaukee and said, "Are you going to play?"

He answered yes, but I insisted, "There's no way you can play a game with all this rain."

He explained, "We've got helicopters coming, and they're going to dry the field. The game was delayed, but it was played, and the club salvaged a big gate.

Milwaukee would play in any kind of weather. Once when I was there for a night game, the temperature was 31 degrees, and it was snowing - they were playing "Jingle Bells," but they were also playing baseball.

Cleveland was also a hotbed that year, because the Indians were in the middle of the race for the American League pennant, which they eventually won. Cleveland had a great pitching staff, with Bob Feller, Bob Lemon, Mike Garcia and Early Wynn as starters, plus a great bullpen.

We were there to do the first game of a doubleheader with the New York Yankees, and they had 86,000 people on hand. Fans were even standing in the bullpen area. I think two people at the game died of heart attacks.

THE GREAT TED WILLIAMS

However, even more enjoyable for me was the doubleheader between Boston and Detroit at Detroit the week before. Ted Williams had just returned from army duty in Korea, and he had a great day. Williams had eight hits in ten times at bat, and his two outs would normally have been base hits, but they had the "Williams shift" on and had fielders in the right places.

One of Ted's eight hits that day was a grand slam home run that landed on the right field roof, prompting the spectators to give him a standing ovation.

I worked the final game of that series on Monday afternoon, and Williams reached safely in his three appearances at the plate. In the top of the ninth Boston trailed the Tigers by one run, with two outs and the bases empty. When Ted came to the plate, the Detroit manager, Freddy Hutchinson, had seen enough of Williams with a bat in his hands.

He ordered the pitcher to give Williams an intentional base on balls, which went against the so-called "book." In that circumstance you never intentionally put the tying run on base. The next batter, Jackie Olsen, hit a hanging curve into the left field seats, and Boston held on to win the game.

The media and fans jumped all over Hutchinson for his strategy that backfired, but it clearly indicated the respect everyone had for the "Splendid Splinter." He was in a class by himself.

I went to the ballpark early just to watch Williams take batting practice. In fact, players from both teams would just stand there and watch him take his cuts. It was exciting, even to the veteran players.

Williams would also go up and help batters on his team and on opposing teams. Give them tips on what might improve their hitting. He probably made Al Kaline, who led the American League in batting for Detroit the next year, the hitter that he was.

Bob Fulton "My Career My Life"

Williams had great vision - could see the stitches on a pitched ball. I later was talking to an American League umpire, and he said, "I'm going to tell you something that, if you quote me on, I'll call you a liar. Ted Williams is not a 'guess' hitter. If he takes a pitch - doesn't swing at it - as far as I'm concerned, it's a ball. He has better eyes than any umpire in the game today, and I'm sure that I'm not the only one who feels that way. If he lays off a pitch, it's a ball - even if the count is three balls and no strikes."

Every announcer would like to call at least one no-hit, no-run game, and I had that chance. We were supposed to do a Cubs game, but the Phillies, who were playing well, were in Milwaukee. Helfer called New York and had them switch games.

About the seventh inning Helfer told someone to call New York and make sure that they were taping the game, as they normally did.

We later found out that they hadn't taped the game, which turned out to be a no-hitter. A friend of mine later told me that he was stationed in North Korea and listened to the game on the Armed Forces Network. He thought it was going to be a no-hitter, so he taped the last five innings. He sent me the tape, but, unfortunately, in moving around I have lost that tape.

A BAD BET
The 1954 World Series became the subject of rather strained relations between me and my father-in-law, Floyd Terrell. Floyd liked to place small wagers on games - particularly big events like the World Series - so he decided to go to an expert for advice. Cleveland had won the American League pennant, and the New York Giants were champions of the National League.

When Floyd asked me my opinion, I said, "There's only one team to pick, and that is Cleveland. Look at their pitching staff. It's obvious. The Giants were scrambling at the end of the season."

Floyd took that expert advice and bet heavily on the Indians. I couldn't have been more wrong. The Indians not only didn't win, but the Giants swept the series, four games to none. My father-in-law continued to speak to me, but I'm sure that it wasn't easy.

I didn't attend that World Series, because Mutual didn't broadcast it, and I had seen enough baseball to last me awhile. I had tickets, but my wife was expecting, so we headed back home to Columbia. Dody flew, and I packed all the pots and pans and drove from Chicago.

A BIG DECISION
I broadcast the Carolina football games the rest of the fall, and in January I got a call from Paul Jonas. He told me that Al Helfer had resigned, and that certainly didn't make me mad.

Then he said, "You might think we're gonna make Art Gleason the top man, but we don't think he's a heavyweight." That's exactly what he said. "We think you're doing an excellent job, and we want to bring you to New York and make you the number one man," Jonas added.

He told me the date they were going to spring training, and he told me to make up my mind and let him know by a certain date. He said he would call me at one o'clock on whatever the date was. It happened to be two days before Dody went to the hospital, but she didn't have the baby right away, so I don't have the exact date clear in my mind.

When Dody had our first child in Little Rock I had to leave that day for my new job in Columbia. I felt bad about that, and here it was about to happen again. That put me in a real bind.

At the time, as far as prestige was concerned, this was the best baseball job in the country. I knew that, yet I didn't feel comfortable, plus the fact that the traveling had been so bad - and working with Helfer. Then there was the tense situation between Helfer and Dizzy Dean. I felt that it would be better to work with just one ball club, rather than the network. However, I knew that this was a great opportunity.

I was all by myself in our apartment, thinking about what I should do, and I knew that I'd be talking to Jonas in a matter of minutes. The phone ran, and it was Jonas. He asked, "Are you all set to go to St. Pete?"

I said, "Paul, thank you, but I've decided not to go," and explained why. A lot of people have told me I made a big mistake, and maybe I should have stayed another year. But I turned it down. I went back to my job at the radio station and also became a partner in an open air market on Two Notch Road in Columbia.

I'll never forget. Art Gleason came by on his way to spring training. I'm sitting outside the store with an apron on, and this Cadillac convertible pulls up. It's Art Gleason on his way to Florida. Two Notch Road is actually the through-town leg of U.S. Highway One, which goes from New York to Florida, so Art didn't have to detour one bit to find my place of business.

Art said, "I can't believe you. I can't believe you're not coming back." He just kept shaking his head. "What are you doing here?" he continued. "I know guys who would give their right arm for this job. I would love to have had it. And here you are running this dump."

That made me feel great. But there I was, although I still had my job at the station, along with doing Carolina football and basketball.

The guy who replaced me was Mel Ott, the Hall-of-Famer, who had played for the New York Giants and led the National League in home runs in five different seasons. Mel didn't make it, and the following year they gave the job to Bob Feller.

Ott came through Columbia and called me up and said, "I want to have lunch with you. They told me that this is the only place I could find you." I had never met Ott, and I jumped at the invitation.

At lunch he told me, "You know what my trouble is in this thing? They think I should get excited when someone hits a home run. Honestly, Bob, I hit so many home runs, and I've seen so many home runs from the dugout - especially in the Polo Grounds - that I can't get excited."

I told him that what Mutual should have done was to make him an analyst, instead of doing play-by-play. Feller had the same problem. He just wasn't a play-by-play man. But what a nice guy Mel Ott was. It really made me sad several years later when I heard that he was killed in an automobile accident.

Mutual's Game of the Day went on for several years after I left, but the major leagues were having more and more night games, television was becoming an increasing factor, and most clubs were developing their own networks. So the Mutual concept died sort of a natural death.

Ironically, after I decided to stay in Columbia, one day Bill McKechnie, Jr., who was general manager of the Cincinnati Reds, came to Columbia. I had done a lot of games in Cincy, and I liked their people and the people I had met from that organization there and in Columbia during the time the Reds had their Class A farm club here.

McKechnie said, "Bob, I want to tell you this story. I don't know if I ought to tell you. It will make you feel good, but it may also make you feel bad. He went on to say, "We lost an announcer, and we wanted someone to work with Waite Hoyt, and your name was the first one that came up. We had been in Columbia, and we had seen you with Mutual, and we thought that this is the guy we want. But somebody in the group said, 'We can't afford to pay him what Mutual is paying him.'"

I told him, "Bill, I wasn't making that much money with Mutual. Everybody thought I was making a lot of money, but I was a rookie, and Paul Jonas was pretty tight fisted." If they had just called me, I would have said, "Here I come. I'm on my way."

I would love to have had the job at Cincinnati. I liked the town, the idea of following just one ball club, and I liked Hoyt. It would have been a great situation for me.

That was water under the bridge, and I have never liked to dwell on what might have been. If I had gone, I might never have had the great experiences, made the wonderful friendships and lived the satisfying life I have spent in Columbia.

What I did store away from 1954 was a great experience and fond memories. The old style ballparks with character and mystique, such as Ebbets Field in Brooklyn; rides with Brooklyn cab drivers, with whom the expression, "Wait till next year," really originated; all the great stars I saw perform around the two leagues; and the off-the-field associations with such characters as Dizzy Dean.

It was the last year that major league outfielders left their gloves in the field when they came in to bat. That marked the end of an era that I felt grateful just to have had a taste of.

So I left Mutual and settled down with the Gamecocks.

Al Helfer died. Art Gleason died. Dizzy Dean died. Paul Jonas died. Only Buddy Blattner is left. The rest are gone. Blattner is retired and lives in Missouri and still is a top-flight tennis player.

Announcers come and go. Players come and go. But the world of sport continues on, without missing a beat.

As for me, I considered myself fortunate to continue doing something I really loved, wherever it might have taken me.

~BASEBALL - MINOR AND MAJOR~

During the previous ten years I had become an expert on adapting to new towns and new situations, so I had few misgivings when I made the move to Columbia. That came well in advance of the Columbia Reds baseball season, so I had a little time to settle my family, which included my wife and newly-born daughter, Robin, into an apartment.

Columbia and Little Rock have their similarities. They are both state capitals, are about the same size, and the people have similar values, likes and dislikes.

I had no idea what this new move would lead to. It could have been another one-year stand, and that would have been nothing new.

Actually, the first sports broadcasts I did after coming here were University of South Carolina boxing matches in the old Carolina field house. Boxing was a popular sport at many colleges then, and Carolina Coach Jess Alderman had assembled a talented team of fighters. One of the most exciting events I broadcast was the Southern Intercollegiate Boxing Tournament held in Columbia. As I recall it drew teams from Maryland, Virginia, Miami, Louisiana State, Clemson, The Citadel, and, of course, Carolina.

Boxing matches would easily draw more spectators than would home basketball games. However, the lasting effects of boxing on some of the participants became a matter of concern among the colleges, and, one by one, they abolished the sport from intercollegiate competition.

That helped me bide my time until baseball season arrived, and it also allowed me to meet a number of people in the Columbia sports community.

The Columbia Reds were in the South Atlantic League, which included Savannah, Montgomery, Charleston, Jacksonville, Macon, Augusta, Columbus and Columbia. It was a very good class A circuit and was a prolific developing ground for future major leaguers. The Reds were in the Cincinnati organization, and they showed a lot of interest in bringing good baseball to Columbia.

The field manager was Ernie White, a likeable veteran with hair to match his last name. He had pitched in the major leagues, was very knowledgeable, knew how to work with ballplayers and was a professional in every sense. Personally, he was what you would call "of the old school." He had a great sense of humor, knew every baseball cliché and story and was very cooperative. Ernie was a delight to work with, and we got along well together. In my business you always consider that a plus.

There was a lot of talent in the Sally League, but the Reds won the pennant by 11 games and did it with only one player batting over .300. They did have great pitching, led by Barney Martin, who grew up in the Olympia section of Columbia and had major league potential. He moved up the ladder to AAA ball, and then to the Cincinnati Reds, but he missed Columbia and came back to settle down. Barney died several years ago and is missed by all former Columbia Red's fans.

Baseball was in the early stages of integration, particularly in the South, and some fans still didn't accept the black players. Jacksonville had three talented black players, Hank Aaron, Horace Garner and Felix Mantilla, all of whom moved up. I remember the first time Aaron came to bat in Columbia; we had a pitcher with the last name of Schoonover, who hung a curve ball to him. Aaron hit it over the top of the flagpole in centerfield, which is about 375 feet from home plate.

Bob Fulton "My Career My Life"

At that time black spectators were relegated to bleachers along the leftfield line, and they pulled for black players, even if they were playing against the home team. When Aaron slammed that home run, the leftfield bleachers went wild. I said some nice things about Aaron on the air, and the next day I got about 50 phone calls about it. The essence of the calls was, "We like you fine, but stop applauding those black players."

Columbia's first black player was Frank Robinson, a picture athlete who came here from the University of Southern California. He went up in a hurry and is the only person ever to receive the Most Valuable Player award in both the American and National leagues. He received it at Cincinnati in 1961 and when he played for Baltimore in 1966.

Even though he was a great prospect playing for the home team, a few of the fans still couldn't accept the advent of the black athlete. When Robinson developed an infection in his right shoulder it affected his ability to throw the ball, so he was moved from his natural outfield position to first base. There would be no need for long throws from that position. It still affected Robinson's overall play, and in the sports vernacular of today, "he was struggling."

One night we were televising a Columbia home game. I was positioned right even with first base behind a cyclone fence waiting to do a post-game interview. Robinson was on first base, having drawn a base on balls, and several rude fans - mostly winos – came down from the right field bleachers to where I was located and began to heckle him - really working him over. It was the worst I have ever heard, and I've heard a lot.

To make matters worse the batter kept hitting foul balls, which kept him at the plate for what seemed like an eternity. When he finally made an out, which ended the game, Robinson made a beeline toward the hecklers, grabbing a baseball bat from the bat rack in the dugout on the way. As Frank started to leap over the fence Ernie White, who had been coaching at third base, raced across the diamond and tackled Frank just as he was clearing the fence, perhaps saving the hecklers from being beaten to a pulp. Frank was enraged and you couldn't blame him.

Ernie told the fans doing most of the heckling, "I want you down at the Jerome Hotel at eleven o'clock tomorrow morning. I'll have a room ready, and I'm going to put you in there with Robinson." The two hecklers said, "We'll be there." As you might have guessed, they weren't!

After that ugly incident Robinson disappeared, and nobody knew where he was for a couple of weeks. Bill McCarthy, the general manager, finally located him, and he returned to Columbia and completed an impressive season.

Robinson was one of the strongest hitters I've ever seen, and that includes many of baseball's all-time greats. Ernie White told me about an incident that occurred when Columbia was playing a series at Jacksonville. The Reds "owned" the Braves, holding a big edge in their games played this season. In this particular Sunday afternoon affair, the Reds were leading by eight runs in the seventh inning, when Robinson came to bat.

Frank hit a ball toward left field that cleared a light tower by 15 feet. It looked like a comet leaving the park. It was obviously foul, but the umpire declared it fair, and Robinson circled the bases, knowing that he has just received a gift!

Jacksonville manager Ben Gharity, who was having a rough afternoon all the way around, charged out of the dugout and was right in the face of the umpire, telling him in no uncertain terms what he thought of the call. The umpire, I believe his name was Parks, was a likeable guy and had a great sense of humor. He tolerated the tongue lashing he was getting, then calmly took off his mask and said, "Ben, anybody who can hit a ball that far deserves a home run." Who could argue with him?

Although the Reds had good ball clubs in Columbia, attendance wasn't as good as the parent club in Cincinnati would like for it to be. So, by the time I had spent a year with Mutual's Game of the Day, the Reds were pulled out of Columbia and, I believe, Cincinnati concentrated on Savannah as their Sally League entry.

However, a "save baseball" movement, led by Columbia businessman Julius Love, resulted in a new ownership and affiliation. Love's club was nicknamed "Gems," and an affiliation with Kansas City was arranged. The field manager was Hank Biasetti, and Bill Herring was the general manager.

The club was not a winner, the fans didn't turn out, it was inevitable that baseball was doomed in Columbia, and the city was without organized baseball until the Bombers came to life a few years back.

A great positive for me out of this new arrangement was working with and getting to know Julius Love. He was a great person to work with, a person who loved this community and a died-in-the-wool baseball fan. Julius died several years ago in Florida, but he is indelibly etched in my memory. We need more people like him.

The Gems were way down in the standings and not drawing well at all. Julius was looking for anything that could be done to sell tickets, so I came up with an idea that we tried. I bet Al Jennings, the broadcaster for Savannah, that Columbia would outdraw his team during the next two weeks. The loser would have to sit on the roof of his ballpark until 10,000 tickets were sold. Jennings gleefully accepted, because he knew that I would become the "fiddler on the roof!'

A nine-game losing streak by the Gems did nothing to help my cause, so I lost the bet, as we had planned. I packed my bags and set-up housekeeping on the roof of Capital City Park, and, believe me, that's one helluva place to spend your summer. I believe my residency on the roof spanned the hottest weather of that summer, but it paid off.

Dixie Youth baseball players conducted a drive that sold 10,000 tickets, so I could put a roof over my head, instead of under my feet. I've often said I would try anything once, but once is enough for something like that - perhaps too much. But the Gems had some much needed cash in the bank, and I had paid my dues.

One story about Julius: When the Gems were playing away from home I would re-create the game from Western Union reports, and, of course, the broadcast lagged behind the actual game by two or three innings. Often games would last up until the late hours on the air, if not on the field.

Julius would listen to the games, knowing that in the latter innings the outcome of the game had been decided, while he was still sweating it out in his bedroom. He couldn't go to sleep without knowing the result. So, I worked out an arrangement with Julius that would signal to him the winner of the game as soon as I knew it.

This is how it worked. If the Gems won the game, I would say, "The wind is now blowing in from right field." If they lost it would be, "The wind is coming in from left field."

What if the game was going into extra innings? The wind would be "blowing in from center field," of course. I got that idea from my experience with the gambler in Hornell.

With that, Julius could cut out the lights and go to sleep!

123

Bob Fulton "My Career My Life"

~ THE BEGINNING OF MY RETIREMENT~

In 1994, I was informed by a "friend" that if I retired during that year, I, like many others, would receive a $7,000 bonus from the University. During my years at Carolina, my salary was never more than $29,000 a year and a large portion of that came from marketing the George Felton TV show.

When Dick Bestwick became the AD, he requested that I receive a substantial pay raise. His request was turned down.

In addition, the network, which had the rights to Carolina football and basketball broadcasts, paid me $200 per game. If you figure the hours I spent on each broadcast, I was receiving $10 or less per hour.

I was having a difficult time trying to decide what to do – so I called the AD Mike McGee for some help. He immediately told me to call Tommy Suggs – why Tommy – I don't know or perhaps didn't want to know - so no call.

Prior to all this, Jim Host whose company had now owned the rights to Carolina football and basketball broadcasts flew down to Columbia to see me. He told me I was free to do what I wanted to do but that he thought it would be wise for me retire and take the $7,000 bonus. I finally decided to resign. I called McGee and we set up a time for a meeting in his office. When I arrived at the appointed time, John Moore, the Assistant AD, was also there. This was a very difficult time and I felt that perhaps I was making the wrong decision. But when Mike McGee said to me, "you don't have to resign," I knew it was all over. Had Mike said to me, we would love to have you stay, I would have probably stayed several years longer.

Now the University started a search for my replacement. They invited sportscasters to send to the University an audition tape covering their play-by-play in football, basketball, and baseball. A committee of four was selected to make the final choice. I was asked to serve on this committee, but relented as many of my friends were seeking the job. I told Mike that I would be glad to listen to all the tapes and eliminate those that were not even close for consideration.

After much deliberation, the committee chose Mick Mixon who had worked with me on baseball broadcasts at Carolina and later was involved at the University of North Carolina as an assistant to Woody Durham on all major sports. Mick is now the football voice of the Charlotte Panthers.

But as it turned out, the committee's choice was not the broadcaster selected. To my surprise and the surprise of many others, the University announced that Charlie Mac Alexander would replace me. I had known Charlie Mac for many years and considered him to be a very good play-by-play broadcaster who would do an excellent job as the Voice of the Gamecocks. Charlie had a most impressive resume, which included Broadcaster of the Year awards in Mississippi and also Tennessee, where he handled the Vanderbilt play-by-play. Jim Host's firm in Lexington, which had the rights to the University of Kentucky sports broadcasts, had offered Charlie a position on the broadcast team of the Wildcats – a position which he accepted.

Shortly after Charlie Mac was hired, Mike McGee told me that he would like for me to become a consultant in the athletics department. I asked him what my job would entail, and he replied that I should just schmooze the important Carolina people I met. I dislike that word "schmooze" but was thankful to earn some extra money. However, it did not take me long to realize that I would do nothing – more or less disappear – I was out and Charlie Mac was in and that's the way it should be.

Two things happened that confirmed this. Several months before this Coach Eddie Fogler had invited Carol and me to make the trip with the basketball team to the Holiday Basketball Tournament in Hawaii. When Fogler told McGee we were going to make the trip, Mike cancelled our trip for the reason that my going would detract from the attention given Charlie Mac. I think Mike gave me more credit than I deserved. I had previously made three trips to the Islands, but this decision was very disappointing to Carol who had never been to Hawaii.

The second confirmation came when Jimmy Collins, a former Carolina basketball star who had become the manager of a group of stations in Columbia, wanted me to do a four-hour show on Saturday mornings before the Gamecock football broadcasts. I knew I would enjoy getting back on the air and, of course, the extra money would be a real bonus. When Collins told McGee what he had planned for me, McGee said that I could not do the show because I was from a different era – in plain words – forget the past.

As I said in my book, Athletics Director Mike McGee did so much in taking Carolina's athletics program to new heights. I thank him, as do many Gamecock fans, for the job he did. But where I disagree with Mike was in his attempt to write off the past, including the McGuire years, which built a tradition that had been sorely lacking at Carolina.

Although Columbia Mayor Bob Coble had declared March 21 as "Bob Fulton Day" in the city, the real climax of my final year came on January 21. The University sponsored a tribute dinner for me that night at the Sheraton Hotel on Broad River Road. Gene McKay was emcee for the affair, and Carolina President John Palms and his wife Norma were among the head table guests.

Those chosen to make comments about me were Carolina coaches Brad Scott, Eddie Fogler and June Raines, former football coach Paul Dietzel, former football players Alex Hawkins, George Rogers, Jeff Grantz and Tommy Suggs, former basketball player Alex English, Clemson broadcaster Jim Phillips and Don Barton, who is co-author of the book *"Hi Everybody! This is Bob Fulton"* Among the some 450 people in attendance were my two daughters, Robin and Nancy.

McGee announced that a scholarship bearing my name would be established at Carolina and that my wife and I would receive a trip to Europe as a gift of appreciation from the athletics department. He also announced that I would continue to serve the University as a consultant to the athletics department and that Carol and I would receive tickets to Carolina football, basketball and baseball games in the years ahead.

There was still another surprise ahead. A group representing the Columbia Tipoff Club invited us to dinner and presented us with a check to help defray extra expenses on our trip to Europe, and they also gave us a beautiful silver tray as a permanent memento from the Tipoff Club. At the dinner were Coach Eddie Fogler, Skip Kickey, Casey Manning, Dennis Powell and their wives.

Our European trip in the summer of 1995 took us to Germany, Austria, Italy and Switzerland.

In the spring of that year I had attended a number of Gamecock Club meetings around the state, and that gave me a chance to meet more and more Gamecock fans – who are the best in the country. This was climaxed later in the year at the Alumni Association banquet, at which I received an honorary membership in the Association.

Of the 43 years I spent broadcasting for the Gamecocks, I must say that the entire Carolina community made the 43rd special and unforgettable. My next 43 years are being spent in appreciation for all the special moments and all the athletes, coaches and others who made my work exciting. I'll always remember those who helped me along the way and especially the fans. Without the fans, there would never have been a need for Bob Fulton.

~BROADCASTERS ARE MADE, NOT BORN~

As a result of circumstances surrounding my birth, I have no documented proof that it actually occurred, except for the fact that I am here.

Weather records for Philadelphia will reveal that on December 21, 1920, the city experienced one of the worst blizzards in its history. As the snow accumulated, Mary and Robert Fulton were welcoming into the world a baby boy with a rather deep crying voice. My mother made it to the hospital for this occasion, and so did the doctor, but because of the deepening snow, he was unable to turn in the record of my birth. My 53-year broadcast career has provided millions of witnesses to the fact that I was born, but I've never had a birth certificate to prove it.

That does present a problem in life when you need a passport or other things that require proof of age - or birth.

My family moved several times during my early years - from Jenkintown to Chester to Ridley Park, all located near Philadelphia. My school days were spent at Ridley Park, about 12 miles from town but close enough to relate to things taking place in the City of Brotherly Love.

I was nine years old when the Great Depression occurred, and my father had to go about four years without a regular paycheck. He was treasurer of a brick business, which went under, and he could never recover from that financial setback. We were forced to take in boarders for a source of income, and I tried to help out by delivering newspapers in the mornings and afternoons.

I also did a few other jobs, such as working at a drug store soda fountain, but my school work suffered, as a result. To make matters worse, my sister, who was six years older, never made anything but A's, and people expected the same of me.

For years I had taken violin lessons, so when I was a sophomore in high school several friends of mine formed a dance band with me, and we earned some extra money by playing at proms and dances around the area. I had learned to "slap base," which fit right into the popular music of that day.

My high school class was graduated in 1938, as Adolph Hitler tightened his stranglehold on Germany and set the stage for World War II. There wasn't a lot in my high school experience that predicted that I would make a career out of sports, although, for some reason, the class prophecy had me becoming a major league baseball announcer. I did play a lot of basketball and a little football, but not well enough to attract the attention of college recruiters.

There were no high profile sports figures in Pennsylvania at that time. That's an interesting fact about a state that later produced more than its share of stars. Like Stan Musial in baseball, Arnold Palmer in golf and Joe Namath in football, to name a few.

It was my lot to become a Philadelphia Phillies baseball fan, and they were the worst team in the National League. I also would go to Shibe Park to see the Philadelphia Athletics, but their glory days under legendary Connie Mack were over.

The Phillies played in Baker Bowl, which was a pitcher's nightmare, because it had such short fences. Phillies pitchers were bad enough in any ballpark.

I recall a game in which a guy named Beck was pitching for the Phillies, and he was having a terrible day, even for a Philly. Opposing batters were having a field day, sending balls either over or against the fences. The Philadelphia centerfielder, having become weary from chasing balls all over the lot, hung his head after watching one of Beck's pitches knocked well over the centerfield wall.

When Beck had a new ball delivered to him, he eyed the batter then turned and threw the ball as far as he could in the general direction of centerfield and well over the still bowed head of the centerfielder. When the demoralized fielder heard the ball make contact with the wall, he instinctively sprang into action again, retrieved the ball and fired it in to second base, as he had done following so many other fence-rattlers during the game.

From that day forward the pitcher was known as "Boom Boom" Beck.

Visits to Shibe Park were exciting, not for the quality of the A's but because of the stars on visiting teams. Dad and I would stand in line to buy 75-cent bleacher tickets, and it was well worth the wait and the price. The Athletics did have Hall-of-Famer Lefty Grove, and it was a special treat to watch him pitch. Especially when the New York Yankees came to town with Babe Ruth, Lou Gehrig, Bill Dickey and other members of "Murderers Row."

Even at the age of seven I had a secret ambition to be a baseball announcer, because I loved to listen to broadcasts of Philadelphia games. All games were played in the afternoon in that era. Often I would throw a tennis ball against the stoop of the stairs of our house and would pretend to broadcast a baseball game. Perhaps I would have recorded some of my efforts, but tape recorders were non existent.

When I was a teen-ager I would go to Shibe Park and position myself behind the box of Athletics play-by-play man Byrum Saam. His box jutted out toward the playing field, so he wore a big Stetson hat to shield his head from the summer sun. In 1954 when I was broadcasting Mutual's Game of the Day, I met Byrum Saam and told him about eavesdropping on him as my model for doing baseball play-by-play.

He smiled and said, "You should have told me, because I would have made it possible for you to get in without buying a ticket." A little late but an indication of what a nice man he was.

After finishing high school I attended West Chester State Teachers College, and I took a course in speech, but my teacher was not impressed. I was so bad that my teacher wanted me to come back after class for special instruction. I couldn't do that, because I was earning money for my tuition by driving several high school students to and from West Chester, which was 25 miles south of Philadelphia.

That teacher gave me a big fat "F" in the speech class, a fact that I never mentioned in my resume for broadcast job applications.

After a year at West Chester State my passengers no longer needed a ride, so I had to look elsewhere for my higher education. That elsewhere turned out to be a small college in Clarksville, Arkansas. It was called College of the Ozarks, the name of which has now been changed to University of the Ozarks. I later became a member of that institutions board of trustees.

Why did I go there? It was because the school was supported by the Presbyterian Church, and my parents were devoted Presbyterians. Through their efforts I was able to get jobs to pay my way through college, and I received my degree in speech in 1942. My jobs included waxing floors in the administration building, driving a truck to transport dirt and washing pots and pans in the kitchen at night. That was tough work all the way around!

My work scholarship had me working four hours a day, for which the NYA (National Youth Administration) paid me nineteen cents an hour – seventy-six cents per day. Yes, times were tough.

I owned a 1929 Model A Ford, which provided fun and also enabled me to pay me expenses for a trip home during the Christmas holidays. The fun part was having some of my college classmates join me on most Saturday evenings to ride down the long hill from the college into town without using any fuel. Then pushing the car from one closed service station to another, collecting fuel from the gas pump hoses which would enable us to cruise around town – then drive back to my dormitory parking space – sometimes barely making it.

Two college students whose homes were not far from mine asked me if I would drive them back east for the Christmas holidays, so we shared expenses. It was not much fun as the 2,000 mile round trip was made in the 1929 Model A Ford through lots of snow and ice. Not exactly fun but it enabled us to spend the Christmas holidays with our families.

However, one of these trips almost cost us our lives. On this particular return trip I decided to go by Kingsport, Tennessee, and make a surprise visit on New Year's Eve to the home of a girl I had been dating in college. Unfortunately, she had returned to college early so around 1 a.m. we continued our trip westbound up the mountains that surround Kingsport. It was snowing and it was bitter cold. My two passengers were bundled up and trying to stay worm in the back seat so I, in need of heat, opened the little door which was located just above the floorboard on the passenger side. This enabled the heat from the manifold to warm the interior. Within fifteen minutes we were approaching a small farm community when I suddenly started to get dizzy and just as I was about to pass out I stopped the car, threw open the door, and rolled out into the snow. I pushed my face right down into the snow and slowly my mind cleared. Then suddenly I realized my friends were still in the car. I would have called for help but the closest farm house was some distance away and no lights were on. What followed, I don't clearly remember but somehow I was able to get my two friends out of the car and put them face down into the snow. It seemed like an eternity, but we finally came around – cold, wet and exhausted, but still alive – thankful that we had not all died from carbon monoxide poisoning.

My major extracurricular activity at the Ozarks was the debate team, and my partner and I won a number of meets. We even defeated the Baylor Law School team, one of the top teams in the country, at an event in Oklahoma. My roommate was one of the best debaters in the country, and that was a big help. One of our work-scholarship assignments was washing the pots and pans in the college kitchen. It was there where we used the chopping block as a lectern as we would go over our notes for our next debating meet. That was as close to a lectern as we could get.

Along with my paying jobs and the debate team, I still found time to get a pilot's license and play basketball. I even played on an "all-star" team that advanced several rounds in an AAU tournament. I was a guard with deceptive speed - slower than I looked. I made up for lack of speed with shooting accuracy. I once won a foul shooting contest by making 45 out of 50.

Looking back at my senior year in college, it appeared I was majoring in basketball. First of all the high school in Hartman, Arkansas, twenty miles from Clarksville, asked me to coach their boys' and girls' basketball teams. I was able to rearrange my work schedule at the college and took the job, which I enjoyed immensely, and was very pleased with our teams. My college could not afford to field a team that would play a full-time schedule so I chose the top eight players from our intramural teams and we became the Clarksville All Stars.

RED HICKEY, who lived in Clarksville and had been a star performer in football and basketball at the University of Arkansas, was a friend of mine, and I asked him to join our All Stars – which he did. We did very well defeating some of the better teams in the state. Red Hickey completed his career, eventually becoming the head coach of the San Francisco 49ers in 1960. With a four and four record, the 49ers were practicing for a game against the two-time defending champion Baltimore Colts when Red decided to scrap the traditional T-formation, hoping to cope with the Colts' rush. He had his quarterback stand about five yards behind the line instead of taking the snap while under center, and he spread his backs to the sides. That alignment gave the offense an extra second or two to develop a play. The quarterback could run, hand off to a crisscrossing back, or throw. This was the beginning of the shotgun offense, which is used by so many teams in college football today. The 49ers beat the heavily favored Colts 30 to 22. Red died in April of 2006, at a Hospice in Aptos, California.

I should mention that for several years I served as a member of the Board of Trustees at Ozarks with Helen Walton, the wife of the late Sam Walton who was the founder of Wal-Mart and Sam's. Helen was one of the finest people I have ever met. I am sure she had much to do with my receiving the Ozarks Alumni Achievement Award a few years ago. Helen Walton's support of Ozarks was incredible. She has given the College, through her foundation and from her personal funds, over one hundred million dollars. Because of these donations, the beautiful campus at the foothill of the Ozarks now has several new buildings, one of which includes a complete TV and radio studio for students who want to pursue careers in communication. There is also now a complete theatre for Little Theatre productions. Helen Walton died peacefully in her sleep in April 2007, at the age of 87.

University of Ozarks President Dr. Riece and his lovely wife Sherri`, are role-models of what a college president's family should be. I love this school. Without the help I received from Ozarks, I probably would not have had a college education. I am proud to tell you that the University is now rated as one of the leading Liberal Arts colleges in the southwest.

After I finished college, with World War II in full force, I worked at a Philadelphia shipyard while waiting for the inevitable draft notice. There I received a severe injury and lost a toe when a large pipe fell on my foot, requiring surgery.

When I was called for the draft my foot was in such bad shape that they said they couldn't use me. I guess feet were very important to the military at that time, because they turned down Joe DiMaggio (New York Yankee great) because he had a heel spur, and rejected 1942 Heisman Trophy recipient Frankie Sinkwich (Georgia) on account of his flat feet.

FIRST JOB IN BROADCASTING
Near the end of 1942 I noticed an ad in the PHILADELPHIA ENQUIRER for a job as a radio announcer with WCAM. I reasoned that male voices were getting scarcer and scarcer, as the armed forces grew. I arrived at City Hall at nine o'clock in the morning, and a large crowd had already gathered. So much for the scarcity of male voices!

I said to myself, "I can never get this job," so I went back down the elevator and across the street to get a cup of coffee. The coffee must have heated up my confidence, so I decided to return to the audition. "What have I got to lose?" I asked myself. I auditioned and was terrible on the straight stuff, but there must have been something in my voice that they liked. One of the people said, "We need a sports announcer. Can you ad lib some sports?"

That's something I could do, so I did. They called me back later, along with eight others, for a final "talk-off," and I got the job. It paid a whopping $25 a week!

I looked at this job as a stepping stone. If you can make it in Camden, you can make it in Philadelphia.

While at WCAM, in addition to doing newscasts and regular studio broadcasts, I had the opportunity to cover horse racing at Garden State Park, wrestling and boxing at a small fight club in Philadelphia – where most of the bouts were fixed – and also ice hockey.

The races at Garden State Park were taped and played back later, because if you didn't delay at least an hour, you were aiding and abetting the gamblers in New Jersey. I remember that one guy lost his job because he put on the wrong race, and the numbers racket paid off thousands of dollars as a result.

A SHORT LIVED COACHING CAREER

After an illness, I decided to get out of broadcasting for awhile. I had coached basketball and football at Hartman, Arkansas, while I was in college, so I applied for and landed a job at Pulaski Junior High School in Little Rock. I didn't know much about football, so I got a book on the single wing offense by Fritz Crisler, the great Michigan coach. I jazzed it up a bit, which, I'm sure, would have been appreciated by Crisler.

We drew big crowds for these junior high school games, particularly when we played one of the other junior high teams in town. We won the city championship in 1944, and that paid off with a great thrill - but little money.

It may be hard to believe, but it is true, that in recent years our junior high football and basketball teams have held our 54th and 59th reunions. A writer at the ARKANSAS DEMOCRAT Newspaper in Little Rock was so amazed that a junior high team would be celebrating their 59th reunion that he came to our dinner, took notes, wrote a feature in his paper, the story of which got on the internet and ultimately gave us national publicity.

It seemed that fate was still drawing me toward broadcasting. The father of the fullback on my junior high team was chief engineer at KLRA, the CBS station in Little Rock. He told me

KLRA would give me a job doing sports in the evening, and I could still hold my coaching job, if I wanted to. I accepted the offer and began doing a daily 15-minute sportscast. At the end of 1944 I became a full-time staff announcer, which found me doing a morning show, the news and sports. My coaching career had ended.

Shortly after joining KLRA I was approached by the Magnolia Oil Company's advertising agency in Dallas, Texas. They wanted me to broadcast a high school champion football game in Arkansas. Naturally, they assumed I had previous experience broadcasting football. Of course, I hadn't, but I practiced many hours sitting in stadiums far away from the fans doing play-by-play of the game I was watching. This was my first experience lying my way into a play-by-play job. Fortunately, the producer and the agency were pleased with my broadcast so when the high school championship basketball game was scheduled I went through the same process with the Magnolia Ad Agency. Now I was lying my way again. Glad to report, all worked out just fine.

Soon I began doing play-by-play for some of the University of Arkansas football games, as there were no exclusive rights. I also did games involving Central High School, which made national headlines in 1957, when President Eisenhower ordered federal troops to Arkansas to supervise the admission of nine black students to the previously all-white school.

The first Arkansas game I broadcast was against Texas in Little Rock High School Stadium, and a crowd of 10,000 turned out. That wasn't bad, considering wartime circumstances.

My years at KLRA gave me a broad base of experience. In addition to sports, I covered a number of events such as rodeos, horse shows, auctions, elections, man-on-the-street interviews; and back in the studios, I did newscasts, record shows, sports shows, and a feature that was different for me but one I thoroughly enjoyed. At 11:30 each evening, KLRA would leave their CBS programming and bring an organist to the studio that would play very sentimental ballads, as a background while I read poetry. I was very pleased with the listener response and the comments that were "very interesting" - particularly those from women.

When the war ended, Frank Page, a returning service man whose home was in North Little Rock, was hired as an announcer by KLRA. Frank, an outstanding broadcaster, and I became close friends.

During the war years there had been a freeze on building materials that were necessary in constructing new radio stations. Now with the war over, hundreds of stations were being built across the country and there was a tremendous need for announcers. So Frank and I decided with the GI Bill available that we would open a school to train announcers. We had one of our engineers install turntables, etc., and we auditioned all applicants and accepted only those whom we thought were able to make the grade. We were fortunate to place all thirty-seven of our students – so the school was a real success.

Since Frank and I had enjoyed success with our radio school, we decided to broaden our business ventures by buying the Broadway Diner on a main street in downtown Little Rock. This was a disaster. We spent our time off from the radio station trying to run a business about which we knew nothing. The cook and his wife we hired were stealing us blind – sometimes showing up for work drunk or not coming in at all. To compound our problems, Frank had become involved in a confrontation with the program director at KLRA, which resulted with his being fired. I had a friend who owned station KWEM in West Memphis, Arkansas. I knew he was looking for announcers and he immediately hired Frank. Frank and I had worked together on a listener participation show which had the highest rating in the Little Rock area. I was very upset with the way my friend had been treated, and the following week, I resigned. Yes, I went to work with Frank at KWEM. Frank's wife Helen, who had been helping us from the time we bought the diner, remained in the Little Rock area, running the diner which by this time we had put up for sale. The irony of all this is that my partner and I were flat broke and we were several weeks away from our first paycheck. So to sustain us in our small one-room apartment we lived off bananas and milk while some ninety miles away there was our diner just loaded with plenty of food.

KWEM was a daytime station with a signal covering several states, including Louisiana. The manager of KWKH, a fifty thousand watt station in Shreveport happened to hear Frank and liked what he heard and offered my friend an announcing position which was the beginning of an outstanding career for Frank. Later on KWKH, Page was the emcee of the Louisiana Hayride Show which featured Elvis Presley every week. Frank wisely saved many tapes from this show and to say that they are valuable is an understatement. So was buying the diner a disaster for my friend – of course not. At the height of his career, he was named "Man of the Year" in Louisiana.

With my friend gone, I decided to move back to the Little Rock area and joined the staff at KXLR in North Little Rock, which had become the flagship station of the University of Arkansas football and basketball games. This was a perfect fit for me as I had already been the Voice of the Razorbacks when the games were carried on KLRA. I really had a busy schedule on this station. In addition to studio shows, which at one time included an all-night record show, I would do a junior college game on Thursday, a high school game on Friday night, an Arkansas game on Saturday afternoon and an Arkansas Intercollegiate Conference game on Saturday night. As if that were not enough, on Sunday afternoon I would do re-creations of the Philadelphia Eagles games, whose star was former Arkansas All-American Clyde Scott. He was a great running back who had grown up in the little Arkansas town with the intriguing name of Smackover.

During my three years at KXLR I observed a man who would be a strong candidate for my choice of "most unforgettable character." He was Jimmy Karam, coach of Little Rock Junior College and an absolute wild man. His team played in what they called the "Little Rose Bowl" in California, and that would determine the national junior college champion, which Karam's team won.

I was told that during the season when his team was behind at halftime, he would detour into the stands on his way to the dressing room and place a bet with one of the fans that his team would come back and win, and they did most of the time.

He sometimes predicted that his team would win by 40 points, and he was usually right.

He would call me up and invite himself to come down for an interview, and it was hard to turn him down, because he was so colorful. He called Harry Wismer, Mutual's Sports Director in New York, and told him that he would fly to New York to be interviewed on Wismer's sports show, and, by golly, he did!

When the head coaching job at Arkansas was vacant in 1951, Karam ran a full page ad in the ARKANSAS GAZETTE promoting himself for the position. That didn't work. When I came to Columbia I showed the ad to Carolina head coach Rex Enright, and he said he had never seen anything like that in his life. He couldn't believe it.

Karam later left the coaching profession, changed his ways and went to work for evangelist Billy Graham.

The year was 1948, and I was about to discover, as Frank Page had, that buying the diner turned out to be a blessing not a disaster. The attorney who handled the purchase of the diner was Floyd Terral, the top criminal lawyer in the state, whose brother had been Arkansas' Lieutenant Governor and for a short time, Governor. Floyd and I had become friends through our mutual interest in University of Arkansas sports. He and his lovely wife Wade had four daughters, one of whom was Dody, living with her parents in Little Rock. She had attended Iowa State for a year. Tired of all the snow, she transferred to

SMU where she, with her sister Janet, graduated. Dody, who was a Phys Ed major, joined the faculty of the high school located in a suburb of Dallas. Two years later she decided to return to her home in Little Rock and went to work in the city library. She loved her new job as she always had spent much of her time reading there. She began to work toward a degree in library science by taking a course at Little Rock Junior College.

My attorney friend, Floyd Terral, realizing I was single, asked his secretary who had been a classmate of mine at Ozarks just what kind of a person is this guy – obviously she gave me a good report. So Floyd gave the news to his wife Wade. Wade arranged it where I would by chance run into them at Franke's Cafeteria in Little Rock. So there I was eating dinner when Mrs. Terral walked in with Dody. Wade asked me if I would mind sharing my table with them. Of course, I wouldn't. Dody was very attractive and the minute I met her, I fell in love with her. She was intelligent, had a good personality, and was not involved in any relationship. I waited a couple of days, and then called her, asked her for a date, and she agreed. We dated for two weeks at which time she was scheduled to leave for Denver, Colorado, to work on her library science degree at Denver University. We were very much in love and decided to become engaged before she left for the summer and would marry sometime in the fall after her return. During the summer we wrote to each other every day and I would call her once a week.

Dody returned in September and we were married November 28, at the First Baptist Church in Little Rock. A beautiful wedding and reception, all planned by her mother. Unfortunately we never had any pictures of the wedding or the reception. A "friend" of mine who owned a photo studio in Little Rock told me that for his wedding present to us he would take the pictures at no charge. However, he just forgot to show up - thus not even one picture of the wedding or the reception. Our honeymoon was fun and also work. I broadcast an Arkansas game at Fayetteville two days following the wedding. Then two days later, I broadcast the Razorback's game at the University of Tulsa. Finally, back to Little Rock and to a small apartment, very close to the Terral residence where we were only a few minutes away from the wonderful meals Wade Terral insisted we have with the family.

I was very fortunate to have Dody as my wife.

Dody was an avid follower of sports, particularly SMU football, as she had attended SMU at the same time that Doak Walker and Kyle Rote were responsible for the Mustangs gaining national recognition. Dody was an outstanding tennis player. Her dad had built a tennis court next to the Terral residence and had her take tennis lessons from the time she was seven years old. She won quite a few tennis tournaments including some AAU sponsored events. When we played singles, it was "love – love" for me all the way. When thinking of Dody she reminded me of the person entering a crowded room – she could say here I am but Dody was always "there you are."

Our marriage was blessed with two children, Robin and Nancy, each having a son and a daughter.

A SHAKY START IN COLORADO

My entry into broadcasting baseball was really a fraud! This is how it happened. Someone from an ad agency in Denver, Colorado, called me and wanted to talk to me about doing baseball play-by-play. They handled the Columbine Network out of Pueblo, Colorado. "You have done baseball?" he asked. I muttered in the affirmative. "I thought so," he added.

A friend of mine told them I could do baseball, and they accepted that. My friend had just assumed that I could do it. The agency man told me, "The broadcaster we have now just doesn't have any experience, and we've got to make a change." He added that he would like to have a tape of a game I had done, just for the record. "Send me a tape of a live game," he said.

I faked a game between Little Rock and Chattanooga and sent it to the agency. They never checked with the Little Rock ball club to ask about me - otherwise I would have been a dead duck. They called me and said, "You've got the job. We like what we hear."

My wife, Dody, and I went down to watch the announcer re-creating Little Rock games, and, frankly, he wasn't all that good. I told myself, "I can do better than that." So on my way to Pueblo to talk to my new employers, Dody and I were going through the baseball rules book to get up to date on everything. Of course I had seen a lot of baseball games while I was growing up, so it was definitely nothing strange to me.

When we finally arrived at Pueblo, much to my surprise - and shock - there was a full page ad in the newspaper, heralding my arrival. It said, in effect, "One of the nation's finest baseball play-by-play announcers is coming to Pueblo. Tune in tonight and every night and hear Bob Fulton calling the play by play for all the Pueblo Dodgers games, both home and away, sponsored by Walters Beer. Fulton comes to Pueblo with seven years of topflight sports announcing to his credit, working with some of the nation's best."

If they had only known, they would have needed something stronger than Walters Beer! I had never done a game and was living a lie out there.

What's just as funny was the reason the job came open. The guy I replaced was named Johnny Special. It was his first year, and he was having some problems. The incident that led to his firing took place in a game in which Pueblo's starting pitcher, Ray Hathaway, was really getting shelled by the opposition. Hathaway, who later managed at Asheville in the old Tri-State League, doubled as manager of the Pueblo club.

After being hit so soundly, Hathaway decided he was getting out of there and bringing in a relief pitcher. Special, in telling his audience what was happening, said, "Hathaway has decided to relieve himself on the mound." That on top of everything else was all they could take, and Special was on his way out.

I must admit that when the agency man came down from Denver to check me out, I was scared to death. I was living a lie that I had seven years experience broadcasting baseball, and this was the first game I had ever done. To make things worse, this guy sat in the booth with my statistician, Dody, and me. Of course, Dody had never done a game either.

We went on the air 15 minutes before game time, and I had written a lot of things to use in the introduction. I was well rehearsed for my first venture into baseball play-by-play. When the game was about to start, the lights in the park went out, but I was still on the air. While they worked on getting the lights back on, I was in the dark and trying to ad lib my way through.

All I could talk about was beautiful Colorado and how Dody and I loved it. Doty had been to Denver, but this was my first visit to Colorado. I talked about how we liked the people of Pueblo, how happy we were to be there, and so forth.

Finally, the game began, and things seemed to work out pretty well. It was a win for the Dodgers, and the manager didn't have to relieve himself on the mound!

We were off and running - or talking - and the season went well for me. Unfortunately, it didn't go so well for the Dodgers. Pueblo had a great outfield prospect named Bill Sharman, who had just been graduated from the University of Southern California. He was a good ballplayer, and the parent club, the Brooklyn Dodgers, wanted to take a good look at him.

So rather than fly out to Pueblo every time they wanted to see Sharman, they moved him to Elmira, New York of the Eastern League. Incidentally, Bill later played in the National Basketball Association with the Boston Celtics.

His loss to the ball club might have had something to do with the tailspin in which it went. The frightening prospect for me was that Pueblo was within one game of tying the record of 26 straight losses held by the Little Rock Travelers. If they should tie or break the record, it was bound to make the SPORTING NEWS. Then it would be inevitable that the people in Pueblo would ask me about that Little Rock club, and it would have come out that I had never done baseball in Little Rock.

Talk about sweating it out. We went to Denver with the prospect of tying the record, and that probability was still very much alive as the teams went into extra innings. In the 12th our catcher, named Merv Dornberg, hit a grand slam home run, and the Dodgers held on to win the game and break their streak. I could have kissed Dornberg. My sordid past remained a secret.

BACK TO ARKANSAS

That was my only season at Pueblo, because I needed a full-time job. At the conclusion of the baseball season at Pueblo, the radio station offered me a full-time job. However, I wanted to return to Little Rock so I could continue covering University of Arkansas sports. Since I had left KXLR, my studio job was no longer available so all I had were the Razorback games and some free-lance work. Money was tight, but I still wanted to land another baseball job. In the spring of 1951, I answered two ads in Broadcasting Magazine – one was for a play-by-play job in Williamsport, Pennsylvania, in the class A Eastern League and the other for play-by-play in the class D Pony League in Hornell, New York. I knew it was competitive for the jobs and I would have been happy to land just one. Much to my surprise I was offered both positions. I decided to take the job in Hornell because they were covering all the games, while the station in Williamsport was carrying only three games per week. Ironically on my way to Hornell, I passed right past the station in Williamsport. Hornell was located just across the Pennsylvania line in New York. This league was comprised of teams in New York, Pennsylvania, and Hamilton, Ontario – thus the name Pony League.

What follows here is really unbelievable but is absolutely the truth. For the second year in a row, I was replacing a play-by-play man because he had made a huge mistake. However, nothing like the person I had followed in Pueblo – this man was a first-class baseball broadcaster. He had been hired when his predecessor decided to work in another league. He was so thorough in his preparation for the start of the season that he listened to some of the tapes of the announcer he was replacing and heard on one of them a broadcast of the game in Bradford, Pa., where this man had used the sound effects of a locomotive rolling along beyond the right-field fence. This certainly would add credence to a re-created broadcast. Unfortunately, in the first week of the season he used the locomotive train sound effect. Hornell was a railroad town. It seemed everyone worked for the railroad. As a result, what the listeners knew, and the new play-by-play man didn't know was the fact that in the off season the railroad decided to use diesel engines. Thus the re-creation that was intended to make the listeners believe that the broadcast was live from Bradford had failed, so the new man was fired and I followed.

Like Pueblo, Hornell was a Dodger farm team. The fans packed the ball park every night. There was only one town, Wellsville, New York, not far from Hornell, where we would do live broadcasts.

One night we were broadcasting at Wellsville, and it was so foggy in the late innings that you couldn't see beyond second base. It was an important play-off game, so they didn't call it, as they probably would have done under other circumstances.

In the top of the 12th inning we scored two runs, so all we had to do was get them out in the bottom of the inning with one run or less. Foreseeing a possible crisis and considering the poor visibility, each of our outfielders put a baseball in his pocket, and this strategy paid off.

The home team loaded the bases with two out and their clean-up hitter at the plate. He hit a towering drive, and the ball disappeared into the fog, apparently on its way out of the ballpark. The 4,000 spectators began a wild celebration, which came to an abrupt halt when our centerfielder, Andy Greener from Macon, Georgia, came running in from out of the fog, waving a baseball, as the batter rounded second base. The cheers turned to screams of outrage, as the umpire declared the ball caught and the game over.

Those fans knew that the ball couldn't have been caught, and they were nearing riot status, as the umpires ran for the safety of their dressing room. The road leading out of Wellsville winds over a large hill that overlooks the ballpark. As Dody and I headed out of town, we could see a crowd of people, many with flashlights, trying to find the baseball that should have represented a game-winning home run. The problem was that the area beyond the fence was very swampy and capable of hiding a baseball forevermore. Later, Greener confessed to me that the ball he was waving coming into the infield was the one that he had stored in his pocket.

There were several bars across from the station at Hornell, and I developed a friendship with one of the owners, and we even played golf together occasionally. In the back rooms of these places they had a big board, posted with all of the different games and things in those games that people could bet on.

One day he said to me, "Bob, I want you to know we do a lot of betting on baseball games in a room behind the bar. We bet on everything from the score of the game to home runs, singles, doubles, triples, strikeouts - you name it." He made me feel good by telling me that I was bound to move up the next year, because I was too good for Hornell.

"Here's a chance for you to make some money before you leave," he said. He knew that the re-created broadcasts lagged several innings behind the actual game and that I knew in advance what was going to happen, before it went on the air. He said, for instance, if it was a home run, I would say the wind is blowing in from left – for a triple, wind is blowing from center – a double, the wind is blowing from right, etc. The odds were set according to the probability of something happening. He said there were of course long odds on a homerun; and if I gave him the wind signal from left, he would hold up for a few minutes, than place his bet. He would lose some bets to legitimize the whole process. There was no way anyone would ever know what was happening. He would split the money with me. 'Think it over,' he said. Incidentally, the station where I would be broadcasting was directly across the street from Frank's Bar and Grill.

I didn't want to embarrass him with an immediate rejection, so I waited until the next day to call him and tell him that I couldn't do that. It just wouldn't be right.

He paused a moment, then replied, "Well, I know that. I just wanted to check you out!"

You know how much I believed that.

When I took the job at Hornell, the Dodgers were still wearing the shorts and featured three players who would later star in the majors. Maury Wills, who led the majors in stolen bases for several seasons – Don Zimmer, who for many years following his beaning accident was a fixture as an assistant coach in the Yankee's dugout – and Carl Spooner, a pitcher who later pitched for the Brooklyn Dodgers. Oddly enough, the final game I did for Mutual was a Brooklyn – Pittsburg game. Carl Spooner was the starter and winning pitcher. Spooner later developed arm trouble and wound up in the Sally League, where I worked a few games in which he was involved. Incidentally, I was hoping that the Brooklyn – Pittsburg game would be rained out, which would have given me the opportunity to watch Caroline upset Army at West Point. I was never able to get the score of this game until I returned to Chicago.

THE MOVE TO COLUMBIA

The following year, 1952, I saw two ads in BROADCASTING magazine seeking sports announcers in Columbia, South Carolina and Columbus, Georgia. I applied for both and was one of three finalists for the job in Columbus, but another broadcaster was chosen. The manager told me I would have had the job, but the man they chose had an uncle who was on the team's board of trustees.

I had also sent a tape to Moody McElveen, manager of station WNOK in Columbia.

They had rights to games involving the Columbia Reds of the South Atlantic League and were trying to get rights to University of South Carolina football games. I got a call from Moody, and he invited me to come to Columbia for an interview. We met for awhile at the station, which was in the old Jefferson Hotel on North Main Street. Then we walked about six blocks to the other end of Main to the Jerome Hotel, where the Reds office was located. Both the Jefferson and Jerome hotels were demolished years ago.

After meeting with Reds General Manager Bill McCarthy, Moody and I began walking back up the street toward WNOK. All the way up the street Moody didn't say a word to me. No word to indicate any hint that I had the job, so I figured it was a no go. As we got to the Jefferson and were ready to enter the station, he suddenly turned to me and said, "You've got the job." He told me that they had received about a hundred tapes but that mine was easily the best.

My relatively short career in broadcasting had taken me from town to town and station to station, so little did I suspect that those four words, "You've got the job," would be the beginning of a 43-year love affair with the City of Columbia, the University of South Carolina and the entire state.

I had really intended to return to Little Rock at the end of the baseball season, but when WNOK asked me if I would stay and do University of South Carolina football, I decided to stay.

~COACHES WITH WHOM I WORKED~

I had the experience, and usually the pleasure, of working with a lot of coaches during my five decades as a sports announcer. Their personalities were as varied as snowflakes, and they covered the spectrum in coaching techniques and relationships with the media and the public. There were no two alike, and that's what makes life interesting - variety.

If, as is said, "Variety is the spice of life," I have led one spicy existence!

THE FOOTBALL COACHES

I'll discuss the Carolina coaches in order of appearance, starting with football, because that's where I started, and then move into basketball and baseball, plus some non-Carolina coaches, such as Frank Howard of Clemson.

REX ENRIGHT
There has never been a more respected coach at Carolina, or anywhere else, than Rex Enright. He was first and foremost a gentleman, and that sometimes was a handicap in the cut-throat world of athletics.

Rex seemed too prone to compromise in his dealings with people, especially his adversaries, but he used to say, "Sometimes you have to lose battles to win wars." Rex did win the war. I'm saying this 36 years after Enright died, and I remember him for the fine person that he was and not for his won-lost record.

Rex would have made a great politician, but he played for Knute Rockne at Notre Dame, and you didn't get football out of your blood after that. He had a law degree and this afforded him credibility in the academic community at the University.

In contrast to the corporate approach to college football today, it was a lot of fun back then, win or lose. Everybody involved operated like a family, and that included media people who followed the Gamecocks.

Can you imagine a sports writer or broadcaster today confessing to be in support of a particular college? Media people of Enright's day weren't ashamed of hoping the Gamecocks would do well, as compared to many of today's sports reporters who too often assume the role of critics, or even prosecuting attorneys.

After home games, win or lose, assistant coaches, professors, friends and sports reporters would gather at Enright's home to either celebrate or drown their sorrow. Rex's wife, Alice, had to be prepared at all times for a bunch of people to drop in, and she always had refreshments on hand.

Contrary to the "don't get too personal" relationship that exists between coaches and the media that exists today, it wasn't that far fetched for a coach to ask a favor of someone, or vice versa. People who weren't around during the Big Thursday era of the Carolina-Clemson rivalry really have no idea of how hard tickets were to come by. They never ever went on sale. Like tickets to the Masters Golf Tournament, you almost had to inherit them.

A good friend came to me shortly before the game, and he said he was desperate for two tickets - sounded as if his life depended on it. So I went to Rex and told him the situation, and in true Enright style, he said that if it were really important he would find two for me. And he did.

I delivered the tickets to my friend, and he expressed his appreciation. I thought no more about it, until I was in the press box prior to the game on Big Thursday. I just happened to look out of a window that overlooked the parking lot, and I saw the friend for whom I obtained the precious tickets. I felt good about what I had done, because there he was heading into the game.

I didn't feel so good, when I saw him walk up to another guy in the parking lot, hand him the tickets and receive money from the guy. My friend then headed away from the parking lot, and back toward his car.

I never mentioned it to my friend, but I never saw him that I didn't think of that incident. As the Good Book says, "be assured that your sins will find you out."

Rex was a great storyteller, and occasionally I would have lunch with him and several others at the Elks Club in Columbia. I found it to be especially interesting to hear him tell stories about Rockne and the "Four Horsemen" of Notre Dame. He was a personal friend and teammate of the "Horsemen," Harry Stuhldreher, Don Miller, Elmer Layden and Jim Crowley. I might be showing my age, because there are probably not too many people who know about that famous backfield for the Fighting Irish. The Notre Dame football players know.

When you looked at the facilities at Carolina when Enright was coaching, you wonder how he did as well as he did. The athletic department offices were two tiny rooms and a small reception area at the end of the swimming pool building in the middle of Sumter Street, behind what is now Longstreet Theater. The football team practiced at the corner of Sumter and Green Streets, where the Cooper Library now stands.

When I arrived in Columbia in 1952, there were no Sunday coaching shows on television. In fact WIS-TV had not even gone on the air at that time. On Monday evening Rex would show the film of the previous Saturday's game to anyone who wanted to come and watch. He either showed in the old field house or at a hotel ballroom, if that was available. Of course, he did it for free. Can you imagine a modern day coach doing something like that?

When there was finally a Sunday TV show, there was no fee to Enright, but a local men's clothing store did donate a suit of clothes each week. Rex would give the suit to one of his assistants.

As a coach, Enright will be remembered for several things. First, he was able to beat Clemson most of the time, and that will be to his everlasting glory among Carolina supporters of his day.

He was also remembered for two of the bigger victories in Carolina's history, both coming in enemy territory. His Gamecocks beat a great Army team, 34-20, in 1954, and upset West Virginia's unbeaten Sugar Bowl team in 1953.

If you rated football coaches by the number of friends they have, Rex Enright would no doubt be in the Hall of Fame.

WARREN GIESE

Warren Giese was about as different from Rex Enright as night is from day.

Rex was getting old; Giese was young. Rex had a warm personality; Giese could be considered rather cool. Where Rex had questions, Giese had answers. And paradoxically,

Enright coached a wide open brand of football, while Giese was the ultra conservative. Enright courted the media; Giese challenged them.

However, Giese was Enright's chosen coach, and Rex based it on the recommendation of his good friend Jim Tatum, the highly successful Maryland head coach. Giese was an assistant to Tatum at Maryland and had played for him at Oklahoma.

I can't verify the accuracy of it, but one story said that when Giese played at Oklahoma, the pronunciation of his last name was "geezie." Tatum supposedly didn't like the sound of that and had Warren change it to "geezay." Clemson's Frank Howard always stuck to the former pronunciation and always referred to him as "geezie," because that sounded like a "put down."

When Giese made his first public appearance in Columbia, a friend of mine told him that I did a good job and always put the right "spin" on the Gamecocks' performance. I was told that, in response to that, Giese threw his head back and chuckled, as if to imply, "I won't need that kind of help."

Media people, who always found an open door to Enright's office, found it difficult to adjust to the hard-to-reach Giese.

With that, I must say that Warren was a good football coach, sound in fundamentals, a tireless worker and a disciplinarian. One could not hold his conservative approach against him, because that is what he learned under Tatum, and it was winning national championships at Maryland. The challenge at South Carolina was to accumulate the high level of talent that was winning games for Maryland.

Tatum once made the statement that, if he could have an All-America player at any position of his choice, it would be at offensive tackle. That's because the Tatum-Giese offense lined up behind a huge offensive line and sent running backs behind them with the idea of picking up four or five yards at a clip. As long as they did that, they would maintain possession of the ball and ultimately cross the opposing goal line.

Giese would point out that, if their running play worked perfectly, it would not result in a long touchdown run, because it was not designed for that. The problem at South Carolina was that opposing coaches took him at his words and had all eleven of their defensive players in close proximity to the line of scrimmage. They knew they didn't have to worry about a forward pass, particularly on first or second down.

Giese's attitude toward the forward pass was that when you put the ball in the air, three things could happen, and two of them were bad. A completion was the good, while an incompletion or interception was bad. Of course, another possibility would be a pass interference call, which happens with about the same frequency as interceptions.

The fans became bored with Giese's conservative offense, but not as long as he was winning with it. He could have run quarterback sneaks all day, and that would have been fine, as long as he won. However, losses are boring in whatever form they come, but particularly if your offense is one that doesn't seem to be able to get you back into the game, once you get behind. Coming from behind was not Giese's strong suit, and he pointed out that while he was at Maryland, a team that was behind by at least two touchdowns never came back and won a game.

When Giese posted 7-3 records in two of his first three seasons here, 1956 and 1958, he was popular among most of the fans. When he defeated Duke in his first season here, for the school's first victory in that series since 1932, he became popular with the administration, too. He was placed on tenure, with the same job security as a full professor.

Carolina fans were nervous after his good start, because the University of Houston invited him to come to Texas and interview the job of head football coach at that institution. It was a much publicized trip, and the media waited to announce the outcome.

Giese had his pets among the sports writers, and somehow Johnny Hendrix, sports editor of the AUGUSTA CHRONICLE, caught his fancy. When Giese returned to South Carolina, the story that he had "turned down" Houston's offer broke in the CHRONICLE. There was no news conference, such as they hold today, whenever a coach or athlete has a major thought.

Jake Penland, sports editor of THE STATE in Columbia considered himself as close to the University athletics department as Damon was to Pythias. When Giese had the audacity to break what Penland considered an important story in an out-of-state newspaper that was tantamount to treason. From that moment on, as far as Penland was concerned, Giese was persona non grata. That is the way it remained as long as Giese was head football coach.

The feud that persisted from 1957 through 1960 was bad for Penland and Giese, and the public grew weary of it. It didn't help Giese with his recruiting or public relations, and it didn't help Penland with his readers. Both were replaced in their primary jobs, and, ironically, they later let bygones be bygones and became friends.

Giese held his tenure at the University as a member of the Department of Physical Education, later getting into politics as a Republican and gaining a seat on the Richland County Council and, subsequently, in the South Carolina State Senate.

If the bowl set-up of today had been in place during Giese's tenure, he would have taken his Gamecocks to three bowls, but the number of post-season games was limited then.

One year when Warren's team had a bowl-worthy record, I did an interview for the Columbia Touchdown Club with George Olsen, executive director of the Gator Bowl in Jacksonville, Florida. I asked George if the type of offense used by Carolina would be a problem for the team in getting a bid to the bowl. George said that it would be.

Giese called me and was terribly upset about that interview. He said that I had set that up, but I assured him that I didn't. I lied.

For some reason I was teed off with Giese, and it could have been for any number of reasons. For instance, I'd go to interview him, and he would lie down on a couch he had in his office, and I'd have to go over and stick the microphone in his face. We media people were accustomed to being catered to, and that was not good for the ego.

Giese would not have interrupted a practice session for a visit from the President of the United States. However, contrary to his austere coaching approach, he loved a gimmick.

In 1959 Giese was contacted by a television production company that had a contract to do a commercial for a mattress manufacturer. Their storyline was to have two charging football teams run a play on top of this mattress to show how tough it was. Giese welcomed that little interruption in his schedule.

On the practice field behind the Roundhouse, Warren had two teams dressed out, one wearing garnet, and the other, all white. They walked through the motion of how the play would work. It would be a handoff to the fullback, who would go crashing into the middle of the line - or mattress, in this case.

The camera was ready to roll, the quarterback barked the signal, and 22 football players met head-on over one of the prettiest mattresses you could imagine. Well, it was-

Bob Fulton "My Career My Life"

n't pretty for long, because when the players came to rest, the mattress had been ripped to shreds, with several springs protruding. Twenty-two players were rolling on the ground in uncontrollable laughter.

What the production company hadn't counted on was the players being equipped with sharp aluminum cleats on their shoes. There wasn't a mattress alive that could have stood up under that.

However, the director of the commercial was unperturbed by it all. He simply surveyed the scene, pulled himself together and said, "I think that will be fine. We'll just have to do a little editing!"

They never contacted Giese for another commercial shoot.

I don't know that you could call this a gimmick, but in 1957 he came up with the idea of placing a television camera in the press box and a monitor on the sideline, so that they could give players a coach's box view of what was taking place.

The TV set was in a tent, and during a game, the assistant coaches would have players gathering around to discuss strategy on various developments. I don't know how much it contributed in a tactical sense, but it caught the attention of the media.

The main problem was that, when the Gamecocks were hopelessly out of a game near the end, it was always a temptation for a sports writer to point out that "Giese folded his tent."

I was the host for Giese's Sunday television show, and I must say that he did an excellent job in that capacity. He was good looking, well groomed and articulate. He was also good at bringing out the best points, even in the worst situations. Guess that is what has helped to make him a successful politician.

He liked to play little jokes, however, such as waiting until the last second to appear on the set for the Sunday show. He would wait outside until we were introducing the show, then sneak into the studio and take his place on the set. It got to the place that I just expected it.

When they first come to Carolina, I don't think coaches can appreciate the rivalry that exists between Carolina and Clemson. You have to experience it to catch the essence of it, because there is no other situation like it in America.

Giese expressed his misunderstanding of it, commenting that it was "just another game." It might have been to him, but to people who support the program, it is THE game. When the Atlantic Coast Conference was formed in 1953, Maryland had started playing Clemson each year, and it was no big deal, so that was the attitude that Giese brought with him to Columbia.

However, Warren was no dummy, and he caught on fast. At Carolina, when you lose to the Tigers one time, you learn all you need to know about losing to them. In his five years as coach of the Gamecocks, his team beat Clemson only once - that coming in 1958 - but that gave him a chance to receive the accolades and benefits of winning that game.

After the 1960 season, when Carolina's administration determined that Giese was not the future of the football program, Warren left behind one of the better won-lost records in the school's history. He was a fine coach, with a lot of positives, but as it is in so many cases, a few negatives can drag you down in the job of coaching a major college sport.

MARVIN BASS

Just as Giese was given a lot of credit for the success Jim Tatum had at Maryland, Marvin Bass was in that role in Giese's first four years in Columbia.

Marvin was a man's man, and one who assistant coaches and players looked up to and sought for counsel. He was also the first Southerner to hold the permanent head coaching job here since 1934. Marvin grew up in Virginia, played football at William and Mary and spent his career as an assistant coach with colleges in the South.

This gave him a leg up in identifying with people in South Carolina, and he knew how they thought - their likes and dislikes.

When the trustees selected him to succeed Giese, he had been an assistant to Bobby Dodd at Georgia Tech for a year. However, when he moved into the top job with the Gamecocks, he had already been well schooled in the magnitude of the Carolina-Clemson rivalry. His biggest accomplishment as head coach was defeating the Tigers three times in five games.

I had more rapport with Marvin than any football coach that served at Carolina during my years of covering sports here. He didn't have a super ego, such as too many coaches have today, with their big contracts, television contracts and endorsements. The only thing Marvin would have endorsed was the school that was paying his salary.

Marvin was easy to work with, and the kind of guy who would sit down, have a beer with you and talk about something besides football. He was also very superstitious, but that is not unusual among coaches, because they are looking for anything that will help to eke-out a victory.

Marvin told me something once that made a lasting impression on me and affected my philosophy of broadcasting football games. He told me that during an out-of-town game to which his wife, Audrey, didn't go, she was listening to the broadcast and was down on her knees in the kitchen praying. This was important to her, because it was her husband's livelihood. It was very important to win, and people didn't understand, if you lost.

I became more aware than ever of saying anything that might be construed as criticism of a coach or second guessing. I always assumed that the coach's wife was listening to the broadcast, and I didn't want to say anything to upset her. That might sound corny in today's world of sports, with all of the analysts and self-styled experts who can make all of the right calls - after the play is run or the game is over.

Marvin was a kind man, and I never felt that I had to be unkind to anyone, in order to report a football game in an interesting and accurate manner. So, why should I go out of my way to say something to hurt someone, just to appeal to the base instincts of a very few frustrated fans.

Bass was a "hands on" coach, and if he felt that a player wasn't getting a point, he would get down in the trenches with him, and show him what he was talking about. Marvin was a big man and could hold his own, even at an advanced age.

He had a handshake that really got your attention, and his big smile - he had a great sense of humor - was enough to melt an iceberg.

However, Marvin never received the support of the administration that was needed to be a big success in his job. When the trustees hastily came to him, so that they would have a man ready to step into the job when Giese was moved out, he just wanted the job. He wasn't in a position, and probably didn't care to go into hard-nosed negotiations.

144

His contract was sort of year to year, and that was not conducive to recruiting or long-range planning.

The best known of his recruits was Dan Reeves, former head coach of the Dallas Cowboys. When Dan left his job as assistant coach of the Dallas Cowboys to take the head job with the Denver Broncos, he went to his former coach, Marvin Bass, and made him his right-hand man. You couldn't ask for a higher compliment. Dan closed out his coaching career in the NFL with the Atlanta Hawks.

His most famous assistant? That was Lou Holtz, former Notre Dame's head coach, whom Bass lured from the University of Connecticut.

Midway through spring practice of 1966, Marvin resigned at Carolina to accept the job as head coach of Montreal in the new Continental Football League.

He's back in the Columbia area now, where he is living in retirement in Blythewood.

Marvin didn't go down as a coaching legend, and not many do, but he had a rewarding career as a coach on several levels, and he is remembered at Carolina, and by me, as a man of integrity and compassion. The world of sports needs more like him.

PAUL DIETZEL

Had it not been for Paul Dietzel, I probably wouldn't be doing this book, at least from a Carolina football perspective. It would be featuring, perhaps, 20 years as a play-by-play man for the Georgia Tech Yellow Jackets.

During Marvin Bass' final year at Carolina, I had been hired to do the games for the Tech football network. It was a big network for a school with a national football reputation under Bobby Dodd, and they played in bowl games every year. It was exciting football, especially compared to that played in the Atlantic Coast Conference at that time.

I continued to do the Tech games in 1966, when Dietzel had come to Carolina, following Bass' resignation, and Dodd, who was also athletics director at Tech, offered me a ten-year contract to do the games there. I would still be free to do Carolina basketball, continue to make my home in Columbia and commute to Atlanta, or wherever Tech was playing on football weekends. Tech didn't play many games away from home.

Incidentally, I was really feeling good at the time, because I had also been offered the job of doing games for the University of Georgia Network. It was an even larger group of stations than the Tech network had.

Dietzel had never heard me do a football game, but I'm sure that he talked to people around the University and Columbia who liked my work. Paul wanted to have the best possible program, and that included everything to do with the athletics set-up at Carolina.

One of the reasons I took the Georgia Tech job was that the University had awarded the rights to the Sunday coach's TV show to someone else, and I was out in the cold, as far as that income source was concerned.

Dietzel met with me and made me an offer that I could have refused, but Paul was a super salesman, and it was hard to say "no" to him. He said that I could have the Sunday TV show back, and that he would make me a member of the athletics staff, with all the benefits of being a state employee.

Carolina was always where my heart had been, and now he was bringing my pocketbook closer to home. So, I turned down Dodd's generous offer of a ten-year contract and the overture from Georgia and became a full-time Gamecock.

Dietzel was always supportive of me and most cooperative. He also knew the importance of the media in shaping his public image.

As I mentioned in the chapter on football, he took the trouble to call me and give me the details of a new spread offense that he planned to use against Tennessee at Knoxville. Most coaches would keep such things a deeply guarded secret from anyone outside of the immediate staff.

Paul was a class act in every sense of the word and probably the most positive thinker I've ever been associated with. He was a good coach, with a national reputation, having won the national championship at LSU in 1959. He had played collegiately at Miami of Ohio and was named to what they then called the "Little All America" team at center. Miami was not a major college football school at that time. However, Miami was nicknamed "the cradle of coaches," because so many outstanding coaches had either played there or begun their coaching careers there.

Ara Parseghian, who was head coach at Notre Dame for a number of years, played for Miami, and Paul Brown, legendary coach of the Cleveland Browns of the NFL coached at that Ohio institution.

Dietzel had great ambitions for Carolina, and a number of them were accomplished. The stadium was expanded to seat 54,000 and included a new press box and greatly improved accommodations for spectators. As they say today, "more user friendly!"

Dietzel was an avid supporter of the Fellowship of Christian Athletes, and this brought him in touch with another enthusiastic member, Bobby Richardson. Paul hired Bobby as baseball coach, and I doubt that anyone else could have lured Bobby into the job. Paul and Bobby had a lot of principles in common, and Dietzel knew that the players would have a coach who would be the right kind of leader and role model.

Paul had a sense of humor, but it had its limits. For instance, he once said to me, "We've got to stop this drinking that's going on in the stands."

I replied, "Paul, the way the football team has been playing, maybe we should let them keep on!"

He didn't laugh, and I learned to stay away from humor that might relate to his football team. That was serious business to him. So was the matter of alcoholic beverages around the stadium. He promoted strict enforcement of South Carolina's laws on drinking, which prohibited alcoholic beverages being consumed in non-licensed public places. That included the trunks of automobiles.

Paul used the Sunday television show for things other than strictly reporting on the previous game. It was on his show that he announced that the stadium playing field would be replaced with artificial turf, and he promoted it by asking fans to purchase pieces of it, symbolically. In other words, send money to help pay for it. It was a very successful promotion.

As Carolina fans of the Dietzel era are well aware, it was Paul who changed the design of the Gamecock logo to the one that is now in use, and he prompted band leader Jim Pritchard to obtain rights to the tune of Carolina's fight song. The melody was from a Broadway musical, "How Now Dow Jones," which featured music of Elmer Bernstein, and Dietzel supplied the words. Paul didn't miss a trick.

Near the end of one season - I've forgotten which one - Dietzel's name was being mentioned as a possibility to fill the head coaching vacancy at Baylor University. When we went to a commercial break before concluding the Sunday TV show, Paul turned to me and said, "When we come back on the air, ask me about the rumors that I might be going to Baylor."

Bob Fulton "My Career My Life"

The cameras lit-up again, and I asked Dietzel about the rumors concerning him and the coaching vacancy at Baylor.

He gave a surprised look and replied, something like, "Bob, I don't think this is the proper time to discuss things like that. I am only interested in doing the best coaching job I can for the University of South Carolina."

That made Paul look very noble in the eyes of the viewer, and it was another example of his skillful use of the show to make a point or impression.

Freddie Zeigler, the record-setting wide receiver who played on Dietzel's 1969 ACC championship team, tells a story of another such incident, when Paul was left speechless. Paul called a squad meeting in the big circular room at the center of the Roundhouse, and when the players had gathered, he addressed them.

He told them that President Dwight Eisenhower had offered him the job as Director of the Selective Service System. Before he could continue, Zeigler had jumped to his feet and yelled, "Take it, Coach, take it!" That took away the drama of Dietzel's follow-up that he had already turned down the position. Of course, Zeigler wasn't serious, but he had a quick sense of humor and just couldn't resist the temptation of that moment.

Under Dietzel's leadership the Gamecock Club was expanded greatly, both in numbers and total contributions. He raised the school's sights and had the administration "thinking first class."

I doubt that anyone else could have sold the trustees on the idea of building the beautiful athletic dormitories and dining facilities, known as the Roost. That and adjacent facilities, including an improved baseball park, are part of Dietzel's legacy.

Although his football program never achieved what he aspired to, it did produce the school's only ACC championship and first authentic trip to a post season bowl.

The bottom line is that the University of South Carolina's athletic program was far better off when Dietzel departed in 1974 than it was when he arrived in 1966.

JIM CARLEN

Jim Carlen was a fine football coach but his poor relationship with the fans and the media led to the end of his college coaching career.

I first knew him when I was broadcasting Georgia Tech football games, and he was an assistant coach under Bobby Dodd.

Jim came to Columbia loaded with confidence, as he had been a winner as head coach at West Virginia and Texas Tech. He came here with an attitude that seemed to say to the people, "How lucky can you get!?"

When he first came to Columbia he decided to use someone from WIS to do his Sunday television show, although he knew that I had done it in the past. "The past" didn't seem to mean a great deal to most of the new coaches that came to Carolina. Carlen even got rid of films of Carolina football games that had taken place before he arrived. After he left the school had to borrow game films from past opponents in order to put together historical or highlight videos.

Back to the Sunday show, I think that Jim got some feedback from people about not using me as the host of his show, so he changed his mind. I found out later that changing Carlen's mind wasn't exactly a piece of cake.

It was a real experience to do a TV show with Carlen. It wasn't in the same hemisphere with the approach taken with Paul Dietzel, who gave a lot of advance thought to what was going to be included.

When we started we would go down to the studio on Sunday, take a look at the game film and do the show "live." Later we began taping it on Saturday night, and copies of the tape would be sent to all of the stations carrying the show, so they could fit it into their schedules. Many times I would wait a long time for Jim to show up. He would then walk into the studio and say, "Let's go."

We would sort of wing it, because we would have other commitments and needed to get the show finished, so that we could go from there.

Toward the end of the program, Carlen would turn to the producer and say, "Give me this camera." He would turn to his right, and that meant he was going to let someone hold it! He had a little sermon at the end, and he did his thing.

Sometimes it seemed that he was anticipating questions or criticisms that might be on the mind of the public and answer them on the show. Quite often he was not so diplomatic, and that was translated by many as "blunt."

Jim didn't care what kind of appearance he made on television. After a game with Florida State in Tallahassee in 1979, some guy came out of the stands and blindsided Jim and gave him a world class black eye that was swollen and very dark.

Before we taped the TV show I tried to get Jim to put some makeup over it, but he said, "I don't want that stuff on me." And that's the way he looked on the air. Perhaps it was against Jim's personality - makeup is phony, black eyes are not. He presented himself to the public, warts and all.

Once he came into the studio wearing an orange sports jacket. I told him that he was going to get some feedback, if he wore it on the show. He said, "This is all right," and he wore it. The next week he got a lot of letters and phone calls, objecting to his wearing the colors of the arch rival Clemson Tigers. That didn't bother Jim, because he really didn't care what people thought. He was his own person, and that was good enough for him.

Jim certainly wasn't the easiest person to interview. I had a lot of respect for him as a coach - we probably never had a better one. But on the post-game radio show or Sunday TV show, no matter what I said, he would say, "That's wrong," or "That isn't the way it is." As a result, I just started asking him generic questions, like, "What did you think of the ball game?" And he could take it and run with it, and he always did. He was never at a loss for words.

Carlen was toughest to handle after Carolina had won, because he felt that he was dealing from strength. After a loss it was a lot easier.

When we upset third-ranked North Carolina at Chapel Hill in 1981 - Carlen's last year here - as he was coming off the field, a Gamecock fan rushed up to congratulate him. Carlen just pushed him out of the way and kept on walking. Things like that catch up with you.

Once he said, "Bob, I get a lot of mail from people who say that I'm not nice to you, and it shouldn't be that way. I didn't think it should be that way, either, but I didn't write him a letter about it.

One thing, outside of his coaching ability, that I respected about Jim, was that he never talked out of both sides of his mouth. If he wanted to tell you something, he would tell you to your face. If he didn't like you, he would let you know it. He never tap danced around. That is not always the case with coaches - or other people.

Carlen had a "thing" about sports writers. The first time he met with the media in Columbia, he opened it for questions, and it was a frosty situation. At the end of the session, he came to me and named several writers that he wanted to know more about. They

148

had asked what he considered hostile questions. Right away, I knew he had great concerns about the press.

I had to work with both Carlen and basketball coach Frank McGuire, and they were both strong personalities. Rightfully, each thought his sport was the most important. Therefore, I had to be careful not to show any hint of partiality to either.

Dexter Hudson, editor of SPURS AND FEATHERS, the newspaper that goes to members of the Gamecock Club, did an article featuring me, and it was basically concerning McGuire. So, I bent over backwards to avoid saying anything that might bother Carlen. Dexter did a good job on the story, and it was very fair.

The next week, Ken Shipp, one of Carlen's assistant coaches, called me and said, "Bob, you've got the big man all upset."

I asked why, and he explained, "Carlen saw the article - you talked about McGuire - and he is mad as hell."

I said, "Ken, I knocked myself out to be fair, and if he doesn't like it, there's not much I can do about it."

About four days later I was going to a meeting at the Roundhouse with the people from WOLO-TV, because they were interested in getting the Sunday TV show. As I was going in the door, Carlen was coming out and he grabbed me by the arm. He let me hold it for about twenty minutes, charging that I was not loyal to him. I told him that Ken Shipp had gone over all that with me, and that I tried to be as fair as possible.

One thing about Jim - you might start talking, but you soon become a listener, and that's the way that conversation ended. That's the only thing Carlen ever blamed me for, and, looking back, that's getting off pretty light. I also warned Dexter to be very careful in the future, because he was dealing with two people who didn't hit if off too well.

Jim Holderman, Carolina's president at the time, found that out, too, and he tried to calm the issue by appointing Carlen, athletics director for football and McGuire, athletics director for basketball. He also named Bo Hagan athletics director for the other sports and Dr. Jim Morris as assistant to the president for athletics. I don't know how that worked, but it quietly evaporated down the line.

Eventually, Carlen fell from grace with Holderman because of disagreements the two had over athletics affairs, especially how the department's funds should be allocated. History tells us that in confrontations between college presidents and football coaches or athletics directors, the won-lost record is very one-sided in favor of the presidents. This would be true in the Carlen-Holderman situation, as it would later when Carlen's successor as athletics director, Bob Marcum, became at odds with Holderman.

One of Carlen's strengths was his relationship with his football players. He was a good recruiter - very persuasive - and he treated them all fairly. That was true with fourth-stringers, as well as starters. His players were also very loyal to him, and that is something that all coaches do not command. Jim was a very good motivator.

I'll never forget a talk he made to the Carolina squad prior to the game with Michigan at Ann Arbor in 1980. This was a great Michigan team that won the Big Ten championship and the Rose Bowl that season.

He told them that he didn't want them to be intimidated by Michigan or the 104,000 people in the stands. He told them that Michigan's team entered the field from the same tunnel that the Gamecocks would use, and they liked to come out at the same time as the visiting team and knock them around and talk trash to them, as they poured up the tunnel.

He told the players, "We're going out there and bump them and talk trash to them. And, if that doesn't work, I'll go out there and bloody Schembechler's nose!" The team just went bananas. Bo Schembechler was the Michigan coach.

Carolina upset the Wolverines in what many consider the greatest victory in over 100 years of Gamecock football. It also was a great boost to George Rogers in his successful quest for the Heisman Trophy.

On the post-game show, Carlen made the remark that the fans should come out to meet the team when it arrived at the Columbia Airport, and a big crowd showed up there. To the crowd's disappointment, Carlen walked right through them without stopping to address them or join in the celebration.

Carlen did a great job with George Rogers, because he had to be both coach and father to him. George's father was in a Georgia prison for much of his playing career. Jim was very protective of George, shielding him from the media and limiting the amount of contact he had with sports reporters. He figured Rogers' running did all the talking he needed.

The only time I can remember Carlen making a move as a reaction to outside opinion was when "people" were saying that his offense was too conservative. In response he hired Ken Shipp, who had a wealth of experience as an offensive coach, including positions with the New York Jets, Detroit Lions and Houston Oilers of the NFL.

Ken was the only assistant that didn't call Carlen "Coach," and he didn't hesitate to speak his mind. When he came here he asked Carlen, "Do you have a screen pass in your offense?"

Carlen confessed that he didn't, so Ken immediately added a screen pass. But as I recall, it was never used.

The last time I saw Ken Shipp was when I took him to the airport one day. He turned to me and said, "Bob, Carolina will never have anything in football, until they go out and buy a good quarterback."

The expression that someone "can't stand success" can be supported by many examples, and Jim Carlen just might be a good one. As I mentioned earlier, Jim was toughest to handle in an interview when he had won.

That attitude seemed to affect his dealings with others, also, including people in positions to either help or hurt Jim's career as a coach. In 1979 and 1980, when he presented the University with its first eight-win seasons, plus a Heisman Trophy winner, he seemed to think that he was indestructible. He even made remarks to the media that weren't exactly flattering to the president of the University.

At the same time Carlen was having personal and family problems that were leading toward a divorce from his wife, and the rumor mill around town was not kind at all to Jim. As long as he was winning big and going to bowl games, he survived all of that.

However a 6-6 record and season ending losses to Clemson and Hawaii was just the opening the USC administration needed. Shortly after the season ended Carlen was called and informed that he was being terminated as head coach.

Because he had been given extensions after his bowl seasons, Jim still had considerable time remaining on his contract. He took the school to court over a settlement that would include his annual salary and outside income that related to his coaching job. Carlen won that round and departed from the school with a sizeable amount of money. Not sizeable in the world of sports today, but a big hunk of change in 1981.

Carlen ultimately left Columbia and now resides at Hilton Head, South Carolina, where he operates a business and serves as a volunteer high school coach.

RICHARD BELL

Carlen's departure created openings in positions of head football coach and athletics director, and the University made the decision to separate the two for the first time since Rex Enright died. The first move was to hire an athletics director, who would be responsible for selecting the head football coach.

Bob Marcum, who was in that position at the University of Kansas, was Holderman's choice, and he came aboard in January of 1982. Marcum didn't accumulate a lot of mileage in searching for a successor to Carlen. He elevated Carlen's top assistant, Richard Bell. When Marcum approached Bell about the job, Richard said that he would take it on a one-year basis, but Marcum insisted that he should have some kind of contract. So he signed Bell to a three-year contract, and that would prove to be very important within the next year.

Richard was a popular choice. He had a good football background, including a fine reputation as a defensive coach at Carolina. He was also clean cut, friendly and always a team player. I had known Richard as a player at Arkansas and as an assistant coach at Georgia Tech.

When Marcum "introduced" Bell to a Gamecock Club gathering, he told an interesting story about the football coach at Kansas. Marcum had brought back a former Kansas coach, Don Fambrough, and made him the head man. Fambrough was an instant success, reviving a struggling program and producing, I believe, an 8-3 won-lost record. Marcum told the audience that after the season he was showering Fambrough with accolades and saying what a great guy he was.

Fambrough smiled and asked Marcum, "If that record had been 3-8, would you still feel that way?"

Marcum's reply was, "Yes, we'd still love you. We would just miss having you around!"

Those in attendance laughed heartily, and so did Bell. Little did he know.

During his one season as head coach at Carolina, I found Richard to be very easy to work with. He was a person of outstanding character and integrity, and he would soon demonstrate another admirable trait - loyalty.

Bell's season produced only four wins against seven losses, but one of the defeats was probably a fatal blow to Bell's job security. He probably could have survived a 5-6 season, but his team lost to Furman, 28-23, and that was hard for Carolina fans - and Marcum - to take.

At the end of the season, Marcum "evaluated" Bell's job performance and came up with this proposition for Bell. Fire four assistant coaches - and he named the four - or be fired yourself.

Bell didn't have to give that much thought. First, a coach has the choice of and authority over his own staff. The head man is the one that gets the credit or the blame, so however he achieves it is up to him.

And think of it this way, how can you go out and hire four competent assistant coaches at a school where the athletics director has just made the decision to fire assistants? In other words, "Whom am I working for?"

Of course, Richard stood his ground, refused to fire his assistants and paid the price.

In the law suit that followed, over settlement of Bell's contract, Marcum insisted that the coach was being fired because of insubordination. Witnesses in the coaching profession supported Bell's position that a head coach has control over his staff, including their hiring and firing.

The court agreed with Bell, and the University had its second sizeable payday in two years.

I always felt that Bell wasn't really afforded the time necessary to prove himself as a head coach. He may have been a winner, and maybe not. We'll never know for sure.

When Bell left Carolina, he went to Duke as an assistant coach and was later on the staff at East Carolina, then Georgia, then the United States Naval Academy and closed out his career at Air Force Academy at Colorado Springs.

JOE MORRISON

It could be a long time before any coach at Carolina can match or surpass the 10-2 record that Joe Morrison established in 1984. It was just his second season with the Gamecocks, as he had been hired away from New Mexico State, where he had won ten games and lost only one in 1982.

Morrison's coaching and public relations were pretty much the same as you see in professional football, because that is where Joe became established. He was a star for the New York Giants, for whom he played several different positions, and the Giants thought enough of him to retire his jersey number.

I was never able to establish a close relationship with Joe. He reminded me a lot of Bobby Dodd, in that both were loners. Both were also outstanding in their profession, but they weren't much for circulating in public. Joe had his own group of friends, including his defensive coordinator, Joe Lee Dunn, and a couple of former Carolina players, Ken Wheat and Punky Holler. As soon as a game was over, Morrison would go find those guys, and that was it. He was just comfortable being with a small group that he knew very well.

We would go to Gamecock Club meetings around the state, and as soon as the meeting was over, Joe would get out of there. I would stop and talk to people, but that wasn't Morrison's cup of tea.

I asked Joe if he had done that sort of thing in New Mexico, and he said that the school didn't have an airplane, so it was almost impossible. In that part of the country you'd have to travel a thousand miles to find a town.

He didn't like this thing of running around the state, and he didn't particularly like the recruiting that is so important to a college coach.

A coach of an NFL team doesn't have to do all that running around the state to meetings and to contact high school athletes. That's why it always seemed to me that Joe would return to the pros some day. After his big season in 1984 the rumors began circulating that the New York Giants were interested in getting Joe to come back and coach there.

Frank Sadler, who was Morrison's offensive coordinator at Carolina, told me that Morrison liked to handle quarterbacks the way they do in the National Football League. Most of the times pro coaches leave their starting quarterback in the game, even when it is out of reach. The reason is that people pay to see their number one quarterback, so they leave them in the game.

One night at Florida State, Carolina was getting beat by a sizeable score, and the Gamecocks had to play Clemson the following week. Mike Hold was the starting quarterback, and Allen Mitchell was the back-up.

Morrison decided it would be a good idea to take Hold out of the game, rather than take a chance on his getting hurt and missing the Clemson game. So he asked Mitchell if he wanted to go in. Mitchell politely declined, and Hold finished the game.

One of Morrison's former New York Giants teammates was Pat Summerall, who made a name for himself as a network commentator on NFL telecasts. Summerall always narrated Morrison's recruitment film, and that was aimed at impressing the high school prospect. The normal approach would be to get the person that does the school's football network, but Joe was close to Summerall and wanted to take the national celebrity approach.

Morrison did call on me for some help, when he was trying to recruit Todd Ellis, the outstanding quarterback from Greensboro, North Carolina. Quite often they would take prospects and female escorts out to Williams-Brice Stadium to show them around, and they would flash their names up on the scoreboard, and so forth.

We went a step farther for Todd. We took him out onto the playing field and they played a tape I had done over the public address system. The tape was a play-by-play account of Ellis quarterbacking the Gamecocks on a winning touchdown drive against Nebraska. The Gamecocks needed a two-point conversion to win, and Ellis ran it over, when he couldn't find a receiver open. I hope that the tape played some part in Ellis' decision to come to Carolina.

Later ESPN did a feature on that "fantasy tape" during one of their college football telecasts. There must have been a "whistle blower" watching, and he called the NCAA to complain about using such a tactic. Perhaps it was someone close to a school that had tried to recruit Ellis! Anyhow, the end result was the NCAA ruled that a school cannot use such a tape as a recruiting tool.

To illustrate how badly Morrison wanted Todd to come to Carolina, he did something that was completely out of character with the Gamecock coach. On Christmas Eve Morrison dressed up like Santa Claus and went up to Ellis' home to deliver his present - a scholarship to the University of South Carolina.

Somehow Morrison's aloofness had an appeal to Carolina fans. They saw him pacing the sideline during the game, dressed in all black and sometimes even wearing dark glasses. This placed sort of a mystique around him. He didn't mix with them, but he won for them, and that's what they wanted first and foremost. They called him "Coach Joe" and his program had turned into "Black Magic."

Morrison had not tried to create this image or effect, it just happened. When the staff followed through on Tommy Suggs' suggestion that they play the theme from the movie, "2001 - A Space Odyssey," as an entrance for the football squad to the stadium, the package was complete. That pre-game ceremony is still considered one of the best in college football.

Morrison coached the Gamecocks for six seasons, and he took them to three bowl games, the same number that Carlen had generated during his six seasons at Carolina. Of course, none of those six bowl games resulted in Gamecock victories.

When Morrison died suddenly in early 1989, there was a cloud drifting over the Gamecock football program, mainly because of an article in SPORTS ILLUSTRATED concerning the alleged use of steroids by Carolina players. All of this was played-out after Morrison's death, and there was nothing to implicate the Gamecock head coach.

Joe died of a heart attack that followed a game of handball, and it placed the Carolina and national sports communities in a state of shock.

Morrison was a fine coach and a good man, who stuck to his knitting, didn't try to be a folk hero or media super star, and was successful in his profession.

Morrison's teams won 58 percent of their games, and that stands as the best won-lost ratio in the school's history. Sadly, he is also the only Carolina coach to die while still active in the position.

Joe didn't try to make a lot of personal friends, but his admirers in the college and professional worlds were many. On the other side of the coin, I don't believe I ever ran across anyone who could be considered an enemy of Joe Morrison. How many coaches can leave the turbulent world of college athletics and have that said about them?

SPARKY WOODS

In the early part of his coaching tenure at Carolina, Sparky Woods was probably the most popular ever football coach at that point in the school's history. He had great relationships with the fans and the media.

He was a small town Southerner who grew up in Oneida, Tennessee, which sends you searching over your road map to find it. I never did. He "fit in," so to speak with South Carolina lifestyles and philosophy. Family man, Southern Baptist, neatly groomed - all the right things.

Like Bass, Dietzel, Carlen and Morrison, he had served in the position as head coach, having compiled a 39-18-2 record in five seasons at Appalachian State. In 1985 he had given Morrison a run for his money, before losing, 20-13, to the Gamecocks in Williams-Brice Stadium.

He was King Dixon's personal choice to succeed Joe Morrison, and he was from a completely different pattern. Woods was the type of man you would have expected Dixon to choose. The school needed someone to put the so-called steroids scandal behind, rejuvenate the academics approach with athletes and to give the football team a fresh new look. Woods appeared to be the ideal answer.

I'll have to admit that he didn't get off to a sensational start with me - anything but. I respected him, but I vehemently disagreed with him over the way he handled his television show.

He chose to bring in a young man in his early twenties to host his TV show, rather than accept me and my many years with Carolina football. He was also indirectly responsible for my losing the basketball show. I thought that I was entitled to work these shows, but Woods thought differently, and Dixon backed him up.

All of Carolina's football coaches since 1952 are identified with special recruits. Enright brought in Dixon and Alex Hawkins; Giese's highest profile recruit was fullback John Saunders; Bass recruited Dan Reeves; Jeff Grantz was Dietzel's big catch; Carlen attracted George Rogers; and Morrison recruited Todd Ellis. Richard Bell didn't have a chance.

For Sparky Woods it was Steve Taneyhill, the high profile quarterback from Altoona, Pennsylvania. Although they were as different as oil and water, Woods obviously held an attraction for Steve. Perhaps Taneyhill looked over Woods' squad and figured he needed him the most.

When Taneyhill's parents visited with the school president, John Palms, one of their concerns was, "Would Sparky Woods be the Carolina coach during Steve's entire college career?" I guess that was a question that couldn't be answered in the world of sports.

Sparky was a good coach, although his teams won only 24 games in his five years at Carolina. In justice to Woods, you have to consider that his last two seasons, 1992 and 1993, were Carolina's first two in the Southeastern Conference. That elevated the caliber of the opposition to the highest level in the school's history. He was thrust into that competition before he could reap the recruiting advantages that the SEC provides.

He might have survived some conference losses, because fans can understand losing to Florida, Alabama, Tennessee and Georgia, but Carolina lost to The Citadel. That was a big strike against Sparky.

The biggest blow against Woods was that his team revolted in 1992, and that's one of the worst things that can happen to a coach. Some of the players felt that he showed favoritism, and there may not have been many of them, but most of them were seniors, and they got the young players to follow. Perhaps they were players that were recruited by Joe Morrison and wanted to blame lack of playing time on that. Whatever the reason or magnitude of the uprising, it received a lot of publicity. And like a doctor being sued for malpractice, regardless of the outcome of the case, damage is done.

Some felt that Sparky just didn't have a staff that lived up to Southeastern Conference standards. Most SEC schools had assistant coaches who could have been head coaches, but Sparky's staff was young and didn't have experience in the level of football being played in the Southeastern Conference. Sparky considered his staff to be great, and his loyalty was to be admired.

However, some times a coach has to make some tough choices to attain the goals set for him, and friendship can't stand in the way. Behind Sparky's low-key exterior dwelled a determination that could be interpreted as stubbornness. He had his own ideas, but there were times when he might have entertained some advice from others. That might have been a problem, and maybe not.

In 1993 Carolina had changed athletics directors, replacing Woods' initial employer, King Dixon, with Mike McGee. The Gamecocks won only four games that season - over Georgia, East Carolina, Vanderbilt and Louisiana Tech. At the end of the season, talk shows were filled with speculation over Sparky's future, and opinions varied as to his fate.

I believe that Sparky felt that he would be given another year, even if it smacked of probation. McGee had other thoughts. At that point he wasn't "McGee's coach," but if he had extended Sparky's life as a coach, he would become "McGee's coach." History has shown that athletics directors do not feel as obligated to coaches that they didn't hire.

So Woods was on the way out, re-creating a scenario that was not strange to followers of Carolina athletics. The entrance to the Roundhouse may not have been a revolving door, but it definitely worked two ways.

Woods had become a victim of cruel reality. As Bob Marcum said, lose and you may still be loved - but you'll also be missed!

BRAD SCOTT
I'll always appreciate Brad Scott for making my final season (1994) of broadcasting Carolina football a good one. It was not only a winning season, but it was exciting football.

I have felt for years that when a school is shopping for a football coach, they should-n't overlook the outstanding talent among top assistant coaches around the country. All of the great head coaches got their start as an assistant somewhere. Bobby Bowden is a prime example. He worked under Jim Carlen at West Virginia, and when Carlen left, Bowden moved into the head job.

It doesn't take a genius to figure that a coach who is successful enough to be a con-tender for a national championship each year has surrounded himself with excellent assis-tant coaches.

Mike McGee played and coached long enough to appreciate that.

Therefore, Florida State was an obvious place to explore, when McGee began look-ing for a replacement for Woods. That doesn't necessarily mean that you can just blindly pick an assistant coach from a championship team and come up with an outstanding head coach. It sure increases the odds, however.

McGee found his man in Scott, who was offensive coordinator for the Seminoles and given much credit for the success of their "fast break" offense. Brad seemed to have all of the other ingredients that a coach needs for long range success. He is very person-able, has a fine sense of humor and seems to know how to get along with people and the media.

Scott was hired before the Seminoles wrapped up their 1993 national championship quest, and it just upped the excitement level in Columbia when FSU downed Nebraska in the Orange Bowl. Brad had already started recruiting and hiring, prior to the Orange Bowl game.

I covered only Brad's first season, but I came to know him well enough to feel that he would build a program that Gamecock fans will enjoy and be proud of. I traveled with him to a number of Gamecock Club meetings around the state, and I saw what a good rela-tionship he was establishing with the fans.

Too many coaches seem to feel that just showing up at such meetings is the impor-tant thing, but if they don't project the right image, they can do themselves more harm than good. Brad knows what to say and how to act. Sometimes football coaches also underes-timate the intelligence and perception of football fans. A lot of them don't know an X from an O, but they can spot a phony a mile away.

Don't get me wrong. I'm not intimating that Scott was a soft touch, because he was not. I believe his assistants knew who was boss, and he could drive a hard bargain in the important things that affected his program and livelihood. He had to make some tough decisions about his staff, following his second season. But he made them. I don't know who coined the phrase, "If it ain't broke, don't fix it." I do know that too often it's hard to recognize when "it's broke," and even more difficult to "fix it."

In Brad's fourth year, the Gamecocks went 5 and 6, and 3 and 5 in the conference. The following year, his team won only 1 against 10 losses and 0 and 8 in the SEC. McGee thought it was time for a change and Holtz came in. Scott later was hired by Bobby Bowden at Clemson, and has played an important part in the Tigers' success.

Scott's legacy to me was allowing Bob Fulton to say that, in his career at Carolina, he broadcast more wins than losses. And, thank goodness, one of those wins finally took place in a bowl game.

THE BASKETBALL COACHES

There were ten different men who served in the position of head basketball coach at Carolina during my years of broadcasting here, if you include Dwane Morrison, who served in that capacity for a half-season. Those coaches presided over a program that moved through the Southern Conference, the Atlantic Coast Conference, a period of "independence," the Metro Conference, and, finally, to the Southeastern Conference.

Little emphasis was placed on basketball in the Southern Conference, of which Carolina was a member, when I first came to Columbia. Everett Case had come down from Indiana and built a program of national status at North Carolina State. The annual conference tournament, which determined the representative in the NCAA tournament, was a mere formality. State won it with boring regularity.

North Carolina was tired of watching the Wolfpack dominate and brought Frank McGuire down from St. John's to do something about it. McGuire ended Case's dominance, and this stirred up Duke, which couldn't stand the success of the arch rival Tar Heels. Wake Forest also upgraded its program in an attempt to keep pace with the other members of what is known in North Carolina as the "Big Four."

Carolina and Clemson were slow to react to this increasing prominence and were the "whipping boys" of the North Carolina schools when the ACC was first in operation, beginning in 1953.

FRANK JOHNSON

While the other ACC institutions had full time basketball coaches, those who headed up those sports at Carolina and Clemson had other coaching duties. Frank Johnson was doubling as freshman football coach at Carolina, and Banks McFadden, an assistant on the Clemson football staff, coached the Tiger basketball team.

Basketball received little media attention in South Carolina. Covering the games at Carolina would be the Columbia newspapers and sometimes a sports writer from the location of the visiting team. State, Duke and North Carolina would have radio stations broadcasting their games away from home.

The Columbia newspapers depended on the Associated Press for coverage of Gamecock games on the road.

I began broadcasting Carolina's games while Johnson was the coach and did practically all of the games the Gamecocks played through the 1993-94 season. Basketball at Carolina went through an evolution during that period and continues to enjoy increased interest and coverage.

Johnson was limited in his ability to recruit by several factors, including time, budget and attractiveness of the school as place to play basketball and get a college education. Players of college caliber were practically non existent in South Carolina high schools, and coaches who headed up big-time programs attracted available talent from basketball hotbeds, such as New York and Indiana.

Johnson therefore did the best with what he had. He came here primarily for football, because he had played at Georgia when Rex Enright was an assistant there. Frank was also a fine basketball player for the Bulldogs, and Enright was doubling there as head basketball coach.

I knew Frank very well, but I probably saw more of him in connection with the football team than during basketball season, because he had additional duties as business manager. In two stages Johnson was relieved of his football duties and basketball duties to devote full time to his role of business manager.

Johnson did not fit the high-tech profile of today's basketball coaches of today, but he wasn't atypical of most of the college coaches in the immediate years after World War II. Like most coaches in any sport, he was about as good as his players allowed him to be.

When he had Grady Wallace, the national scoring leader in 1957, he was a good coach. He advanced to the finals of the ACC tournament, before losing to national champion North Carolina. Earlier in the season his team had taken McGuire's Tar Heels into overtime in Columbia.

The final game of that season was against Clemson in the Carolina field house, and it was monumental for Johnson. In pre-game ceremonies his star player, Wallace, was given a five-minute ovation, as his jersey number 42 was retired. Frank's Gamecocks then went out and destroyed the Tigers, 113-85, in a classic Wallace scoring binge.

When Wallace graduated, Johnson became a lesser coach, and his final season, 1957-58, was a loser. Grady Wallace was the most humble basketball player I ever knew. He was always uncomfortable talking about his achievements. Grady is gone now and missed by all who knew him as not only a great basketball player, but an outstanding person.

Johnson's most notable achievements? For one, he ranks second to Frank McGuire in total number of coaching victories at South Carolina.

However, no Gamecock coach - not even McGuire - can come close to this. Johnson's teams won the first 14 games played against arch rival Clemson. That's 14 straight. And his final won-lost record against the Tigers was 25-5.

By 1958 Johnson's era of basketball was over. Schools now needed basketball specialists, with supporting staffs and recruiting budgets, in order to compete in the ever-strengthening Atlantic Coast Conference. So Enright moved his colleague into the business office, which was one of the two tiny offices at the end of the swimming pool building.

WALT HAMBRICK

Walt Hambrick was Grady Wallace's coach at Pikeville Junior College in Kentucky. The two of them, along with Bobby McCoy, a fine guard, came to Carolina together.

Like Johnson, Hambrick was a busy man. He assisted Johnson with the basketball team and taught physical education classes, while working on his Master of Arts degree. Later he became academic counselor for the football team and coached the golf team.

So when he took charge of the basketball team for the 1958-59 season, it was not on a long term contract - it gave Enright some breathing room while assessing the future of Carolina's basketball program.

With the two mainstays of Johnson's final team - Wallace and McCoy - gone, Hambrick didn't have the firepower with which to face a demanding schedule. Hambrick's teams were always competitive, but seemed to find a way to lose most of the time. They lost several games by two points and lost by respectable margins to the ACC leaders, Duke, State and North Carolina.

The classic loss was the one I described in the basketball chapter. Carolina led State by three points with just a few seconds remaining, had an inbounds pass intercepted and fouled a State player on a desperation shot, resulting in a three-point play that sent the game into overtime.

Bob Fulton "My Career My Life"

The best victory during Hambrick's season came at Clemson, where the Gamecocks defeated the Tigers, 83-69. This was an utter surprise, because the Tigers had defeated Carolina six days earlier in the Carousel Tournament in Charlotte. But Walt's team had it all together this night, before a packed Clemson field house.

The Gamecock coach made an unusual move by calling a timeout with only a few seconds remaining in the game, and the Tigers hopelessly out of it. I don't know what Walt wanted to talk about at that point. Perhaps he discussed where the team would go to eat after the game. I suspect that he just wanted to enjoy that moment of triumph in a season that produced few such opportunities.

The emotion of Clemson fans turned from disappointment to anger during that minute, and when the final seconds of the game were allowed to tick off, a number of fans rushed to the floor to tell Walt what they thought about his strategy. It was mostly expressions of hostility, but a couple of Clemson hands reached Hambrick, ripping his shirt and reminding him to accelerate his departure from the court.

It might have been a scary few minutes in that mob, but Hambrick reached the dressing room safely - and satisfied that he had made his point.

Hambrick was a knowledgeable basketball man, and he loved the game dearly. He just didn't have the tools to compete in his one year as head coach.

Considering his situation, Hambrick did a fine recruiting job in that one opportunity. He brought in Art Whisnant, who still ranks as the school's sixth all-time scorer. He is second only to John Roche among Gamecocks who couldn't play on the varsity as freshmen.

Hambrick also recruited Bobby Robinson and Bud Cronin, who would also be double-digit scorers for Walt's successor, Bob Stevens.

Hambrick was an easy-going person and he loved to tell stories about his years in Kentucky basketball circles. He particularly liked to reflect on the refusal of Kentucky basketball coach Adolph Rupp to consider giving Grady Wallace a scholarship.

After the 1958-59 season, Hambrick served as an assistant to Stevens for two years, before concentrating on his teaching and other duties in the Department of Athletics. Years later he was athletics director and basketball coach at Coastal Carolina, a branch of the University. It was shortly after that Hambrick passed away.

BOB STEVENS

Prior to one of Carolina's home basketball games, I believe it was in 1961, I was talking to Fred Shabel, an assistant coach at Duke. He was there to scout the Gamecocks, who would be playing the Blue Devils in their next game.

Fred said to me, "I don't know why I bother to come down here. They do the same things every game. They run, don't hold the ball and use the same defense all the time. So there's no reason for me to come down here."

Those thoughts probably ran through the minds of a lot of other basketball coaches around the Atlantic Coast Conference. One thing you could say about the teams under Bob Stevens at Carolina from 1959 through 1962 - they were completely predictable. Stevens didn't care. His constant motion offense was going to score, and he was going to use a zone defense, come hell or high water.

Stevens was the first coach hired strictly for basketball by Carolina. He was allowed to add a full time assistant in the person of Gordon Stauffer, who had been at Michigan State when Stevens was on Fordy Anderson's staff there.

Stevens was of the new style of college basketball coaches - young, aggressive, ambitious and confident. He also added a few wrinkles to the style of play he brought with him from Michigan State.

When he arrived in Columbia, the first piece of equipment he looked for was a tape recorder. He used this to fill the locker room before games and practice sessions with the loudest and wildest music he could find. The players would supplement the music by beating on metal lockers and anything else that would produce a noise, along with their vocal contributions. You could hear it a block away.

I don't know what this did for the players' psyche, but I can tell you that they were definitely awake.

Stevens might have been a bit too ambitious in his approach to recruiting. He and Stauffer subscribed to newspapers published in the basketball hotbeds of the nation, and they would compile a list of the top dozen prospects. This is where they concentrated their recruiting efforts.

That might have been feasible at Kentucky, North Carolina or Michigan State, but there was no way that a coach at South Carolina was going to attract many blue chippers. The most highly recruited player signed by Stevens was Scotti Ward, an all-state guard from Indiana. He also landed Ronnie Collins from Winnsboro, managing to recruit him away from college football teams that considered him a fine quarterback prospect. Both Ward and Collins proved to be fine college players.

In spite of the predictability of his teams, Stevens won some big games, including three over Frank McGuire's North Carolina Tar Heels during the three seasons he coached the Gamecocks. Few ACC teams won that often against McGuire.

In his third season he won 15 games against 12 losses and broke even (7-7) in ACC games. That was considered a noteworthy achievement by ACC sports writers, who voted Stevens the conference coach of the year.

That got the attention of the University of Oklahoma, and they attracted Stevens to Oklahoma, where he served as head coach for five years without producing a winning season.

While Stevens was coach, I began to broadcast more of the Gamecocks' games away from home, although basketball was still difficult to sell to sponsors. The atmosphere around the basketball program wasn't as relaxed as it had been in past years, but it still didn't have the life- or-death aura that surrounds the sport today.

Bob's teams were interesting to follow. They were well coached and highly motivated. And they achieved more than they should have, when you compare their personnel with that at other ACC schools. In general his teams raised the level of basketball interest to at least the point it reached during Grady Wallace's two seasons.

Bob played by the rules and was a good example to his players. You would have to say that he was the right man at the right time for Gamecock basketball.

CHUCK NOE

Without fear of contradiction, I can say that Chuck Noe was the all-time most unorthodox character to serve as coach of any sport during my Carolina career. His season and a half at Carolina was a wild ride.

Noe had known Marvin Bass in Virginia, and the Carolina athletics director knew that Chuck had been successful as a head coach at Virginia Military Institute and at

160

Virginia Tech, where he had coached since 1955. Bass liked Noe and hired him to lead the Carolina program, beginning with the 1962-63 season.

Chuck is one of the most intelligent coaches with whom I was ever associated. He was able to take a team with limited talent and put them into a position to defeat teams with far greater talent. He had coached a high school team in Virginia that won 48 straight games.

He walked to the beat of a different drummer, and he is one coach I could never forget. I enjoyed my relationship with him, but he was definitely different - certainly a contrast to Bob Stevens.

Noe installed the "mongoose" offense, which he borrowed from Babe McCarthy, the coach at Mississippi State. It was similar to Dean Smith's four corners offense, which keeps the center open and counts on quickness to create "backdoor" lay-ups. Other teams had a hard time adjusting to it.

Deciding that his players need an extra boost, Noe had them taking "uppers," to give them more energy and drive. At the time there was no NCAA rule against such pills, although they were not considered advisable. Chuck didn't care - he did things his way.

Beating Virginia three out of three games was probably Chuck's most gratifying accomplishment. He was a Virginia graduate, but for some reason, he hated his alma mater. That probably stemmed from playing and recruiting against Virginia while coaching in that state. When the Carolina football team was getting ready to play Virginia, Bass had Noe scout them and help map strategy. Carolina defeated the Cavaliers, 40-6, in 1962 and ended up in a 10-10 tie with them in 1963.

At times Chuck could just disappear, and nobody would have an earthly idea of where he could be. When we played at Virginia in 1963, Chuck went up there ahead of the team, and his assistant coach, Dwane Morrison, brought the squad up later. As the players started up the walk to the Virginia field house, I heard a low whistle coming from between two cars parked there.

It was Chuck, wearing a T-shirt, and it was freezing cold - must have been ten degrees. Chuck said to me in a very low voice, almost a whisper, "Have Dwane take the ball team in there, and I'll be up there later on." Dwane took charge of the team, and Chuck came in about time for pre-game warm-ups. It obviously didn't affect the team, because they won the game. They had grown to expect almost anything, when it concerned their coach.

Midway through that season the University terminated Chuck "for personal reasons" and returned to Virginia, where he did very well as a sales representative. Morrison had to coach the team for the rest of the season.

Chuck was just another case of a good coach allowing other things to be his undoing in the profession. You could say a lot of things about Chuck, good and bad, but nobody could ever say that he was dull.

I've often thought, if I came up with a composite of the coaches I worked with at Carolina, in order to create the ideal head coach, perhaps Noe would be the one I would choose for mapping game strategy. His players will tell you that he would gather the team around him during a time-out and tell them exactly what the opposing team was planning to do when they resumed play. Chuck was right most of the time.

Noe did a good job of organizing his teams, but quite often life's biggest challenge is to control yourself, and therein lay Chuck Noe's problem. Chuck died in 2006.

DWANE MORRISON

It was Dwane Morrison's job to pick up the pieces, following Chuck Noe's departure, and he did a commendable job. He was Noe's opposite in many respects, and a half-season allows no time to demonstrate an ability to be head coach of a college basketball team.

Dwane had been a highly successful high school coach in Anderson, South Carolina, and he was a former Gamecock star who had many friends in Columbia.

His 12-game career at Carolina produced victories over Clemson, North Carolina State, Virginia and Maryland, no small fete in view of the confused state of the Gamecock basketball program. Morrison did stop the use of the "uppers" by his players and tried to get them back into the normal routine that a basketball team should follow.

Dwane was a fine, knowledgeable coach, who was placed on the bench opposite some of the nation's top coaches, after just one season as an assistant coach at Carolina. It was sort of a no-win situation. He was just there, with no promise that he would get the permanent job, nor an assurance that he would not.

You couldn't keep from liking Dwane, and no one will know how he would have fared in a long-range situation at the University. He possibly would have had the chance, had not Frank McGuire made himself available for the job. Getting a coach of McGuire's stature was like manna from Heaven to the USC administration.

Morrison understood that - it was an offer Carolina couldn't pass up - but Dwane was hoping that he could stay on as McGuire's assistant, and he received considerable support from influential people. But McGuire wanted to "pull the curtain" on the past and start fresh with an entirely new staff.

Dwane was thrown for a loss, but he landed on his feet. He coached at Mercer in Macon, Georgia, assisted Whack Hyder at Georgia Tech and became the Yellow Jackets' head coach in 1973.

After that Morrison got closer to the game of golf that he dearly loved, becoming a caddy on the PGA tour.

FRANK MCGUIRE (Continued)

The first time I met Frank McGuire was at a party at a Raleigh country club, following the championship game of the ACC tournament. Someone introduced me to him, and I liked him right off the bat. He had a charming personality, and he seemed to take an interest in what I said. His eyes weren't roaming around the room to see what more important person might be there.

Because we both came from "up East," he from New York and I from Philadelphia, he could relate to me. We talked about basketball in that area of the country, and we got off to a very good start. I never dreamed that I would eventually have an association of almost thirty years with him.

That is the only contact I had with him until he came to Carolina in 1964.

When he arrived here, Tom Price gave him a list of people he should contact. He called me on a Saturday afternoon and said, "I'm looking forward to having you broadcast the games."

Of the many coaches who came to Carolina during my career, he was the only one to make that initial contact. He could appreciate anything that would have a bearing on the presentation of his team to the public.

He was very positive, and that gave me a good feeling about him and the job that he could do for Carolina. There wasn't a trace of doubt in his voice. He was going to produce a winner.

Frank and I just seemed to hit it off from the start, and in just a short time I got to know him better - and become closer to him - than any of the coaches with whom I worked at Carolina.

McGuire was a man of fierce pride, and he couldn't stand for it to suffer. I'll never forget a game we played at Chapel Hill in 1966 - Frank's second season here. He faced his former assistant, Dean Smith, and the Tar Heels embarrassed his Gamecocks, 104-70, as Frank's former supporters looked on in delight. Toward the end of the game, with the Gamecocks long since out of it, Smith had the Tar Heels put on a full-court press, such as you do when you're trying to come from behind at that stage of the game. That infuriated McGuire.

Following the game, I was going through the stands when I ran into Dean Smith's wife. She stopped me and said, "Bob, I think my husband got carried away tonight." I agreed with her.

About an hour after the game, Dean came by the Pines Motel, where we were staying in Chapel Hill, with the intent of speaking with Coach McGuire. He knocked on the door a number of different times and I finally said to Frank, "It's Dean Smith out there again. Shall I let him in?" Frank immediately said that under no circumstances was I to let him enter our room. Frank didn't get over what had happened in that game for some time. In fact, it was about two years before he even talked to Coach Dean Smith. I give Dean a lot of credit for continuing to invite Frank to come up to Chapel Hill to be recognized as the coach who brought the championship to North Carolina in 1957. Finally McGuire accepted an invitation to go to Chapel Hill, and the two ultimately became friends again - perhaps closer than ever – and except when they were on opposite benches, Frank and Dean got along well. In McGuire's waning years, Smith was one of his more loyal and attentive friends.

After arriving at Carolina, McGuire changed the look of the basketball team in many ways. He changed the mode of travel to places of any distance from bus to air, and we stayed in the best hotels. When they traveled, his players were dressed in blazers, coats and ties. The idea was to be first class in everything. If you do that, you take greater pride in other things that you do - such as playing basketball. It was a refreshing change.

I guess it rubbed off on me, too. I even became more cognizant of the way I dressed, because I was traveling around with this guy who looked like he had just stepped out of ESQUIRE magazine.

He once said to me, "When you go out to eat in New York, if the waiter can see skin between your sox and your pants, he doesn't want to wait on you. He figures you don't know how to dress."

He added, "If you wear white socks with anything, they don't want to come near you!"

When we dined at a restaurant, Frank would always tip the maitre de on the way in. Then he would tip the waiter as soon as he came to our table. I asked him why he did that.

Frank said, "You establish yourself, so you'll get good service. If you wait until it's all over, then it's too late."

He would do the same thing at a hotel. Once we went into the New Yorker, and he was met in the lobby by the assistant manager. He tipped the guy right off the bat, so he'd get good attention. He would tip anywhere from fifty to a hundred dollars. He'd tip the man who drove the bus for us, the people who cleaned up the room - he would tip everybody.

McGuire knew New York like the back of his hand. He loved Columbia, but he always felt at home in New York City and maintained regular contact with his many friends in the Big Apple. He knew all of the good places to eat there - not the tourist traps - but places only the insiders were familiar with.

On one occasion Frank and I couldn't find a cab to take us back to our hotel, so we had to walk. Frank knew the shortest route, which took us through a lot of dark back alleys. I thought to myself, "This is really taking a chance. It's scary."

It didn't bother McGuire one bit. I honestly felt that if I was ever stuck in a dark alley in New York City, there was only one way out, and I needed someone to help me - I would choose Frank McGuire. He was fearless.

For most of the 16 years I traveled with McGuire, he would have a suite of rooms, and I would have the room right next to his. During the day we socialized. We wouldn't talk about sports, but we talked about everything else.

When it came to meeting people and mixing in a crowd, there was nobody better than McGuire. However, he preferred to be with small groups of friends, with whom he could relax and be himself.

He rarely ate in hotel dining rooms. Most of the time he would have food sent to his room. Then he didn't have to worry about people coming over to speak and interrupting his meal.

Frank liked things that money could buy, but he didn't care about money itself. Other people always handled his financial matters. Members of his family would tell you that he didn't even know how to write a check. Well, he probably could have, if he had wanted to.

However, McGuire was given a lot of things by friends and supporters. He had a friend who was a Cadillac dealer in Charlotte, and he was furnished an automobile by that man. We used to kid him about how fussy he was about his car - that, as soon as the ash tray was filled, he would turn it in and get a new one.

Friends in the textile business would give him socks, and he had enough pairs to fill a closet. A relative in San Francisco who was in the clothing business furnished his suits, and he was always dressed in sartorial splendor.

A friend once gave him a cashmere coat, and he took it with him on a trip we made together. I said, "Frank, why are you taking that coat with you. You never go outside. All you do is walk from room to room. You don't need a coat."

All he did was laugh, because he knew that was the truth.

Doctors never charged him, and everywhere he went, people were always reaching for the check, and they usually came up with it.

The clothes he wore and the car he drove were very important to McGuire. He couldn't understand anyone who would drive an expensive car and then buy cheap gas for it.

He liked to be around celebrities, but in contrast would spend time with people who had absolutely nothing. He could relate to the latter because of his background in New York City, where he was in a family of 13 children.

When you travel by air as much as we did with the basketball team, sooner or later you're going to have some anxious moments, and we had our share.

164

I remember a trip when the airplane we were on started throwing oil, so it stopped at Bristol, Tennessee to refill. When you take off from that airport, you're flying right into the mountains. It's a nice view, if you aren't concerned with becoming part of the scenery.

I was sitting in the back, across from Frank, as the plane taxied to the runway. The plane made it off the ground, but it began to shutter something awful. I thought, "We're not going to make it!"

We had been off the ground about thirty seconds, when Frank turned to me and said, "I'm sorry I cussed that official like I did tonight." He was obviously thinking the same thing I was. We weren't going to make it.

We were both right, because the pilot turned the plane around and landed it in a field near the airport. Fortunately, it was a level field between the hills.

They told us later that if the pilot had waited a few seconds longer to turn around, we would have gone right into the mountain. There was no way he could have pulled it up. That would have been the end of my story - and McGuire's.

Frank was a unique coach. He depended on good talent, motivation and overall strategy. He gave his players a lot of freedom on the court. They weren't a group of robots that you can manipulate. They were young men with brains, hearts and athletic ability, so he let them use them.

In 1968 we were at Chapel Hill for a game that was most important to McGuire. It was the one in which Carolina upset Dean Smith's Tar Heels, 87-86, when Bobby Cremins made all of those crucial free throws at the end.

Prior to the game, Frank and I were in the dressing room, and I was working on my information for the broadcast. McGuire was just sitting there on the training table.

He said, "You know, all those people back in Columbia and around the state think I'm up here working on a blackboard - putting up X's and O's."

I never saw him pick up a piece of chalk, except one time. We were doing a feature on a television show, where he was going to diagram something to do with offense or defense. He picked up a piece of chalk, got some dust on his hands and threw it down. He said, "I don't want to fool with this chalk." I never saw him pick up another piece.

Donnie Walsh was the X and O coach, so McGuire didn't need to concern himself with that part of coaching. He did the important things, such as handle the officials. He was the best I've ever seen at doing that.

Back to the game at Chapel Hill. As we were walking out of the dressing room, we were confronted by one of the officials for the game. He extended his hand and said something like, "Good to see you, Coach."

Frank never shook hands with him. He simply looked him in the eyes and said, "I want to tell you something. If you drop your guts out there tonight on that floor, I'm coming after you."

The official turned as white as a sheet. Nothing else was said.

Normally when you play at Chapel Hill - there's an expression - the defense plays right up in your jock. The Tar Heels got away with a lot of things on their home court, because most of the time the officials let them get away with obvious fouls.

Down the stretch, the Gamecocks were ahead by one point, and this is where McGuire's little pre-game chat with that official paid off. North Carolina was pressing us all over the court, trying to steal the ball or cause a turnover. But, now, instead of letting the fouls go, as they normally do at Chapel Hill, they were calling them. They were fouling Cremins, because he was the worst free throw shooter on the team, but Bobby made 7 out of 9 in the closing moments, and Carolina held on to win.

The fans thought the game was won right there at the end, and, technically, it was. But I knew when the turning point really occurred. It was before the game ever started - because if Frank hadn't said what he did to that official, we would never have gotten to the foul line in the closing moments of the game.

In 1966, for some unknown reason, we were playing Florida Southern in Lakeland, Florida. It was one of those games in which you have absolutely nothing to gain, and a lot to lose.

Carolina was trailing at halftime, and none of the calls from the officials were going our way. At the end of the half, Frank stopped by my table and said, "I'm not going to the dressing room. I'm going to talk to those officials."

Frank knocked on the door, and the officials let him in. He told them, "I'm going to report you guys to the NCAA. You're stealing this game." And he threatened them with everything he could think of.

In the second half they called the first eleven fouls against Florida Southern, and Carolina won the game by ten points. Actually the game was won during the halftime intermission.

One of Frank's favorite tricks was this. During a game, if he thought he wasn't getting a fair shake from one of the officials, he would talk to the other one, loud enough for the problem official to hear. He would say, "Look, you're a good official, and we're looking for you to control the game, because this monkey working with you doesn't know what he's doing."

Frank was putting the official he was complimenting in his pocket. The other one was thinking, "Here's a man who's a national figure, and maybe I'm not doing the job I should be doing." And that official would usually then start looking after the Gamecocks.

We seemed to have a lot of things happening on airplanes, but all of them weren't life threatening. This incident happened in 1976, when we were flying into Lincoln, Nebraska to play the Nebraska Cornhuskers.

As we were going in for the landing, the pilot announced, "We're now coming in to Lincoln, Nebraska, home of one of the finest football teams in the country - the Nebraska Cornhuskers."

That really made Frank mad, so he called the flight attendant over. He said, "You go up there and tell your captain that the University of South Carolina basketball team is on this flight. And we're not coming here to play football. You've got a basketball game up here tomorrow night, and you tell him to mention it."

The pilot came back immediately with, "We also want to remind you that the South Carolina basketball team, coached by Frank McGuire, is on this flight, and they will play Nebraska tomorrow night."

The Gamecocks got the proper recognition on the flight, but they ended up losing the game by one point, 69-68.

If you've ever traveled with a sports team, you know about the ins and outs of the routines. You board buses and planes, you check in and out of hotels, you eat meals, you hold meetings, and you do a lot of waiting around.

After the team had its pre-game meeting and meal, everybody would go to their rooms to relax until time to head for the arena. Frank and several of us would be in a room together, and the bus to take us to the arena would invariably park under our window. A good while before we needed to leave, the bus would start to warm up, and we could hear the engine droning below.

On one such occasion McGuire turned to us and said, "This is like waiting for an execution." It was bothering me, too - like they're testing the electric chair. You could imagine how the ancient Christians felt, when they were waiting in the dungeon inside the Rome Coliseum. And they could hear the lions roaring in the arena.

Frank said, "Maybe we should tell the driver to go to the other side of the motel, when he's ready to warm-up the bus. So we can't hear it."

That never came to pass, and the sound of the bus warming up became a trademark of our trips to games on the road. It meant it's about time to go fight for your life.

I've never known a tougher person than McGuire. Here's an illustration. I went with him to Hilton Head, where he was the main speaker at some sort of gathering. I've forgotten what it was. When he was getting ready for the affair, he fell in the shower and really hurt himself. He was in agony, so I said, "You stay here, and I'll go cover for you."

Frank said, "No, I came here to speak, and that's what I'm going to do." So I helped him get dressed, although it pained him just to stand up. He went down and made a half-hour speech, never mentioning his injury.

He was tough and had tremendous pride - never wanted to appear weak. However, he never confused weakness with compassion or consideration for other people.

Frank knew my father was in the Presbyterian Home in Philadelphia, so he called me and said that he was going to Philadelphia to coach in an all-star game to be played in the Palestra. He invited me to go along in the private plane that was taking him up there, so I accepted.

When we got to our hotel, I got a call from Columbia saying that my father had died. My sister and brother-in-law came in from California for the funeral, and it was a couple of days before I was ready to go back to Columbia. Meanwhile, Frank's all-star game was played, and his business up there was finished.

However, he said to me, "I know it's going to be a rough trip back for you, so I'll just hold the plane for another day, so you can fly back with me."

That was a side of McGuire that a lot of people experienced, but that wasn't what you saw on the basketball court or in the media.

This is not a criticism of any other coach with whom I worked at Carolina, because they were all fine people, and I got along with them very well. But Frank McGuire was the most successful, the most interesting, the most loyal to me and the most fun to work with. If McGuire had not come to Carolina, I would have missed a great adventure in my life.

Even after he suffered the stroke that confined him to a wheel chair, impaired his speech and limited his ability to do things for himself, he never lost his dignity. He maintained a positive attitude and continued to be well groomed, even in bed clothes. During his final year, I saw him quite a bit, as Don Barton and I worked with him on a book about his life and career.

Never did I hear him utter a word of complaint about his fate. Nor did I hear a word of bitterness toward people who had been his detractors through the years.

I sensed that he was at peace with himself, as well as friends and adversaries. He had played and coached basketball with a passion, but he left it in the arenas and the locker rooms. He played the game of life with the same drive and enthusiasm, but he left that in the hands of the Lord, because he had an abiding faith.

His legacy to the University of South Carolina was an example of what can be done in a sports program, when you have the right direction, the right support and, of utmost importance, the right man. For his day and time, Frank McGuire was that right man.

BILL FOSTER

In hiring Frank McGuire, Carolina had taken the approach of hiring a big name coach, and hope that he could produce a big winner, and that's what McGuire did.

Bill Foster didn't have quite the national image that McGuire enjoyed, but he had been successful at Rutgers, Utah and Duke, and he was definitely in the "big name" category. His Duke teams won three Atlantic Coast Conference championships in six years, and he was national coach of the year in 1978.

He had recruited blue chip players at Duke, and the Carolina administration hoped that he could achieve the same success here. Both President Jim Holderman and Athletics Director Jim Carlen agreed that Foster was the right choice. That was an achievement in itself, because there were an increasing number of things that Holderman and Carlen disagreed on.

Foster accepted the job before the end of the 1979-80 season, and his Blue Devils won the ACC tournament after that.

I always experienced a closeness to Foster, because we had both grown up in small towns in Pennsylvania, only a mile apart. Our high schools played each other every year, and I felt that it gave us a common background.

I never saw a coach more focused on his profession or one who hated to lose any more.

Bobby Cremins had wanted the Carolina job in the worst sort of way, and I wanted to help Bobby any way I could. I went to Carlen to put in a plug for Cremins, but I found out that he was a strong Bill Foster booster. Perhaps if Foster had turned down the job, Bobby might have had a chance, but that certainly wasn't a sure thing. There was some friction between McGuire and the administration over his retirement, and some people at the University didn't want a coach with a Frank McGuire connection. That's a reverse case of the saying, "It's not what you know, but who you know."

However, I had no problems with the hiring of Foster, because he was a proven coach and didn't have any negatives attached.

Here's an example of how much Bill hated to lose. Early in his third season here, we played East Tennessee State in Carolina Coliseum, and they beat us, 88-82. The game was played on a Saturday night, and that's when we always taped Foster's Sunday television show. We were set to do it right there in the Coliseum, following the game.

We waited for an hour for Bill to come out. Only my wife, the engineer and I were left in the place. When Bill finally came out, he walked over to where the East Tennessee team had sat. The chairs that serve as the teams' benches come in sections of four. He was so upset that he kicked three of those sections into the stands. I thought he was going to break his leg, but he didn't.

Then he turned to me and said, "Let's go!" He taped the show and didn't display any signs of the temper he had shown just a few minutes prior.

My thrills relating to air travel weren't confined to the Frank McGuire era. I went to Richmond with Foster in 1984, I believe, and we were traveling in what seemed to be an airplane that looked like a pre-World War II model. I remember the pilot remarking that these planes weren't monitored enough, and we found out later what he meant.

When we were preparing to land, the pilot couldn't tell whether or not the landing gear was down. A red light in the cockpit indicated that it wasn't down, but the pilot didn't consider that signal to be completely reliable. He came back to where I was seated, and was shining a flashlight underneath the plane to see if the landing gear was down. A generator failure caused the cabin lights to go out. Foster and I were standing in the aisle when he said, "Isn't this a helluva way to make a living?"

We circled the airport a few times to burn off as much fuel as possible. They had fire trucks waiting on the runway, and, finally, down we went. We made it, but it wasn't the prettiest landing I ever experienced.

I really wasn't surprised when he had his heart attack during the 1982-83 season. He was completely immersed in his profession. I'm sure that the by-pass surgery that Bill underwent took something out of him, for at least the remainder of the 1982-83 season. Ironically, that was his best season at Carolina, 22-9, although he missed 17 games while he recuperated.

Carolina wasn't facing exactly a back-breaking schedule during Bill's first three seasons here, but it became tougher during his last three, because the Gamecocks became members of the Metro Conference. The Metro didn't rank all that high as a basketball conference, but it presented stronger teams than some of those that the Gamecocks played when they were independents.

Carolina never had a winning Metro record, and in 1985-86, Bill's last year, they won only two of twelve conference games.

I believe that part of Foster's problem was that he was trying to attract ACC type players to an independent, then Metro, program. He could recruit a Mike Gminski to Duke, but even McGuire couldn't lure Gminski to South Carolina.

On top of that, he and Bob Marcum didn't get along very well. Of course, you didn't have to try very hard to not get along with Marcum. The only way a college coach can overcome not getting along with his boss, is to win big. And Foster didn't. Once that 12-16 opening occurred in 1985-86 season, Bill was dead meat.

Bill was a pleasure to work with, as far as his Sunday TV show was concerned. He was articulate, cooperative and had a good sense of humor. Like most successful coaches, he had his share of ego, but I didn't find it offensive. And most coaches who have come to Carolina - as well as a certain play-by-play announcer - have received some great lessons in humility!

As the saying goes, Bill Foster was his own man, and he didn't like to delegate authority. The head man is going to get either the credit or the blame for what happens in a program, so he wanted to make sure that it was done his way.

As I mentioned in the chapter on basketball, when Marcum didn't bother to go by the Carolina dressing room, following the Gamecocks 100-59 loss to Memphis State in the Metro Tournament at Louisville, it was an obvious message to Foster. "Clean out your desk, and get out your resume!"

Foster's resume earned him the head coaching job at Northwestern, and he coached at that Big Ten school for a number of years. He didn't have a winner there, but that is not expected of you at Northwestern. Perhaps desired, but not expected.

Foster's exit from Carolina followed a familiar pattern, established by McGuire, Carlen and Bell. Terms of departure were dictated by a court of law. Bill insisted that his mustering out pay include moneys that he would have received from non-salary items, such as television, radio and basketball camps. The court agreed, and the sum that the University was paying people to "not coach" was growing.

Foster's won-lost record (92-79) was above break even, but it was a far cry from the taste of excellence that had whetted the appetite of Carolina fans during the McGuire era. That's the type of basketball they wanted. Foster came with the right credentials, but he fell short of the new standard that had been set.

Marcum made the decision to terminate Foster, and now it was his responsibility to find the coach that could bring back the "glory years."

GEORGE FELTON

One thing I can say about the 19 basketball and football coaches that have served at Carolina during my tenure, "They have something in common with snowflakes. There are no two alike!"

If Bob Marcum was looking for the antithesis of Bill Foster, he couldn't have made a better choice that George Felton. You'd have to think awhile to find things that Felton and Foster had in common, outside of the first letter of their last names.

Marcum didn't seek Felton. Felton sought him. Ironically, Bobby Cremins couldn't get the Carolina job for himself, but now he was to be responsible for Felton getting it.

The few who knew that Felton was present on the Carolina basketball team under Frank McGuire, had forgotten that he was there and weren't aware that he was an assistant to Cremins at Georgia Tech. Cremins had been a prominent player at Carolina, while Felton's career statistics included one field goal attempt - which he missed.

Cremins talked Marcum into interviewing Felton, and Marcum was impressed. He surprised Gamecock fans and the basketball world with his selection. It was one of those rare occasions when the rumor mill in Columbia was caught completely off guard.

George's prime billing at Tech was that as a recruiter. He had been given a lot of credit for luring Mark Price from Oklahoma, and Tech was getting more than its share of blue chip players from other areas. I'm sure that Cremins had something to do with that.

I got along fine with George, but to say that we had a close relationship would be stretching it. There was more of a generation gap between Felton and me than existed in recent coaches at the University. When such a gap exists, it can be an advantage, if approached in the right way. That is, if the younger person will take advantage of the experience of the older one, and if the senior will embrace the youth and new ideas of the other. It doesn't always work that way.

When George came here and Marcum reminded him that the Sunday TV show was now his property, Felton wasn't at all interested. He said, "I don't know anything about that, and I don't want to fool with it." The show didn't mean much to him, and he didn't care what he was making out of it. He just wanted to coach the team.

George could not appreciate what the exposure on television could do, outside of supplying a supplement to his coaching salary.

Marcum asked me to take it over, and I did. George did fairly well on the show, although he didn't knock himself out. He would sometimes show up over an hour late for a taping, or he would call and say, "I've decided not to come, and I'm going to send Eddie Payne." Payne was an assistant.

I think George was a good coach, hard worker and completely dedicated to what he was doing. Too often, coaches think that coaching is all there is in life, and their families and others have to shift for themselves. He often had problems in his dealings with people.

170

When I was setting-up the network for George's Sunday TV show, one of the stations I had sold it to was WSPA-TV in Spartanburg. That station covered the entire western half of South Carolina and a lot of North Carolina. It was important to us.

Prior to the season George spoke to a Gamecock Club gathering in Spartanburg, and a reporter came to him for a taped interview. George's response was, "If you want to interview me, you'll have to make arrangements through the athletics department."

The reporter got mad and left, and I couldn't blame him. The station then called me and said, "We're not going to carry his television show - we're not going to deal with you anymore. If that guy can't take three minutes to talk to us, to hell with it."

That really put me in a bind, so we had to scramble around and get another station. But it was not one with the coverage that WSPA-TV would have provided for us. And I seriously doubt that the station went out of its way to help George or Carolina in its routine sports coverage.

Felton's coaching record was good. In his five seasons at Carolina his teams won 58.4 percent of their games, which ranks second to McGuire's 66.6 in the modern era of Carolina basketball. He had the distinction of being the only coach, except for McGuire, to take the Gamecocks into the NCAA playoffs, and he never experienced a losing season.

Such a record might provide job security, but as so often is the case, a coach is judged on more than just winning or losing, and the University determined that Felton didn't measure up in some other important areas. He had done a good job of recruiting when he first came to Columbia, but that area had begun to suffer.

When membership in the Southeastern Conference was assured, Carolina decided to look elsewhere for someone to challenge the heavyweights in that league, which was rapidly bringing its basketball reputation toward a level with its football prestige. Bob Marcum was gone, so we'll never know if George would have survived, if he had still been the athletics director.

It was now King Dixon's turn at bat.

STEVE NEWTON

Because of the circumstances surrounding George Felton's departure, and the search for a replacement, I don't think Steve Newton ever had much of a chance to succeed. From the moment he stepped onto the campus, through no fault of his own, the local press seemed to hope that Newton would fail and were more than willing to help him achieve that.

Newton had demonstrated that he was a good coach by taking Murray State and establishing an excellent won-lost record, competing on even or better terms with much larger schools. In six years his Murray State teams won 73 percent of their games, and he took his teams to the NCAA playoffs three times.

He was well educated, possessed a Master of Arts degree and had worked his way through the ranks, from high school coach, to assistant college coach, to head coach. The players he inherited from the Felton program were good, but the best ones were seniors on their way out, and there was only one underclassman, Jamie Watson, with real college potential.

The cumulative total of Felton's last two recruiting classes was two - Watson and Melvin Hartry, a guard from Irwinton, Georgia who was not recruited by any major schools.

The atmosphere surrounding Newton and the Carolina program was not conducive to recruiting quality players, so Steve didn't have a prayer. Newton did recruit a couple of players who would be assets to his successor, Eddie Fogler. They were Cary Rich and Emmett Hall. However, the cupboard was getting bare when Steve took over the coaching job here, and when he left two years later, it was even more bare.

The staff was charged with some picky recruiting violations, such as lending a prospect, who had already committed to the Gamecocks, a pair of shoes. Another publicized sin was a prospect catching a ride with a Carolina player from Athens, Georgia, to Columbia. Declared ineligible to enroll at Carolina, both young men went to other colleges and played basketball.

The school's compliance coordinator watched the basketball program with argus eyes, and most of his suspicions seemed to make their ways into the local newspaper.

When Mike McGee took over as athletics director midway through the 1992-93 season, the handwriting was already on the wall for Newton. McGee moved him into an administrative position in the athletics department, and Newton did a fine job. The move probably came as blessed relief to Steve, because his two seasons here had not been a happy experience.

Two years later he accepted the job as athletics director at Southern Indiana University.

I liked Steve, although my association with him was not very close. For the umpteenth time, I had lost the TV show, so my direct contact with Newton was limited. He was somewhat introverted, and the atmosphere around his program might have made him more so that way.

Now it was Mike McGee's turn. The University was in a pattern. Four straight athletics directors had the responsibility of hiring four straight basketball coaches.

EDDIE FOGLER

In my 43 years at Carolina I was associated with ten basketball coaches, but none whom I have more respect for and genuinely liked more than Eddie Fogler. To me, Eddie was a breath of fresh air, and a great individual with whom to spend my last season of Carolina basketball as a broadcaster.

Eddie had the maturity of his 48 years, the enthusiasm of an 18-year-old and the experience of a coach many years his senior. He was not a miracle worker, nor were Frank McGuire and Dean Smith.

McGuire won six games in his first season at South Carolina, while Smith won eight in his first year as North Carolina's head coach. Eddie assisted Smith at UNC for 15 years, and he has a lot of Smith's coaching philosophy drilled into him. However, he was not without his own ideas.

When I was talking to Eddie at the 1993 SEC tournament at Lexington, Kentucky, I congratulated him on his 25 straight winning seasons. I also told him that Bobby Cremins would be Carolina's next coach. Little did we know that he would be sitting on the Gamecock bench during my farewell season. I'm happy that he was.

There wasn't a phony bone in Eddie's body. He said what he really thought, and some people aren't accustomed to that in this day of spin control. If folks are wanting someone to say something just for the sake of public relations, they should not have looked to Fogler. Not that he was impolite, or anything like that. He was just that honest. You didn't have to stand around wondering where he stands on a particular subject.

I had the pleasure of traveling with Eddie to a number of Gamecock Club meetings around the state, and I think we got along extremely well. We became friends. If we hadn't, Eddie would have surely let me know it. He certainly didn't need me for public relations purposes. But here I am saying all these nice things.

Eddie continues his career as an analyst, covering college basketball on TV, where does an excellent job.

THE BASEBALL COACHES

BOBBY RICHARDSON AND JUNE RAINES

The only Carolina teams that I did play-by-play for were those coached by Bobby Richardson and June Raines. Both were great coaches, good people and had outstanding success in their profession.

Bobby started coaching at Carolina in 1970, but it was 1974 before I broadcast any of his games. That took place in the 1974 NCAA regionals at Starksville, Mississippi, and it turned out to be a good tournament for Carolina, although they lost the championship to Miami.

Richardson coached for two more years after that, and I managed to get some of his games on the radio. We also did Carolina's games in the 1975 College World Series, when Richardson's team lost to Texas in the championship game.

They don't make 'em any finer than Bobby. He has strong religious convictions, didn't mind expressing them, and, what's more, he practiced what he preached. Actually, he was a lay preacher in the true sense of the term.

Bobby was the speaker at a breakfast during that 1975 College World Series, and he made a strong point about the problems connected to drinking alcoholic beverages. In attendance was Jim Brock, whose Arizona State teams won several national championships. Brock was a beer drinker and prone to overdo it, so he listened intently to what Bobby had to say. After the breakfast, Brock went to Bobby and told him how much he appreciated what he had to say and that he was going to take it to heart. Because of Richardson's speech, Brock stopped drinking, and his health and life was greatly improved.

Richardson didn't allow his players to smoke, chew, drink alcoholic beverages, or use profanity. It was a squeaky clean program and then some. When we were in a restaurant after a game, the players liked to sit next to me, so they could order a beer, and if Richardson came in, they could put it on my table. I said, "Wait a minute, I don't want him to see me drinking it, either!"

Once we played at Clemson on Easter Sunday, and Richardson had a sunrise service for the team. It was non-denominational, and I don't think he required attendance, but he most certainly encouraged it.

Jeff Grantz, the outstanding football quarterback for Carolina, was also a fine baseball player under Richardson. He told me one of the funniest stories I've ever heard, and it concerned his coach.

Carolina was playing at Clemson, and the Gamecocks thought the home plate umpire was very inconsistent in calling balls and strikes. Jeff was at bat and got what seemed to be a couple of bad calls, so Bobby called timeout and approached the umpire. He told him that he was making it awfully tough on the batters, and they didn't know where the strike zone was, because of the way he was calling it.

Richardson did this in his usual gentlemanly fashion, and that might have bothered the ump more than if he had just raised hell. He also knew Bobby's background as a major leaguer and might have thought that he was "talking down" to him. Whatever the reason, the ump unloaded on Bobby, not sparing the four letter words and telling him to get back to the dugout, or he would throw him out of the game - or words to that effect.

Bobby thought for a moment, turned around and took about a half dozen steps away from the umpire. Then he turned around and said, "And phooey on you!"

The ump didn't know whether to laugh or cry, and Jeff had great difficulty in controlling his temptation to just fall down laughing.

Talk about a hands-on coach, Bobby even liked to drive the bus for the team, and he sometimes did. I would sit back in my seat and think, "Here's a guy who was a great second baseman for the New York Yankees, World Series Champions, and here he is driving this broken down bus to Statesboro, Georgia." Bobby couldn't have cared less, because that's what he wanted to do.

Outside of Clemson, Georgia Southern was Carolina's biggest rival during Richardson's tenure, and the Eagles had a great program. They drew big crowds in Statesboro, and the people really supported them.

The fans would say some pretty rough things to Bobby and the Gamecocks, much like the third base hecklers of later years said to visiting teams at Sarge Frye Field. Richardson complained about it, and the sports editor of the Statesboro newspaper wrote a column on the subject. The people there were enflamed even more by that, and the rivalry between the two schools intensified.

Richardson belied Leo Durocher's contention that "nice guys finish last." Bobby was a nice guy, and he finished at the top. In seven years at Carolina his teams won 70 percent of their games, and he did it on the straight and narrow.

Richardson raised Gamecock baseball to a high level, and it remained there under his successor, June Raines.

Bobby left Carolina to run for Congress as a Republican, at the special urging of United States Senator Strom Thurmond. I tried to talk Bobby out of it, reminding him that baseball had been his life, and that politics was a different and often treacherous world.

I told him, "In politics, sometimes you have to compromise, and you are not going to compromise." He told me I was right about that, and I thought that he had decided not to run.

However, he went ahead and ran, was defeated, and went on to future careers at Coastal Carolina and Liberty University, before retiring at the home he purchased years ago in his home town of Sumter, South Carolina.

June Raines was an exception to the rule of young men who drop out of school to go into professional baseball. After ten seasons he enrolled at the University of South Carolina as a 30-year-old freshman and earned a Bachelor of Science and Master of Arts degrees. June had enrolled at Furman in 1957 but left after his freshman year to play in the Cleveland Indians organization.

When June came to Carolina, Jackie Powers was coaching the baseball team, and he became an assistant. He served three years with Bobby Richardson, before returning to professional baseball as a catching instructor in the Philadelphia Phillies organization. When Richardson left following the 1976 baseball season, Raines returned to Carolina as head coach.

Raines tenure was not only longer than any baseball coach in the University's history, but no football or basketball coach could match his 20 seasons. He had a great career, winning 763 games against 380 losses for a percentage of .667.

June never had a losing season, but his final one was his worst. Unfortunately, coaches are remembered for their final seasons for a few years. Then their overall records become their measuring stick.

I followed Raines' teams from the outset, and they were always well coached and well motivated. Fifty-three of June's players signed professional contracts, and 11 made it to the major leagues.

He was a laid-back individual, easy to know and very good to work with. He had all the trappings of baseball men from the old school, and he made a few additions of his own to the baseball vernacular. For example, if his starting pitchers weren't rested enough, he would say, "We're going to pitch Johnny Wholestaff," meaning that several pitchers would take short turns on the mound.

When Carolina became a member of the Southeastern Conference, Raines was automatically handed one of the toughest baseball schedules in the country. The SEC is, without a doubt, the strongest baseball conference in the nation.

During Raines' seasons in the league, his won-lost records suffered, and that brought the usual rumors about his career being at an end. It did end after the 1996 season, as McGee re-assigned him to an administrative position in the athletics department. June had baseball and Carolina in his blood, and, whatever his capacity, you may be assured that everything he did will be what he considers best for both.

Following the 1996 season, June was duly honored by the Columbia Dugout Club for the outstanding job he did as baseball coach, and he received the highest honor that can be given by the State of South Carolina, the Order of the Palmetto. That's our state's equivalent of being named a Kentucky Colonel.

Among other things received by Raines were airline tickets to any place of their choice for June and his wife, Elaine. This left one problem to be resolved, however, as Elaine doesn't like to fly. This was a nice gift and subsequently was converted into something of their choice.

June established a great tradition for Carolina baseball, similar to what McGuire did in basketball.

~OTHER COACHES REMEMBERED~

In five decades of sportscasting, it was my privilege to have some sort of relationship or contact with a number of fine coaches. Here's a list of some of those of whom I have special memories - in no particular order.

MARK BERSON Carolina's soccer coach, has done a remarkable job in building the Gamecock soccer program to a position of national prominence which enabled his team to reach the final four in the country. I had the pleasure at one time of having Mark Berson as my analyst on our broadcast of Gamecock basketball. Mark is not only an excellent coach, but one of the good guys.

CURTIS FRYE has been responsible for the women's and men's track teams that have consistently exhibited championship quality. His teams are always ranked among the top ten teams in the country. Coach Frye has also done an outstanding job with the cross country teams.

Coach Frye does not receive the credit he deserves for the remarkable job he has done.

JOYCE COMPTON, a Hall of Fame Coach, for twenty years has had her women's softball teams earning national acclaim. In 2007, she had the thrill of seeing her team play in the national championship playoff games.

KENT DEMARS for many years has done an outstanding job in coaching Carolina's tennis teams.

CLAIR BEE coached at Long Island University for many years and had a lot to do with the growth of basketball in 1940s and 1950s. He had a storehouse of knowledge, and I had the opportunity to attend many of his clinics. He closed his brilliant career as a coach when it was found out that some of his star players were fixing games and making quite a bit of money in the payoff from the gamblers.

PETE CARRILL retired in 1996 after a distinguished career as coach of the Princeton University Tigers. During his long career there, he did more with what he had than any coach in the country.

EVERETT CASE came to North Carolina State right after World War II and brought big-time college basketball into the Southeast. He forced other schools in what is now the Atlantic Coast Conference to upgrade their basketball programs by recruiting from the hotbeds of high school basketball. Case was always gentlemanly in his relationships with the media and the public.

LYLES ALLEY was the first to bring basketball excitement to South Carolina. He recruited Frank Selvy for his Furman team, and the Kentucky native set national scoring records. Selvy led the nation in scoring two straight years, and a teammate, Darrell Floyd, was the top scorer the year following Selvy's graduation. I saw some very exciting games in old Textile Hall, where the Paladins played.

RICK BARNES first recruit when he went from Providence to Clemson in 1994 was my grandson, Danny Johnson. Success follows Barnes everywhere he goes, because he is an excellent coach. He currently is head coach of the Texas Longhorns. My grandson,

Danny Johnson, was Barnes first recruit when he took over the job at Clemson. After two years with the Tigers, Johnson transferred to the College of Charleston.

JOHN KRESSE, a native New Yorker, when he was head coach at the College of Charleston year after year sent his team to the NCAA playoffs. My grandson, Danny Johnson played under John Kresse, and he told me the players loved their coach. John is now a fund raiser for the College. John has always been one of my favorite people.

ABE LEMONS coached at Oklahoma City University, Pan American University and the University of Texas, and was one of the funniest people I've ever met. He could have made it as a stand-up comedian.

One of his teams was playing a game in Madison Square Garden and was far behind at the end of the first half. Rather than go to the dressing room, Lemons kept his squad on the floor, had one group take off their jerseys and had a "shirts and skins" scrimmage. Unbelievable!

One of the media people asked Lemons why he didn't take the team to the dressing room and talk to them. His answer was, "Look, I talked to them before the game, and you see how much good that did." And he made a very good point.

PAUL (BEAR) BRYANT of Alabama is recognized as one of the few best coaches in the history of college football. He was a man's man, and I wouldn't take anything for having sat in on a visit with Frank McGuire in Bryant's office. That made me aware of how alike he and McGuire were.

BUD WILKINSON was not only one of the all-time winningest coaches during his career at Oklahoma, but he was one of the classiest individuals I've ever met. When I was just starting out as a sportscaster, I was doing a high school game at which Wilkinson was in attendance. I met him before the game, and I casually invited him to come by the booth for a halftime interview, if he had time. I had no idea that he would. But as soon as the half ended, he appeared in my booth, sat there relaxed, and answered questions as if he were appearing at halftime of the Super Bowl.

Wilkinson gave the greatest discourse on the kicking game I've ever heard, and when I got back to Little Rock, nobody talked about the game. All they talked about was how much they had enjoyed the halftime interview with Bud Wilkinson. Bud spent this time the night before his big rivalry game with the University of Missouri.

GEORGE WELSH did a fantastic job as head football coach at Virginia. My first look at George came when he quarterbacked Navy against Carolina here in 1955. It was raining hard, and the field was sloppy, but Welsh threw the ball like he was playing on a dry field. He's another one that has shown that any school can succeed with the right man heading up the program.

DANNY FORD won a national championship for Clemson. He is one of the few football coaches who played under Bear Bryant who was successful in emulating him. I admire Danny and value his friendship.

WILLIE JEFFRIES is back in Orangeburg, where he belongs. After a long coaching career including many at South Carolina State where he had many championship seasons, he has now left coaching. It should be noted that he was the first Black Head Coach named at a Division-1 school.

DICK SHERIDAN, ART BAKER AND STEVE SATTERFIELD The reason I list these three together is that they were all on the same staff at Eau Claire High School in Columbia. Sheridan was a success at Furman and North Carolina State. Baker did a fine job as head coach at Furman, The Citadel, East Carolina, along with staff assignments at both Florida State and Carolina. Satterfield had a winning program at Wofford College in Spartanburg, South Carolina, and had great success as a high school coach. All three are first class individuals, as well as fine football coaches.

BILL WILHELM is a legend among college baseball coaches. In his long career at Clemson, he never had a losing season and made the Tigers one of the top college baseball teams in the country. I have great respect for Bill and have enjoyed our friendship over the years.

CHAL PORT With limited player talent and facilities, it is just remarkable what he accomplished with the Citadel baseball program. I miss working the Carolina – Citadel games as they always gave me the time to visit with Chal, one of the nicest and one of the best in the business.

MIKE MCGEE I watched him as an All-American football player at Duke – followed him through his college coaching career and realized the improvements he made as athletics director at Carolina. Under his leadership the Gamecock coaching staff was as good as or better than any previously. He upgraded all the women's sports and the minor sports at Carolina – and the new athletic facilities that he added greatly benefited the athletes, coaches and fans.

HANK IBA In addition to the fore mentioned coaches; he is one coach I will always remember. For many years, Hank Iba was the head basketball coach at Oklahoma A&M, now known as Oklahoma State. Iba, during his career, was known as the top defensive coach in the country. When I was broadcasting University of Arkansas basketball, the Razorbacks would play A&M every year, and when the game was at Stillwater, Oklahoma, I would go to the A&M field house and watch the Razorbacks in their pre-game practice. When I would pass by Iba's small, glassed-in office right next to the basketball court, he would wave to me and invite me to come into his office. He knew I had coached basketball so he would get some chalk and start outlining on a small blackboard the various defenses he and other coaches used. He told me that he would never give a scholarship to a boy unless he could play defense. He also told me that whenever one of his players made a costly mistake, he would take the player out of the game and have him sit at the end of the bench. Then after several minutes passed, he would go down and sit next to this player and explain to him why he had been taken out of the game. By doing this, he was able to calmly instruct the player as to what he should have done; and, at the same time, not embarrass the player by criticizing him as soon as he reached the bench – something that many coaches unfortunately do today.

It was during this time in the late 40's that Iba had a 7 foot center by the name of Bob Kurland, who would on defense time after time swat the ball off the backboard – no goal tending called as he was outside the narrow lane – and as a result of this, the lane was widened, and, of course, that prevented much of the goal tending. At the close of his career, Iba coached the U. S. Olympic squad overseas that had the championship stolen by the timekeeper and the U. S. lost the game. All the players turned back their silver medals in protest. Carolina's Kevin Joyce was on that team, and he liked Iba, but he told me he thought the game had passed Iba by. But what an outstanding legacy Hank Iba left to the college basketball scene.

FRANK HOWARD Although Frank Howard was football coach and athletics director for Carolina's number one rival, Clemson, I always had a good association with him and liked him a lot.

The second bowl game I ever did - the first was Arkansas-William and Mary in the Dixie Bowl - involved Howard. The first Bluebonnet Bowl in Houston, Texas, was played that year, and they asked me to do the play-by-play for the bowl's nationwide radio network. That was before they televised practically everything that moved.

Clemson played Rice in that game and won it by a 23-7 score, so it showed that having a Gamecock on the broadcast didn't do any damage. I enjoyed being with the Clemson contingent out there, and got to know Howard just a little bit better than I had.

He always called me by my last name, as he did with most people. If he called you by your name and not something else, you considered yourself lucky. "Buddy," was a sort of a catch-all he used, and it kept him from having to remember everybody's name.

When Howard died in 1995, I went up to Clemson for the visitation, and I was talking with Brent Breedin, who was sports information director at Clemson in the early 1950s. Brent told me that Howard talked with him about the possibility of getting me to come up and do the broadcasts of Clemson games. I was never contacted about it, so I guess they considered it beyond the realm of possibility, and it would have been. It was still flattering that Howard looked at me from that perspective.

Howard was a coach on the field, but in public, he was an act. He was always on stage and willing to say anything for shock value, especially if it involved Carolina.

When I arrived at Houston for that 1959 Bluebonnet Bowl, I saw a private jet at the airport, and I saw that Nelson Rockefeller was on it. He was going around the country, testing the waters, to see if it would be advisable for him to run for president.

At the Shamrock Hotel, he and I went up on the elevator together, and we were staying on the same floor. He asked me if I knew where Coach Howard was staying, but I didn't know. He told me that he was having a press conference in his room at a certain time and wanted me to attend.

I replied that Howard was having a press conference about the same time and that I would have to go there. As I was getting ready to leave my room, I got a call from Rockefeller, and he said, "I want you to help me. My press conference has supposedly started, but there's nobody here. I'm told that everyone is down at Coach Howard's room. Would you mind if I go down there with you?"

I said, "Of course not," and we met in the hall and went to Howard's room. When we arrived, the room was full of media people, and Howard was holding forth. He recognized Rockefeller and told him how happy he was to have him there.

Rockefeller explained, "I was supposed to have a press conference the same time as yours, but I didn't have anybody up there.

Howard replied, "I can understand that, Buddy." Everybody laughed, and Rockefeller took a seat for the remainder of Howard's session.

The Tiger met his match in Frank McGuire. I witnessed a confrontation between the two, following a basketball game at Clemson, which was won by Carolina in a blowout. After the game, McGuire came back onto the basketball court to do the post-game radio show and talk to the media. Howard was standing there in front of the stage at the end of the court, where he and some of the Clemson people always sat.

Howard said to McGuire, "You sort of took advantage of us tonight, didn't you?"

McGuire didn't like that one bit, and the two got chin to chin in an exchange of words. They were surrounded by a group of Clemson fans, including a number of football players. They exchanged words, and it looked like they were coming to blows, but cooler heads prevailed.

It was the scariest post-game show I ever did, because there must have been several hundred people surrounding us. They were waiting around to hear what McGuire might say about the incident, but he did the right thing and didn't mention it. You could have heard a pin drop throughout my interview with McGuire. The show went on without any problems.

Afterward, I thought, "This is a shame. Both of these coaches are legends, and here they are at each other's throat." That was taken care of, because within a week, they got together on the telephone, resolved their differences, and there was never another problem between them.

Howard could get away with almost anything at Clemson, and he often reminded the media of that. He would say, "I can do anything I want to, because Bob Edwards (president of Clemson at the time) was once the water boy for my football team."

When he heard that I was going to Georgia Tech to do the football games in 1965, he called me and said, "Fulton, that's the first time I've ever seen you show good sense."

There used to be a cocktail lounge near Columbia's Whitehall section, where I lived at one time, and I occasionally stopped by in there. Once I was in there, and I heard this loud voice say, "Fulton." It was unmistakenly Howard, and he growled, "Come on over here."

I went to his table, and there was a very attractive lady sitting there talking with him. I joined them, and a short while later, a Clemson supporter spotted us, and came over to speak to his coach.

He introduced himself, and Howard, without batting an eye, responded with, "Glad to meet you. And I want you to meet Bob Fulton and his wife."

There was a time when I found Howard at a loss for words. Don Barton and I were having lunch in the Market Restaurant, which was at the corner of Assembly and Gervais in Columbia. We saw Howard sitting in a booth alone, so we went over and joined him.

As we were about ready to leave, in walks Lou Cordileone, who had been an All-America lineman for Howard and had just finished his first season with the New York Giants of the NFL.

When Clemson played Houston in the Bluebonnet Bowl, Cordileone had already withdrawn from school to begin his pro career. But he went to Houston and played a whale of a game for the Tigers.

Howard and Cordileone exchanged greetings, and Howard asked his former star, "How do you like pro football?"

Cordileone didn't hesitate and replied, "Fine, Coach, the only thing I don't like is having to take a cut in pay!"

Howard turned red from his chin to the back of his head, and he changed the subject as fast as he could.

The Tiger coach was always proud of having the playing field of Clemson Memorial Stadium named "Frank Howard Field," although the media usually referred to the entire set-up as "Death Valley."

The day prior to one of the Carolina-Clemson games up there, Howard was observing the Gamecocks, as they went through their Friday practice session. As the Gamecocks left the field for the dressing room, one player was late departing, and he passed by Howard. He had no idea who this stranger was, but the Clemson coach stopped him.

"Hey Buddy," he began, "did you know that this place is named after me?"

The Gamecock thought for a few seconds, then answered, "No sir, but it's nice to meet you, Mister Death Valley."

When Carolina played at Clemson, I used to stay at the Holiday Inn there, and I always got a call, telling me that Coach Howard wants to meet you in the dining room. This was his hangout to have coffee with friends, so I would join him and others there.

He would spend some time insulting Carolina, and I would take if for what it was worth - very little. It was not a two-way street with Howard, because he didn't mind kidding you, but he didn't take it too well when you gave him the needle.

Of all the Carolina coaches he faced, I think that Warren Giese was his favorite. I don't know why, because they were like oil and water - little in common. He always referred to him as "Geezie," because Warren was a Gamecock, and that was sort of putting him down. That was for public consumption, not for personal contact.

He thought that Carolina didn't treat Giese right, and I don't know what he based it on. His teams defeated Giese's four of the five times they faced each other, and that might have colored his view of Enright's successor.

181

~MEN IN STRIPED SHIRTS~

As coaches, players and fans well know, officials are most important in the world of sports, particularly in football and basketball. Even more so in basketball, because officials have so many decisions to make.

They are seldom appreciated for the job they do, because most fans - and some coaches - judge calls by the criterion: If it's for me, it's a correct call. If it's against me, it's a bad call.

I heard more than one official say that, after a game, both teams go away mad with him, he feels he must have done a pretty good job.

Personally, I sincerely appreciate officials and the tough job they have to do. I know a number of them personally, and they are not green-eyed monsters. They are just normal human beings trying to do the best job they can in a thankless job. I don't know why they do it, but thank goodness they do.

Here are some officials I consider among the best I've seen, starting with basketball.

RED MAHALIK officiated in the Atlantic Coast Conference in the 1960s and is without a doubt in my mind the finest basketball official I ever watched. He was very intense, and he couldn't have been more impartial. He didn't care where the game was being played, he treated both teams the same, and he was never swayed by the crowd. He was so intense that he had to step aside after officiating for about ten years, because it was taking too much out of him.

LENNIE WERTZ was honored at Clemson several years ago for his many years of outstanding officiating. At that time he was asked whom he considered the best official he had seen, and he named Red Mahalik.

PAT KENNEDY was one of the first officials I ever watched over a period of years. He did most of his officiating in the New York and Philadelphia areas, and he worked a lot of professional basketball and baseball games. He worked the big games in Madison Square Garden and Convention Hall, and when he called a foul, everyone in the house knew it. He would blow his whistle three or four times to quiet the crowd, then he would give the players number and tell what crime he had committed!

Back in the thirties only one official was used in most of the games, and he had his hands full, although the games were not as fast as they are today. Another official, Ab Curtis, told me that he was in Kennedy's dressing room prior to a game, and Pat was putting rouge on his face. Kennedy explained, "I try to be a showman in this business, and people expect me to get red in the face when I call a foul. So that's why I put rouge on my face, so nobody will have trouble seeing it."

For some time Curtis was in charge of officials in the Southwest Conference.

GEORGE CONLEY was not a showman like Kennedy, but he was very professional and very fair. His son, Larry, was a fine basketball player at Kentucky and now does commentary on televised games. George was a fine official and a friend of Frank McGuire, so he often visited with us when we were on the road.

LOU BELLO was another showman-type official. Back when all fouls were shoot-ing fouls, Bello loved to call a charging foul at one end of the court, grab the ball and sprint down to the opposite free throw line and put the ball on the line. Bello's problem was that he often clowned too much.

He was calling a Clemson game in the North-South Doubleheader at Charlotte, and the Tigers were hopelessly behind. Toward the end of the game, Bello was standing at the sideline right in front of me and joking with one of the players on the other team. Choppy Patterson, an excellent basketball player and the Clemson captain, came over and politely said, "Mister Bello, this game may be fun for you, but it isn't fun for me and my team-mates. Stop clowning around!"

For the rest of the game Bello didn't mess around, because Choppy had straightened him out.

Bello died several years ago, but he will always be remembered for the color and excitement he added to the job of officiating college basketball.

JOHN CLOUGHERTY worked a lot of Carolina basketball games that I broadcast, was always involved in the NCAA playoffs and was chosen for the Final Four several times. He is considered one of the top officials in the country. He never loses his cool, so he doesn't have to call many technical fouls, and the coaches have the utmost respect for him.

He made one of the gutsiest calls I've heard about in a game between Vanderbilt and Florida in Nashville. Earlier in the season a Florida player had been accused of hitting a girl with a tennis racquet, so Vandy students recognized this by throwing tennis balls on the court during the game. As time was running out, Vanderbilt had a one-point lead, but Clougherty had to warn the crowd not to throw any more tennis balls onto the court.

As the official went back to the court, here came more tennis balls, so Clougherty lived up to his warning and called a technical foul on the crowd. Florida made both free throws, and that won the game for the Gators. The officials needed security to get out of the arena, but that didn't deter Clougherty from doing what he had warned the crowd about.

CHARLIE ECKMAN could do anything with a basketball game that could be done. We used to call him "Jolly Cholly" for no particular reason, except that it belied his no nonsense approach to officiating. If you were looking for help from an official, Charlie wasn't the one to count on. He called it straight down the middle. He didn't favor the home team, and he didn't try to help the visiting team.

STEVE HONZO worked some of Carolina's games, but he usually did games in the big arenas in the East. He was another excellent official who was color blind when it came to uniforms worn by the teams.

HANK NICHOLS for a time was in charge of officials for the NCAA, but he was one of the best in calling games himself. I've never seen him let a game get out of con-trol. One thing I remember about Hank is that he changed the method of shooting free throws by Mike Brittain, a center who played for Bill Foster at Carolina in the 1980s. Mike had an unusual hesitation when he shot free throws, like a double clutch. Because of this, opposing players would often step into the lane too soon, and if Mike missed the shot, it would give him another try.

Carolina was playing Biscayne College in Miami, and Hank was one of the officials. Mike went to the free throw line, went through his motion, and every Biscayne player stepped into the lane. Nichols didn't call a violation, and he told Brittain that he never would, as long as Brittain used that unusual motion. Mike had to change the way he shot free throws.

DAVID DODGE was never allowed to work Carolina games, because he lived in Columbia. He had coached basketball at Fort Jackson, and he knows the book as well as anyone. Before each basketball season, I would get together with David and go over rule changes. David is now retired from officiating.

JOE AND JIM MILLS, or is it the other way around? They were identical twins who lived near Raleigh, North Carolina, and you honestly couldn't tell one from the other. Don Barton told me the story of his wife, Betty, having a childhood friend named Joan O'Gorman as her guest at a game in the old Carolina Field house. Joan's brother, Louie, was once head coach at Belmont Abbey College, was a prominent high school coach for years and has an annual basketball camp.

On rare occasions, Joe and Jim Mills would be assigned to the same game, perhaps saving travel expenses, and they were officiating this particular Carolina game. Betty, a twin herself, and Joan were busily chatting, as the game progressed. During a pause in the action, Betty asked Joan, "Had you noticed that the two officials are twins?"

Joan looked at Jim and Joe, then replied, "No, but I should have. They are dressed just alike!"

There are a lot of other fine basketball officials, but I could not name them all. I did find out that they had one thing in common – that they hoped every shot goes in the basket! Calls after missed shots are the toughest to make, and the hardest games to officiate are those in which both teams are shooting poorly. That's why today officials just don't call a lot of fouls that occur along the baseline. If they called everything the games would degenerate into a free-throw contest.

Coaches feel that the first five minutes of a game are the most important. That's when officials establish control of a game and let the coaches and players know how it will be called. What coaches want most of all is for an official to be consistent. As long as officials call it the same way on both ends of the court, coaches have no room for complaint.

I'll mention several football officials, although they are not as conspicuous as basketball officials, because they are far removed from the spectators, there are more of them in a game, and they are not as personally involved with what transpires.

JACK LINDSAY was at one time chief insurance commissioner for the state of South Carolina, but he was also a fine official. Other officials would tell me that Jack knew the rule book better than any official in the business. He demonstrated this in 1963, when Carolina played Duke at Durham. Duke kicked a field goal but still trailed the Gamecocks, 6-3. On the kickoff that followed, Carolina returned the ball to its own 35, but a yellow marker was thrown around midfield.

184

The officials huddled for a few minutes, and to the dismay of Gamecock fans, coaches and players, the ball was awarded to Duke at midfield. The ruling, cited by Lindsay, was that a Carolina player had committed an infraction while the ball was still in the air - a free ball - and that it therefore was awarded to the offended team. That is the only time I've seen or heard about that rule being enforced. At that time, no one in the press box or on the coaching staffs along with some of the officials in Jack's crew knew what the ruling was.

I didn't have to worry about seeing it again, because they changed the rule to simply assessing yardage and/or replaying the down. And it was changed because of that situation between Carolina and Duke.

VINCENT PRICE became a referee, because that's the position that the top officials usually hold. He lived in Gaffney, and he introduced himself to me a few years back, when I spoke to the Spartanburg Touchdown Club. I told him that I knew exactly who he was and that I had seen him officiate in a number of ACC games.

WELDON WAITES was from Columbia, but he couldn't work Carolina games under normal circumstances. However, when we played in Hawaii, we were allowed to bring one official. I guess they figured that the visiting team needed all the help it could get. I told about Weldon's trip to Hawaii for our game in 1981, when he tried his best to help the Gamecocks in what turned out to be Jim Carlen's final game as head coach. Weldon definitely favored the Gamecocks on several close calls. The biggest of them all was offensive pass interference in the end zone which cost Hawaii a touchdown. Later in the hotel Weldon came up to me and said "I told you I would help you."

~MEN BEHIND THE MIKE~

People often ask me who I think are the best announcers in the business. There is not an easy answer, but of those broadcasting today I think that Joe Buck does an excellent job on baseball and football. Joe's father was the late Jack Buck with whom I became acquainted when both of us entered our first year as major league broadcasters in 1954 - so Joe had a lot of help in learning the business. For baseball TV, you have to include Vin Scully, who it seems forever has been the Voice of the Dodgers. Vin went right from the campus of Fordham University to the majors. I always liked Red Barber who was a member of the Dodgers' crew and later became one of the broadcasters of the New York Yankees. I remember so well sitting in the booth next to Red and watching him use the egg timer as a reminder to give the score every three minutes. I know some announcers who could improve their broadcasts by simply adopting Red's method of giving the score often. I would also like to include in this category Byrum Saam, long-time Voice of the Philadelphia A's. I alluded to this earlier in the book. Perhaps in a class all by himself is Al Michaels, who teams up with John Madden in their broadcasts of Monday night football.

Dick Enberg gets my vote as the most diverse broadcaster who does an excellent job in his coverage of tennis, football, baseball, and basketball. Dick also does a fine job on game-related commentary.

Going back a few years, Curt Gowdy, long time Voice of the Boston Red Sox, was a very versatile and a top-flight broadcaster. I first knew Curtis when he was doing basketball for Oklahoma A&M and I was doing the Arkansas games. Curtis is gone now, and I miss our long-time friendship.

When it comes to great sports voices, I vote for Mel Allen who for many years covered the New York Yankees – and going back to the 40's – Ted Husing, the best voice of all. He could even make a tennis-match broadcast sound exciting. I first met Husing when he was covering for CBS the horse races at Garden St. Park in New Jersey in 1943. but he had a problem - he would often place bets on the races he was broadcasting. He would be so busy trying to find the horse he had bet on, that he sometimes failed to get the order of finish correct. That was slightly important to a lot of other people who had placed bets and were depending on him to determine win, place or show. Husing was one of the most profane persons I have ever known, and his profanity, unfortunately for him, became a part of some of his broadcasts. For many years, Husing at CBS and Bill Stern (Mr. excitement) at NBC were the radio sports' voices for the entire country. Most people who followed these two said, "If you are a sports fan, listen to Bill Stern, but if you are a coach, listen to Ted Husing."

Stern put real excitement into his football broadcasts. He had a great sports voice, and he was a master of inflection, which added a lot to his presentation. In the late 1940s I heard his broadcast of the Notre Dame-Southern Methodist game, which was of national significance, and I don't think anyone could ever top that broadcast. It was a truly great game, and the people who heard Stern's broadcast probably found it more exciting than those who were at the game.

Years later I met Stern when he was in Columbia for the 1955 Carolina-Navy game, and he was working for Mutual Broadcasting System. At the time he was struggling with health problems, which dogged him in the latter stages of his career. Television also presented a problem for Stern, because it forced play-by-play announcers to be more accurate. Many fans would turn down the sound on the TV set and listen to their favorite radio announcer do the game. If you weren't accurate, you lost your credibility, and a lot of your audience.

There were quite a few other broadcasters I was honored to know during my days with Mutual: Jack Brickhouse, who covered the Cubs and White Sox in Chicago; and Ernie Harwell long-time Voice of the Detroit Tigers, who had the best baseball library in the country.

My apologies to other sports broadcasters for not giving them the credit they deserve.

Husing had an illness that ended his career, but if you are too young to have heard him, take my word for it, he was one of the best ever.

Over the years there have been many excellent play-by-play broadcasters. I will mention a few that caught my attention, but that doesn't mean that there weren't others just as good.

VINCE SCULLY started doing baseball right after he finished Fordham, and he arose right to the top. He started working with the Dodgers at Ebbets Field, and when they went west, he followed them to San Francisco. He has a thorough background, a fine voice and tells excellent stories. He is versatile and can do other sports, but he is recognized most for his career in baseball.

RED BARBER was known nationwide as "the Old Redhead," and he was always one of my favorites. He was one of several Southerners to broadcast major league baseball, and he had a relaxed style to go with it. He developed his own style and became a model that other broadcasters emulated. He was a perfectionist, but had a great imagination. He coined such phrases as "catbird seat," for the team or player in control, and "rhubarb," for hostilities that occurred on the field, particularly in baseball.

I remember so well sitting in the booth next to Red and watching him use the egg timer as a reminder to give the score every three minutes. I know some announcers who could improve their broadcasts by simply adopting Red's method of giving the score often.

Barber spent most of his time with the Dodgers, although he also worked with the New York Yankees. His pleasant voice captivated the listener, and if you were going down the radio dial, when you heard his voice, you knew right away that it was Red Barber.

ERNIE HARWELL did games for the Detroit Tigers, and he was another Southerner who went north. He started out with the Atlanta Crackers of the Southern Association, and did what amounted to a tour of the majors, before settling down in Detroit. Several years ago he was removed from the Detroit broadcasting crew, but the fans protested so vehemently that he was returned as the Voice of the Tigers.

When I was doing Mutual's Game of the Day, Harwell was very helpful to me, and I had him as a guest on our broadcasts several times.

HARRY CARAY became an institution as announcer for Chicago Cubs games, and he got a lot of national exposure through WGN, which is on a lot of cable systems. I came to know Harry when I was at spring training in 1954, and he was broadcasting for the St. Louis Cardinals. We were staying at the same hotel on Treasure Island in St. Pete. At the time he was very much concerned with the amount of alimony he had to pay, but he maintained his great sense of humor and had a lot of interesting stories to tell.

Other announcers have laid claim to the much repeated, "Holy Cow," but it is pretty well established that it originated with Harry. In the jet age of sports, Harry was an anachronism, but I enjoyed listening to him. He had two sons doing baseball broadcasting, and they are good, but they had the good judgment to not attempt to imitate their father. He was unique.

JACK BRICKHOUSE was best known in the Midwest, because he covered the Cubs and the White Sox for many years. He and I worked out of the same office building in Chicago and shared rides quite often to the ball parks. I knew that Jack was one of the more successful announcers, from a financial standpoint, but I was surprised that a large portion of his income came from broadcasting wrestling. Jack passed away several years ago.

MEL ALLEN was another Southerner who made it big, having started out in Alabama. He had a tremendous voice and a great style, which was perfect for baseball. I also saw a lot of Allen during my year with Mutual and found him to be a very pleasant person. He had a great following, was very versatile and fair in treatment of both sides in his broadcasts.

I knew some people who worked with Allen, who was the New York Yankees broadcaster, and they said that it was very difficult to work with him, but you never know the reasons behind such evaluations. Sometimes that booth can get very small! Mel is gone but will always be remembered by New York Yankee fans.

DICK ENBERG, another NBC announcer, has a fine voice and takes care of the people with whom he worked by not hogging the microphone. Enberg does an excellent job in covering all sports. He is one of the most versatile play-by-play announcers in the business.

AL MICHAELS of ABC is also very versatile, can cover any sports and made a name for himself when he broadcasted the United States Hockey victory over Russia in the 1960 Winter Olympics. It was during that game that he popularized the phrase, "Do you believe in miracles?" He and John Madden have become a great team on their coverage of Monday night football.

JOHN MADDEN is one of a kind in the area of football analysis. His authenticity is supported by his background as coach of the Oakland Super Bowl champions, and he has an endless supply of stories to tell. He doesn't take the game too seriously, although for years it was a matter of life or death for his career

JIM NANCE also does a smooth job for CBS-TV, both on play-by-play and in the studio. The role of the analyst has also greatly expanded with the explosion of telecasts of sports events.

TOM HAMMOND, an excellent play-by-play broadcaster on all sports. He and Larry Conley are a great team on their coverage on Southeastern College basketball. Larry

188

played under Adolph Rupp at Kentucky, and his father was one of the top officials in the Midwest for many years. I have known Larry for a long time and consider him a friend as well as a fellow broadcaster.

BOB COSTAS is in a class by himself, if you put the role of play-by-play announcer, studio announcer and interviewer together. He is still young but has maturity and poise beyond his years. He makes the person he's interviewing feel at ease, and he doesn't talk about himself. He keeps attention focused on the person to whom he is talking and the subject they're talking about.

BYRUM SAAM is the Philadelphia broadcaster I discussed in an earlier chapter and one to whom I listened and tried to imitate when I was a young boy.

HOWARD COSELL was in the vanguard of the adversarial sportscaster. He made a name for himself covering professional boxing and Muhammad Ali and on ABC's Monday Night Football. He became very popular with his "tell it like it is" approach, and, unfortunately, a lot of young broadcasters tried to copy him. Cosell's "tell it like it is" seemed to be degraded to "tell it like I think it is," and a lot of people became weary of that.

DICK VITALE may be fine, if you aren't interested in the game he's televising, because he monopolizes the microphone with conversation and observations about things completely unrelated to the game you're seeing. I feel sorry for the people with whom he's working – particularly if they don't get a thrill out of being constantly referred to as "babeee."

AL MCGUIRE'S credentials as a knowledgeable basketball analyst can't be disputed, because he coached Marquette to the NCAA championship. However, in his role as analyst for ABC-TV, he couldn't resist expressing his opinion as to what a coach or player should do in a particular situation, or, even worse, what he should have done, after the fact. McGuire was a likeable guy, however, and a devotee of his former St. John's coach, Frank McGuire.

I would like to recognize sports broadcasters in this area, whom I know, for their excellent work: *Todd Ellis and Tommy Suggs* – USC football announcers; *Mike Morgan* who handles the USC basketball and baseball broadcasts and his co-broadcasters *Casey Manning, Tommy Moody, and Tom Price*; former Assistant Sports Information Director at USC *Tony Cuifo*, who now broadcasts College of Charleston basketball and baseball games, and I congratulate all the other play-by-play broadcasters in this State who do an excellent job covering the teams in their area.

~PHILOSOPHY OF A SPORTSCASTER~

All of us have different ideas of what we like and dislike in a sports broadcaster. What's important to me is to be fair in your assessment of the game and the performers.

The finest compliment I could receive is to be remembered as a broadcaster who was fair. Homers are okay and some of them are very popular. I'm not saying that's not the way to do it, I just don't like it, and I won't broadcast a game that way.

Shortly after Bob Marcum became athletics director at Carolina, he told me that I was too impartial and, in effect, needed to be more of a homer. I told him that that isn't the way I think a game should be done, and that I couldn't take that approach.

Marcum said, "Well, we can find somebody who will."

I told him to go right ahead, but that it wouldn't be Bob Fulton. That's the last I ever heard of that.

I do not like to use a lot of clichés, although there is a lot of that being done in sports writing, as well as sportscasting. Announcers have their own ways of describing a home run or a long run in football, and that's okay, but I think it can be overdone. It sounds like you're trying to embellish the game with phrases that are shopworn.

I'm referring to such things as, "He came to play," "It's not over till it's over," "He doesn't know the meaning of the word, quit," and so forth. He probably doesn't know the meaning of a lot of words!

I think it is important to have a sense of humor. You're not broadcasting a war, although sometimes teams and their fans seem to think that's what it is. It is a game, and it should be fun.

A broadcast team should have good rapport with each other, and your humor should be spontaneous, not something that you planned or contrived. When I was working with Al Helfer at Mutual, he'd say, "Let's talk about the golf game we played yesterday." We never played golf with each other, and the closest we ever came to it was when we went to a driving range at one of the cities where we were broadcasting.

He wanted to superimpose this on our broadcast of a baseball game, and it never came off well, because it wasn't the truth. In fact, if we had played golf, who among our listeners would care?

In my latter years on the Carolina football broadcasts, we used two analysts, Tommy Suggs and Todd Ellis, and they were both excellent. They knew football, and they expressed themselves very well. However, I think there's such a thing as over-analyzing a game, and that takes away some of the emotion of it. It's too much like putting the game into a lab.

You shouldn't give your listeners too much to digest. Perhaps you can do that on television, but it's difficult to do on radio. Don't take away the fans' opportunity to draw their own conclusions and do their own analysis.

Finally, the broadcasters of a game shouldn't talk too much. It's difficult to talk too little, but there are many sportscasters who have too much talk going on in the booth. I've heard many fans commenting on various broadcasts, and they often say, "I wish so and so would shut up!" And I can't help but agree.

Bob Fulton "My Career My Life"

IF I HAD MY WAY

There are some things I would like to see changed in sports play-by-play broadcasting. I realize that times have changed and it has been several years since I was involved in covering games. Yet, I strongly feel there are certain basic things that should hold true for many years. First of all, I believe there is too much homerisim in the broadcasts. I feel that you lose your credibility when you strongly favor one team. Also, by doing this, you take away the listening enjoyment by the fans who have an allegiance to the school that is playing your team. Never once in the 43 years that I broadcast Gamecock games did I say "It's our ball." I always said "It is Carolina's ball." I felt that it was all right to show a little more enthusiasm for the Gamecocks, but even that had an exception. When Carolina played Clemson, I did my best to send the broadcast down the middle as I knew the rivalry divided a lot of homes. To sum this up – let the cheerleaders be the ones on the sideline not in the broadcast booth. To me the booth should have one person reporting the game, the other analyzing. If there is too much analysis of what takes place, then you are not getting the listener into the stadium where he sees and feels all the action.

Some other thoughts: Give offensive linemen credit for key blocks – give defensive alignment. The ball is on the marker from what side line – who are the wide outs – and the Gamecocks are moving toward the north or south goal. Naturally, some of these suggestions do not apply when your team is on the road.

Don't ever second guess the officials or the coaches. After all, they are not telling you how to broadcast. Give the score and time remaining often – with one exception – if your team is far behind, don't give the score quite as much – after all, you need to sell some products to the late tuners-in before they leave you.

Also, when your team has a game-winning lead – the play-by-play report is not important in the final moments. To hold audience, discuss the next opponent and anything else that will keep your audience.

Of course, there are some other things like identifying the snapper, the holder, and the kicker on field goal and extra point attempts. I would also like to see more professionalism in broadcasting. But I've said enough and some may rightfully agree. Too much talking – hey, broadcasters, give the listeners a break!

A final thought: You never stop learning. If you disagree, I strongly suggest that you chose another career. For me, I loved what I did and I miss it and I never stopped learning!

PREPARING TO BROADCAST A GAME

Broadcasting a sports event is much like any job you do - the better the preparation, the better the performance.

You get a lot of help from the team you're working for, including media guides, updates from the sports information office, weekly press luncheons and conversations with coaches.

I always liked to go over offensive and defensive game plans with the coaches, and they were usually most cooperative.

However, the real job is studying the opposing team, because you see it only once during the season, and you change every week. I always tried to memorize the jersey numbers of about thirty of the opposing players, so I wouldn't be completely dependent on spotters. However, it is important to have accurate spotters, and Ree Hart, who helped me, was one of the best.

When we played Nebraska up there in 1987, Tom Osborne dressed 125 players for the game, and there were 25 duplicate jersey numbers. If the game had been one-sided, some of those "duplicates" would have gotten into the game, but it was close all the way, and Nebraska had to keep its top players on the field.

Prior to the game I always reviewed the spotting board with my spotters, so that we could talk about key players, what to look for and any special information on players that should be included. I also discussed the game with the analysts, so that all of us knew what we were going to do, in order that the broadcast would go smoothly. Like a team.

Spotters also watched for key blocks, penalty flags, fumble recoveries - anything that is important to the action. And we have our signals for everything, because it can't be done vocally, while the action is being described.

There are many things you need to inform your listeners about, including scores of other games, weather conditions, wind directions, celebrities in the stands, any bowl scouts at the game, information on upcoming games, and other things that might come up during the course of the game.

In recent years more and more fans bring portable radios to the stadiums and listen to the game while they're watching it. This really keeps a play-by-play announcer on his toes, because if you make a mistake, you have people looking up toward the radio booth, as if to say, "Hey, you really blew that one!"

Preparation for basketball and baseball broadcasts isn't nearly as complicated as football.

In basketball there aren't but ten players to keep track of, and you know the players on your team, without referring to jersey numbers. That leaves a few numbers of players on the opposition, and it doesn't take long to learn the more prominent players' faces.

You are also looking for fewer things in basketball. Shots, rebounds, assists, turnovers and fouls are the five things that are important, and they are relatively easy to follow.

In baseball you are rarely concerned with jersey numbers, because defensive players are identified by their positions, and you're only concerned with one batter at a time. There's also plenty of time between plays and pitches to bring yourself and your audience up to date on a variety of things.

Whatever the sport, an important thing is for an announcer to resist the temptation to second guess coaches, players and officials. The result of second guessing is that you're going to make somebody look bad - either the person you're second guessing or yourself. And it is usually the latter.

RE-CREATING BASEBALL

Believe it or not, a re-creation of a baseball game is easier to do than a live broadcast. When you're doing a game live, you have to keep pace with what's going on, whereas in a re-creation, you can do anything you want to.

You get all the pre-game information, lineups, ballpark information, etc., from the Western Union operator, and the operator puts on the wire what happens on every pitch.

You can speed up the game or slow it down at your own discretion. The toughest thing to call is a three base hit or an error, because you don't want to sound as though you know what's going to happen before it happens.

It's also important to re-create background sounds that are heard in a ballpark, everything from the public address announcer to peanut salesmen.

In 1952, when Western Union went on strike, I learned a new approach to getting the information I needed. I would have somebody at the ballpark, usually a sports writer, call the station every three innings or every half hour and give us the information.

He just told what happened, without going into detail. He wouldn't give balls, strikes, foul balls, and so forth, so I would ad lib that part, including pick-off attempts, conferences at the mound and other gyrations that are prevalent in baseball games. Often we could handle a game by getting just five or six calls.

One of the advantages in re-creations was, if you had a one-sided game on your hands, you could speed things up by having the batter go out on the first pitch, instead of running the count. You could build suspense in a close game, when you knew a big play was coming up, by running a long count, with several foul balls. Then you describe the exciting play, which would often determine the outcome of the game.

In other words, if you had a bad game going, you could "squeeze" it. If it was an exciting game, "milk" it.

1950 was my first year of broadcasting baseball, but the people in Pueblo, Colorado, had no idea that I hadn't been doing it for years. Early in the season I was re-creating a game that was being sent to me by Western Union from Omaha, Nebraska, and involved the Pueblo Dodgers and the Omaha Cardinals of the Class A Western League.

In the seventh inning the bell on the Western Union machine started to ring, and this normally signals trouble. It was trouble! The sound effects man rushed in with the ticker tape, which said that the operator had been giving us the wrong score for the last four innings.

In the second inning, with two outs, there was a play at the plate, in which the runner was safe. However, the Western Union operator thought the runner had been signaled out. He looked down at his keyboard to send the play to us, and when he looked up, the teams were exchanging positions, as they do at the end of an inning.

The inning was over, but it was because, after the play at the plate, the base runner was thrown out at second base, when he tried to stretch his single into a double. That was what ended the inning. The run still counted, but neither the operator, nor we, knew that!

I couldn't figure out how the operator could not know what the score was, but I can assure you that I was scared out of my wits. Here I was, supposedly an experienced baseball announcer, and I had been giving the wrong score for several innings on a broadcast that was supposed to be coming directly from the ballpark, as far as the listeners were concerned.

I could have faked another run, but that would have probably made matters even worse. So, after much sweating, I decided to just tell the truth, so I told the listeners that we were doing the game by way of Western Union reports and what had happened back in the second inning. I'm happy to say that there was no feedback from the listeners, but that is an incident that I will never forget.

For some games in Charlotte, we used to get our information from someone who wasn't even at the game. Dick Pierce, a sports writer for the CHARLOTTE OBSERVER, would sit in the newspaper office, listen to a live broadcast of the games by the Charlotte announcer and call us every three innings.

One year I received a call from someone who wanted me to broadcast games that were played by Hartsville in the Dixie Youth World Series in Gadsden, Alabama. They didn't have a lot of money to sponsor the broadcast, and I really didn't want to travel out there, anyhow. I told him that I wouldn't go to Gadsden, but I would do the games from my home.

I had a coupler telephone installed at my house and ordered a line to the Hartsville radio station and sent a sound effects tape to that station. A man who accompanied the team to Gadsden used a pay phone to call me with pre-game information and then call Gordon Dixon, who was in the house with me, every half hour to give us what was happening in the game.

Hartsville won the championship, and I did all of their games while I was actually sitting in my bed. I don't believe that the people in Hartsville ever knew that we weren't at the ball park.

One night I did an American Legion game in Florence, a Cayce Dixie Youth game in Florida the next afternoon, and a Pony League game in Washington, Pennsylvania that night.

A number of people called me and wanted to know how I could do games in Florence, Florida and Pennsylvania within 24 hours.

People would sometimes say that we were trying to fool them by doing re-creations, but we weren't. We didn't care if people knew that we weren't actually at the games. I felt that we could make the game far more interesting, if we put in the sound effects to simulate actual conditions. For instance, Jim Seay used to talk into a trash can to simulate the PA announcer.

However, it's similar to going to a movie. You know how it's done, but you don't want to think about that. You just want to enjoy the show.

Without a doubt the strangest re-creation I ever did was a high school football game between Little Rock and Pine Bluff. The two high schools were fierce rivals and both had large followings.

In 1951 the game was played at Pine Bluff, and my station wanted to broadcast the game, but the people at Pine Bluff said that they would not allow it, because it would hurt the attendance. They told us that they wouldn't let us into the stadium.

I was determined to broadcast the game, so I drove to Pine Bluff and found a house directly across the street from the stadium where the game was to be played. I went to that house, talked to the people who lived there and got their permission to install a telephone line back to the Little Rock station.

I had two high school boys working with me, and when the game started, they would alternate going across the street to write down what happened in the game, while the other delivered his notes to me. I was sitting in that house with the window open - and it was freezing cold - so that I could pick up the crowd noise.

I did the game without a hitch, and nobody - not even the people in Little Rock - knew how I had done it - nor did the people in Pine Bluff, who were terribly upset with me. They obviously didn't talk to the lady who owned that house. Bless her!

~TALES OF A SPORTSCASTER~

If you broadcast sports for five decades and don't have some interesting incidents occur, amusing and not so amusing, something must be wrong with you. To establish my case against the latter, I'm relating some "war stories" in no special order, because there wasn't really any "order" connected with them!

NOCTURNAL ANIMAL - In the 1972 football game in Columbia, Carolina quarterback Bill Troup had about a half dozen of his passes intercepted, as the Gamecocks lost, 7-6. I was exhausted when I got home that night and was fast asleep, when the telephone woke me up. It was a physician calling from Georgetown, and it wasn't to inquire about my health. He sounded like he had been drinking, let's say, some strong medicine.

He said, "I have a complaint. On your broadcast of the game, you said that Troupe threw six interceptions, instead of saying that Clemson intercepted six passes."

I would never indicate that I'm disturbed by such a call, because you then make the caller feel like he has succeeded.

I said, "Yes, I remember saying that, and you have a very valid criticism."

"You really feel like that," he followed, and he sounded disappointed.

I said, "Yes, I appreciate things like that."

"Did I wake you up," he added, almost hopefully.

"No," I answered, "I really can't sleep after a ball game, so I was doing some reading."

Before hanging up he said, "You know, Fulton, you aren't such a bad S.O.B., after all."

After he hung up, I cussed him up one side and down the other, but I never let him know that he had gotten under my skin.

EXECUTE THE MESSENGER - I'm not revealing any secret when I say that a lot of people place bets on football games, and Carolina fans are no different from those who follow other teams. They win some, they lose some.

The problem is when they lose, they want to vent their frustration on someone, and the coaches have unlisted numbers. Unfortunately, I didn't!

After one game that didn't turn out to their liking, there were three guys, obviously drowning their sorrows, who found my name in the telephone directory and decided that I should be their object of contempt. Luckily, I wasn't home - but my answering machine was.

These guys alternated yelling into the telephone, taking turns of about five minutes, and they called me and the Gamecocks everything bad that they could think of. And they had great imaginations. It sounded like the drunker they got, the louder and more profane they got, but they gave up after thirty minutes. Or perhaps the tape ran out.

That tape is not among my recorded memoirs.

Bob Fulton "My Career My Life"

FOREIGN AFFAIRS - I said previously that the sport I enjoyed broadcasting most was basketball, and if I had to name a runner-up, it wouldn't be soccer. I only have one soccer game in my resume, and that took place some years ago. I don't remember the exact year, but it was when Clemson won the NCAA championship.

Carolina and Clemson played each other at The Graveyard - the nickname for Carolina's soccer stadium - the Sunday after the two schools met on the football field. The game received a lot of advance publicity, so one of the Columbia stations decided to broadcast the game and asked me to do the play by play.

I had witnessed a few soccer games, but I'll admit that I had difficulty trying to figure out what they were trying to accomplish. Anyhow, I told them that I would do it, if they would provide someone with a good knowledge of soccer to help me. That help was the coach of the soccer club at Carolina before it was added to the school's team sports.

I got along fine in the broadcast, except for one thing. Most of Clemson's main players were from the country of Nigeria, and they had some of the most unpronounceable names I've ever had to pronounce. When I had to keep up with the passing - or kicking - of the ball from one to the other, it turned out to be problem.

When I was growing up in Pennsylvania, I had friends with ethnic backgrounds and names that were slightly difficult to pronounce, but nothing like this.

COMMERCIAL BREAK - During the 1982-83 basketball season, Coach Bill Foster missed 17 games, following by-pass heart surgery, and Steve Steinwedel was in charge of the team during Foster's absence. One of the games was at Notre Dame, and the Irish won it by ten points.

Assistant coaches alternated on the post-game show, and after this game, it was Ray Jones' turn. Ray was about five feet, five inches tall, but he had enough enthusiasm to fill up a seven-foot frame. Notre Dame Coach Digger Phelps hadn't endeared himself to the Carolina coaches, because he seemed to be controlling the officials and everything else in the game.

Jones and I were just chatting, during a commercial break, but we went back on the air before Ray realized it. As we went back on, all the audience could hear was Jones saying in no uncertain terms, "Digger Phelps is a jerk!"

Perhaps I should have added the disclaimer, "The views expressed my Mister Jones are not necessarily those of this station."

DRY RUN - When I was living in Arkansas, I traveled to Monroe, Louisiana, to broadcast a game involving Little Rock Junior College. It was an important game, and Little Rock had a lot of fan support, but they didn't follow the team that far away from home. This would be a large radio audience.

I only had one person working with me, and we had a little trouble checking out our line from the stadium, but we determined everything was fine, and I did the entire game, giving it my best shot.

196

When I got back to my hotel, I received a call from the station in Little Rock telling me that none of the game had made it on the air. They had tried to call me at the stadium to tell me, but the call never got through.

Broadcasts are like trees falling in the forest. Unless there's someone there to hear it, there is no sound!

LANGUAGE BARRIER - My radio booth for a broadcast of a high school game in El Dorado, Arkansas, was located right next to the coaches' box, and there was no glass separating us. The language being used by one of the coaches was unbelievable, and I hoped that it wasn't getting on the air. But it was.

At halftime I received a call from the station, and they said that if I couldn't get the guy to stop, they would have to terminate the broadcast. I had asked him once to stop, but he told me that this was his stadium, and he would do what he wanted to.

After the call from the station, I went to the coach and said, "I've got a problem. As you know, your language is terrible, and you told me that I can't do anything about it. But I've got to take care of my audience, so next time you come out with some bad language - I know your name - I'm going to say, 'The voice in the background belongs to coach so-and so.'"

I had no trouble with him during the second half. He was mad, but he didn't want to be identified.

Wonder if he ever found out that I had no idea what his name was?

PHANTOM VOICE - During one of my football broadcasts, an unidentified voice kept interrupting, with statements such as, "Hi mom, I'm here at the football game, and I'm having a good time." Such mumblings continued during the first half, and we had no idea where they were coming from.

Our engineer finally discovered the source. We had a microphone on top of the press box to pick up the crowd noise. A guy, who had more than his quota of alcohol, had climbed up on the roof and discovered the microphone. In his condition he couldn't resist the temptation to become a broadcaster, and he took full advantage of this golden opportunity.

To his credit, the guy used language that was suitable for family audiences.

IMPROVISATION - Male High School in Louisville, Kentucky, is one of the finest schools in the country, but when I went to broadcast a game there, I found their football facilities to be less than ideal. I went to the stadium in the afternoon to check out the situation, and I found that someone had used my radio location for a bathroom. I cleaned that up and went down to inspect the field. There were no yard markers, and no scoreboard.

I went to a store, purchased a bed sheet and hurried back to the field. I tore the sheet into strips and placed a strip every five yards - by my calculations - so that I would have some idea where the ball was located.

The officials kept the time on the field, so I had no idea what it was, and I was busily keeping track of what down it was, the timeout situation and other things that you normally see on a good scoreboard.

I was doing the game live, but with those conditions, it was the closest I could have gotten to a re-creation.

A HORNETS' NEST - An old booth from which we were broadcasting a game between Little Rock Junior College and Arkansas Tech at Russellville had a hornets' nest in a corner. The inhabitants were peaceful during the first half and didn't seem to be bothered by our description of the game.

However, some halftime guests came to the booth, and one of them bumped the nest, and the booth became full of angry hornets. All of us exited in a matter of seconds, and we were not about to go back in there, with all those creatures buzzing around and looking for human targets. We never figured a way to clear the booth, so the hornets prevailed, and our version of the second half never reached the airways.

The audience only got half a game, so you might say, "They got stung!"

QUICK CHANGE ARTISTS - If jersey numbers are not a broadcaster's best friend, they would rank among the top two or three. Without them, at times, we would be lost, and I had two experiences that underlined the importance of these digits.

The first was in a game between Arkansas and Southern Methodist, when the playing field was a quagmire. By the end of the half, all the players looked like walking mudballs.

When they appeared for the second half, Arkansas had changed to fresh jerseys with correct player identifications, but SMU didn't have a spare set. So the Mustangs came out in jerseys of several different colors or shades, and none of the numbers corresponded to the ones the players wore in the first half.

We simply had to guess who was doing what on the field, as far as our visitors were concerned.

Another time, in the Atlantic Coast Conference Basketball tournament, Maryland Coach Lefty Driesell had his team switch jersey numbers right before the game. He thought that would give his team a tactical advantage, but I don't think it worked. All it did was to put me and others who were not familiar with Maryland players at a big disadvantage.

Because of that, a rule was passed that prohibited the changing of jersey numbers without giving ample notice to the opponents and the media.

Bob Fulton "My Career My Life"

FREE DELIVERY - When Carolina played Wisconsin at Madison during George Felton's first season as basketball coach, our broadcast location was in a balcony that had spectator seats behind it. During the broadcast, this guy who must have weighed at least 280 pounds was making his way back from the concessions stand. He had a bunch of stuff, including soft drinks and popcorn.

As he was walking behind our location, a plank gave way, and he fell, tumbling down on top of me, food, drink and all. It looked like a Mac Sennett comedy, and my broadcast crew was in convulsions of laughter. I wasn't laughing at the time.

They did record the game, and I listened to it when I was back in Columbia, and it sounded as wild as it had seemed.

That is not the most satisfactory way to have refreshments delivered to you.

TIMING IS EVERYTHING - When I was working in New Jersey, it was against the law to call wrestling a "match," it had to be an "exhibition." Whatever they called it, wrestling had a large following, and the station I worked for decided to broadcast a match by tape delay.

I met with the participants prior to the bout and explained to them that we had to end at a certain time, so that it would fit into our broadcast schedule.

The match progressed, and our closing time neared, I gave a signal to the two wrestlers in the ring, the appointed winner did a body slam with his opponent, and the bout ended right on schedule.

PERSONAL FOUL - In one of Arkansas' basketball games with Southern Methodist in Fayetteville, I was broadcasting for both the Razorback and Mustang networks.

As usual, my broadcast location was right at courtside, and too close to the action on this occasion. A fight between players broke out right in front of where I was sitting, and several players came crashing over my table. Equipment went everywhere, and I ended up on my back, with players on top of me. They broke my nose, and I was lucky that it was all they broke, because they were a load!

Order was restored; several people came over and helped me back to my chair, while others restored our equipment to working order. We finished the broadcast, but I was ready to move away at the slightest sign of hostilities.

BLIND ALLEY - The University of Louisville is a great basketball school, but there was absolutely no interest in baseball there when Carolina was in the Metro Conference. We went there to broadcast a baseball game, and they had some stands, but they had no more than fifty people at the game.

Their broadcast facilities were nil, so we had to set-up wherever we could find space for a table. The only place our telephone line would reach was a small space between the stands, and this is where we had to locate. The problem was that we couldn't see home plate from there.

I could see the pitcher deliver the ball, and I could get the balls and strikes from the scoreboard. Everything else was left to my imagination, until a ball was hit to the deep part of the infield or anywhere in the outfield.

Tom Price did position himself in one of the nearby seats, so that he could signal or tell me if anything unusual was happening. Otherwise, someone could have dropped dead in the vicinity of home plate, and I would never have known it.

PLANE SCARY - Paul Dietzel wanted us to broadcast a game between the Carolina and North Carolina State freshman teams at Raleigh in 1968, so Joe Petty and I went there in a private plane of questionable durability. The plane made it there, and we did the game, which was won by Carolina.

On our takeoff to return home, the pilot's seat collapsed, and he ended up in my lap, as I was seated behind him. The plane swerved off the runway, and the pilot recovered soon enough to get it stopped.

We got the seat repaired, lowered our blood pressures and made it back to Columbia without further incident.

WAKE-UP CALL - Once we were broadcasting a football game at Athens, and Carolina was trailing Georgia by several touchdowns. Carolina finally scored a touchdown and was ready to kick the extra point, but they couldn't locate the tee. They hadn't needed it up until this point. They determined that it was in an equipment trunk on the sideline, but they had a delay in getting to it.

The equipment manager had fallen asleep on top of the trunk, and they had to wake him up, in order to get the tee.

It wasn't the most exciting game I ever saw, but that was ridiculous.

CLOSED FOR REPAIRS - Not long after I came to South Carolina, the Arkansas basketball team was invited to play in the Poinsettia Basketball Classic in Greenville. My friend Bob Cheyne was the broadcaster for Arkansas, but he had to do the Razorbacks' football game in the Sugar Bowl. Bob asked me to do the basketball game, and I was happy to do it for him.

During the first game, the Arkansas trainer collapsed - fell to the floor, as if he were suffering a heart attack. The Greenville Auditorium grew silent, as people rushed to the trainer's aid. I didn't know the trainer, and I didn't want to say anything on the air that would alarm his family or friends back in Arkansas. The game was held up for about 20 minutes.

I explained the delay to my audience by saying that they were playing on a portable floor, and part of it had come loose. They had people working to repair the floor, so that they could start playing again.

The problem with the trainer was taken care of, I explained that the floor had been repaired, and the game continued. The problem was that the trainer had had an epileptic fit, but I couldn't say anything about it on the air.

Meanwhile, spectators who were within ear shot of my broadcast looked at me as if I were crazy, as I described the problem with the portable floor.

CALM BEFORE THE STORM - George Rogers was not only the most accomplished football player for Carolina during my time there, but he was also one of the most likeable. He was also very much "laid back."

Prior to Carolina's game with North Carolina at Chapel Hill in 1979, the team stayed at a motel halfway between Durham and Chapel Hill. When we boarded the bus for the ride to the stadium, George took the seat directly across the aisle from me. This was an important game, and everybody, including myself, was uptight about the game - everybody except George.

We hadn't been on the bus five minutes, and Rogers was already fast asleep. He slept all the way to the stadium. I thought to myself, "No wonder you're good. You're the most relaxed person here."

On the return trip from a game with Georgia Tech in Atlanta, I was again sitting near George, and he said to me, "Mister Fulton, do you think I played all right today?" Rogers had gained 148 yards on 21 carries for an average of seven yards a try. He wasn't fishing for a compliment; he just didn't realize how good he was.

SMOKE SCREEN - Coaches often know a lot more about what is going on than athletes give them credit for. Coaches see a lot of things that may not be exactly what they like but are not worth creating a scene or confrontation.

When the Carolina basketball team was returning from a game at Auburn, I was sitting beside Frank McGuire near the back of the bus, which had a small toilet provided in that area.

Tom Riker, the All-America center, was in that little room for what seemed to be longer than normal, and as the bus bounced around on some rough terrain, the door to the toilet swung open and shut several times. Each time it flew open, smoke came drifting out.

McGuire said in a loud voice, which could be heard all over the bus, "That guy in there thinks I don't know what's going on!"

Within seconds a sheepish Riker came strolling out, avoiding eye contact with McGuire, as if nothing had happened.

PAUSE THAT REFRESHES - The Arkansas Chamber of Commerce advertises the climate as "mild," but it can get as cold there as anywhere in the country. It was one of those penetrating cold nights that found me doing a high school football game at Blytheville, which is located in the northeastern part of the state.

My broadcast point was practically in the stands, and, as a long distance telephone service once suggested I could "reach out and touch someone!"

As the game moved on, and the weather got colder, I was sipping on a cold drink, of all things. During a commercial break, I made the remark, "What I really need is a hot cup of coffee."

A spectator turned around and said, "I've got some coffee, so you can have some." And he passed me his cup. I took a big swallow, and it must have been about three-fourths bourbon. Because I was so cold to start with, it hit me like a ton of bricks.

For about 15 minutes I was in deep trouble and had difficulty in telling one team from the other. Through the years, perhaps my listeners have had occasions to ask, "What has that guy been drinking?"

On this night, it would have been a legitimate question.

MANY HAPPY RETURNS - My career in radio took me into many areas outside of the world of sports. For years I did a morning show on a Columbia station, along with having other duties, including commercial sales.

The station didn't have a large staff and only one person was assigned primarily to news. When political elections came around, every radio and television station in town would promote their coverage, each claiming to be first with the best. Those stations would send people out to the poling places to gather results and report them.

My station didn't have people to cover the precincts, so here's what we did. We put four radios and a television set in our studio, and tuned each one to a different station covering the election results. We would use information from the station with the latest results, and that would vary from time to time.

Consequently, we would beat most of the stations with the results and could truthfully say that we were the "fastest in town."

There's a saying, "If you copy only one source, its plagiarism, but if you copy two or more, its research!

COCKY DUCKS OUT - Once when the Carolina basketball team was playing in Memphis, we stayed at the beautiful Peabody Hotel in the middle of town. Every day, as part of the Peabody tradition, they bring to the lobby some small ducks who resided on top of the hotel.

Amid fanfare, the ducks are brought to the lobby by way of an elevator, and they proceed to a large fountain, where they take their daily swim. Visitors look forward to this ceremony, and you can see cameras flashing throughout the crowd.

Bob Fulton "My Career My Life"

On this particular morning, as soon as the "ducks were on the pond," Cocky, the Carolina mascot, made his appearance and began running around the fountain in true Cocky fashion. He wasn't to be upstaged by some lowly ducks!

To the ducks, Cocky looked like a monster, and they didn't want to become his midday meal, so they took flight, circling the lobby like aircraft on a bombing mission. And they released a few of nature's bombs during their frantic maneuvers.

A hotel custodian rushed out, grabbed Cocky and escorted him out of the lobby, with instructions not to ever come back. However, the damage was already done, and I thought of how lucky I was not to be the one with the responsibility of cleaning up the lobby. What a mess!

WORTHY ADDITIONS:

When the New York Mets were so bad, they would have a relief pitcher warming up in the bull pen before the game started.

When broadcasting a baseball game with Hornell, a foul ball came up in my booth, and as I turned around to see where it went, it hit the back of the wall and then hit me and broke my nose.

A studio announcer friend of mine at a CBS station in Little Rock was fired because he was unable to pronounce properly the phrase, "your ESSO reporter."

A Columbia Reds baseball manager, throughout the game was being heckled by one of the fans. At the conclusion of the game, he raced out to the parking lot and punched out a fan. However, he hit the wrong fan and the ball club was sued.

At Hornell, New York, the Hornell catcher was arguing with the umpire on the ball and strike calls. The Hornell manager raced out to home plate, asked his catcher where that last pitch was and the catcher answered that it was in the strike zone. The umpire ejected the catcher because he was lying. Wow!

Bob Fulton "My Career My Life"

~THE WAY I SEE IT~

The routine definition of an expert is "someone from out of town carrying a brief case." However, you also qualify as an expert when you retire from whatever you did to make a living. Telecasts are full of retired coaches, who are now experts, because they aren't held accountable for their decisions. They also have the advantage of hindsight, as a rule, and that is a position that I now enjoy! I have officially qualified to be an expert in many things, because my career was involved with such a broad scope of institutional and athletics matters.

KNOWING WHEN TO CHANGE

There are a lot of things in sports and at Carolina that are exactly as they should be, and I wouldn't like to see changed. I have never believed in change for the sake of change, but there are some things that change might help.

I'm not like the guy who reached his hundredth birthday and was asked by a reporter, "You've seen a lot of changes during your life, haven't you?"

His answer was, "Yes, and I've been against every one of them."

That is not my philosophy, but I believe that when you change things, you should make certain that the change is for the better.

First, I feel that too much pressure to give money is placed on supporters of college athletics teams. I know that it takes a lot of money to operate a big-time program, but you shouldn't have to be independently wealthy to follow a college team. Hopefully, a lot of people with money contribute to a college because they love the school and want it to succeed, not because they are responding to a menu of benefits. However, I realize that to be able to compete with the Tennessee's, the Florida's, the Slues, etc., it takes a lot of MONEY.

Priorities are fine, and I can understand that, but people who place other priorities on what they do with their money, shouldn't be looked at as second class supporters. They shouldn't be made to feel guilty, if they don't do everything the institution tells them to do. Suggest, yes, but order, no.

Over the years some of the new coaches who come to Carolina seem to think they need to change uniforms. That should be a decision directed by the administration, not by the coach. Could you imagine Lou Holtz going to Notre Dame and changing the uniforms? What coach could go to the University of Michigan and do away with those ugly striped helmets? The school should make uniform decisions. It's the coach's job to put the right people in them.

I was told that Carolina had 100 brand new uniforms that were never used. They had been ordered, and then Joe Morrison came in, ordered a completely new set and never used the others.

Coaches coming to a school should try embrace what is already in place, rather than make changes to suit their personal whims. Most coaches remain at a school until one of two things happen - they either get a better offer somewhere else, or they get fired. In my 43 years at Carolina, only one football coach - Rex Enright - and one basketball coach - Frank McGuire - retired in their positions here.

204

All schools have their traditions and ways of doing things, and you don't want to mess with the ones that are acceptable to the fans. They are the ones for whom the games are being played, not the coaches or the players.

When Carolina entered the Southeastern Conference, some people began referring to the school as "South Carolina," for fear that people in other states would get us confused with North Carolina. That didn't fly, because for a century students and alumni had been referring to the school as "Carolina," and they were not ready to concede that name to the state north of us.

A lot of fans are irritated when they see the Charlotte team in the NFL referred to as "Carolina" in the Columbia news media. In Columbia, Carolina is the University of South Carolina.

I guess the change I'm suggesting here is to stop changing so often.

Coaches and athletics directors are hired by institutions to administer and coach, not to change everything, from uniforms, to mascots, to fight songs. However, there are exceptions to this and one of the exceptions is Steve Spurrier's choice of new football uniforms, which I think look so much better than the old ones. Of course, building and enlarging facilities are things that are in line with what athletics administrators should do, and that constitutes progress. The bottom line of all this is that if a change is made in any area pertaining to Carolina athletics, the change should be an improvement - then let's keep it that way. That's the way you build tradition.

Here's an example of a change that I thought was good and overdue. When Hootie Ingram came to Clemson as football coach in 1970, Henderson Advertising in Greenville was retained to recommend changes in the Tiger graphics. They made two changes that were great, including the design of the tiger paw symbol. The other change was to drop the purple and orange color combination on uniforms and stick to orange and white. Those are examples of changes that should have been made.

One of the best changes ever at Carolina was the creation of the mascot, Cocky. The first attempt at a living mascot was "Big Red," but that version looked too much like a rooster and didn't have the personality or mobility of Cocky. Cocky has been acclaimed as the number one college mascot in America, and there are a lot of them out there.

The way that Cocky is introduced prior to Carolina home games is also big time. He appears in a puff of smoke onto a special platform on the playing field, wearing his magician's cape.

Most things that catch on with students just happen, rather than being contrived. After a Carolina home victory, as he was going into the tunnel that leads to the dressing room, Brad Scott tossed his cap into a group of celebrating fans. They loved it.

The over-commercialism of college sports bothers me. I say this with the understanding that my income as a broadcaster came from one aspect of this over-commercialization.

In the 1950s the broadcast of a college football game would begin 15 minutes prior to kickoff, giving time for an introduction, starting lineups and a few commercials. Now, we have what is affectionately called the "tailgate show," which starts several hours ahead of kickoff and before the tailgaters have loaded their trunks and vans.

Bob Fulton "My Career My Life"

Everything from the weather to the coach's pulse is analyzed, creating many more commercial positions to pay the schools for broadcast rights.

The network sells everything it can. I'm sure you have heard many times, "This kickoff is brought to you by so and so." So and so really gets its money's worth on the University of Florida network!

Nowadays when you attend college sports events, you're likely to see many advertisements in the stadiums and arenas. I don't particularly like this, but I am well aware that it takes a lot of money to run an athletics program, and these signs are a good source of revenue. These messages should be kept in the best possible taste, because these are college facilities, not professional arenas or ballparks.

There's nothing wrong with an athlete going into professional sports and making as much money as his talent will allow. Still, I think that the modern day money grab has gotten out of hand, particularly when high school baseball and basketball players begin looking at college as a second alternative to signing a pro contract.

There were a lot of changes I liked, and here are a few. The practice of dressing basketball and football players in blazers when they traveled was a very positive move. That has now been outlawed by the NCAA, and you can't even lend them a necktie.

I like the way sports teams travel by air, when they have to go some distance, rather than the bus and train travel that was the mode when I arrived in Columbia.

Staying in hotels, rather than dormitories of the home team, is one improvement Frank McGuire made for the basketball team. I remember sleeping on bunks in Keenan Fieldhouse at the University of North Carolina, when we went there to play the Tar Heels.

WOMEN'S SPORTS ON THE RISE

I might be slightly biased toward women, because I have two daughters and have been blessed with marriages to two great ladies. So I am delighted to see the increase in emphasis place on women's sports on the college level.

Mike McGee did a fine job in enhancing the level and number of women's sports at Carolina, and they are competitive, even in the SEC.

FOR THE LOVE OF THE GAME

This may sound corny in this day of playing sports for whatever benefit might be derived, such as a college education, big professional dollars or personal prestige. But I still get a thrill out of seeing athletes who appear to be playing primarily for the love of the game they're playing.

An example of what I'm talking about was Keith Schmidt, who was a catcher for the Columbia Reds in the 1950s. Keith was not a major league prospect, but he was satisfied with playing in the minor leagues. It certainly was not for the money.

One night the Reds were playing in Savannah, Georgia, and Schmidt was hit by a bat, opening a big crease in his head. Keith plugged the gap with dirt and was ready to play again.

The Savannah batter told Reds manager Ernie White, "You'd better get Keith out of here, he's bleeding to death."

Ernie couldn't get Smitty to leave until the game was over. They took him to a doctor, and he wouldn't allow him to do anything to deaden the wound. The doctor took eight stitches in Keith's head without using a pain killer. It hurts me just to think about it.

Keith Schmidt was just one of those guys who liked to play, anytime, anywhere, and he couldn't have cared less about what he was getting out of it.

A CLASS ACT

One of my favorite football players at Carolina was Todd Ellis, the quarterback from Greensboro who broke most of Carolina's passing records. Todd was probably an NFL prospect until he suffered a severe knee injury midway through his final season.

Todd was already moving toward law school at Carolina, and his alternate career was in great shape.

While he was completing work on his law degree, Todd became an analyst on the Carolina football TV broadcasts, and did some other radio sports and television. Todd is now the play-by-play broadcaster for the Gamecocks on their football radio network, and his analyst is former Gamecock star quarterback Tommy Suggs.

MIXED EMOTIONS

When Carolina pulled out of the Atlantic Coast Conference, I looked at it with mixed emotions.

On one hand, it was a blessed relief, because in my travels with the basketball team throughout ACC territory, I saw a lot of things I didn't like. The competition was so intense, and the attitude of the other schools toward Carolina was so bitter, it made it very unpleasant.

On the other hand, the ACC was a conference growing in prestige in all sports, and the teams in the conference had a lot in common with Carolina. I had a lot of friends throughout the league.

As it turned out, it was an unwise move for Carolina to leave, because it severely weakened the Gamecock basketball schedule. It didn't bother the football schedule, because Carolina continued to play the ACC teams in that sport - but not in basketball.

In the long run, as the saying goes, "Carolina has come out smelling like a rose." Becoming a member of the Southeastern Conference has been one of the greatest - if not THE greatest - things that has happened to athletics at the University. King Dixon was athletics director, and Arthur Smith was interim president, when this was achieved, and this will go down as a monument to their performance in those positions.

The SEC is the finest conference in the nation, and to be competitive in any sport in the conference, means competitiveness on a national level.

CONDUCT OF ATHLETES

I realize that college athletes are youngsters, just like any other college student, and they are prone to make mistakes - just like all of us, young and old.

However, I think there is a limit to what we should overlook or condone in the behavior of college athletes. Too often they consider themselves exempt from abiding by

207

rules of acceptable conduct. I'm not talking about violating curfew or getting a parking ticket. It's some of the more serious incidents in which too many athletes are involved from time to time - such things as drugs, rape, theft and physical assault.

A person is innocent until proved guilty, but once a school is convinced that an athlete has overstepped the bounds of acceptable behavior, I think that the school should deal with it appropriately, regardless of how good the athlete may be. Perhaps a school should set higher standards than even a court of law, because more should be expected of athletes who represent an institution of higher learning and are role models for young people.

It's a case by case situation, but I think that, much too often, coaches and schools go too far in rationalizing misconduct by athletes. When they enroll at a college, athletes should be told in no uncertain terms what is expected of them, and they should be held accountable for what they do.

PERHAPS THIS WOULD HELP

Scholarship athletes have far more pressure on them than the rest of the students at a college, and they often need help with their problems. I think that schools should have a psychologist or other qualified person on the staff that can counsel the athletes and help them with their problems.

There are people available to help with academic and physical problems, but quite often they could use help with personal, emotional and psychological situations.

Many coaches are good at this, but they are busy coaching athletes and handling the many other requirements of their jobs, so they do not have the time to devote to this specialized field.

Having someone to aid athletes in their many adjustments to college and problems that present themselves would be a great asset to the team and to the young people who perform on them.

PREVENT WHAT?

While I'm on the soap box, let me point out something that I personally don't like, although I guess it could be characterized as second guessing. That's PREVENT DEFENSES.

I have seen more games lost in the waning moments, because the leading team went into a prevent defense. That's when a team leading by a touchdown or less concentrates on preventing the long touchdown pass by deploying more players in the defensive backfield. They play deeper and looser on defense.

I've seen even mediocre quarterbacks pick a prevent defense to pieces, relying on short and sideline passes to preserve the clock and take advantage of the shorter gains that are practically conceded by the defense. In other words they have to use several plays to score, instead of just one.

I'm not saying that it isn't appropriate in any situation, such as when you have a two-touchdown lead with time running out. However, in the times I've seen teams try it with small leads, the thing that it has done in too many cases is PREVENT WINNING.

~*FANTASY TAPES*~

When I did a tape for Joe Morrison back in 1985, at the time Todd Ellis was being recruited, I wasn't thinking about other possible applications. It was just a one-time shot that had Todd leading the Gamecocks to a winning touchdown against Nebraska, with all the accompanying sound effects.

Bill Foster asked me to do several of these, when he was coaching the basketball team, but the NCAA ultimately squelched the recruiting applications of such tapes.

One day a friend of mine, T.C. Connell, called me and asked if I would make a fantasy tape featuring him, as he leads Carolina to a winning touchdown against Clemson. T.C. hadn't played football, but on the tape I did for him, he was an All-American quarterback.

He later told me that he had never had more fun with anything in his life. Friends would come from out of town, T.C. played the tape for them, and they were amazed that he had been such an accomplished football player. But there it was - on tape.

A week prior to Connell's death in 1995, he called me and told me that he had this tape by his bedside and played it frequently. Beside it he had a copy of a column, written by Bill McDonald in THE STATE shortly after I produced the tape, and describing the production.

I went to the visitation for Connell's family, and I talked with Reggie Thaxton, pastor of Trenholm Road United Methodist Church, of which T.C. was a faithful member. Reggie told me how much the tape had meant to Connell, and Reggie mentioned it in the funeral service the next day. He said that T.C. had always wanted to be a sports hero, and now he was. He had reached the pinnacle of his life. And that made me feel very good.

Since I did that first tape for T.C. Connell, I've had many requests, and I've produced them for people ranging in ages from 3 to 87.

One of my favorites was a fantasy CD for a guy whom I made into a relief pitcher that entered a College World Series baseball game, saved the game and hit the home run that won it. You don't get much better than that.

For me these CD's are fun to do, and they are not difficult to produce. Jim Seay works with me on producing them, and he does a fine job.

Several years ago, when radio station WSCQ-FM was celebrating an anniversary, I did a "reverse" fantasy tape involving the three principals at the station, Dave Wright, Gene McKay and Bill Benton. I had fun making them mess-up something awful, and they enjoyed it, too.

Years ago in Arkansas I did something akin to that on a high school football game broadcast. My wife had dated a guy named Jack Gulick, who played football for SMU, so I decided to have some fun with this situation.

We were a long way from Dallas, so I made Jack Gulick a player on the opposing high school team, as the broadcast wouldn't be heard in that town. I would have Jack fumbling, jumping off-sides, missing tackles and everything else he could do wrong.

When I got home, Dody would be as mad as a wet hen, telling me what a terrible thing I had done. I would say, "Nobody knows who Jack is, and I was just having a little innocent fun!"

I've never had a complaint about any of the fantasy tapes or CD's I've done, and I get regular requests to do them.

Through my fantasy CD's, I can make people anything they want to be, although I don't recommend overdoing it. You should at least want yourself to be human.

This is also one area in which I don't have to worry about competition from video tape. It is much easier to paint pictures with your voice and sound effects, than to produce two teams and an arena full of people.

Bob Fulton "My Career My Life"

~THINGS (AND PEOPLE) I MISS~

Of course, I miss broadcasting, the preparation, the excitement of the competition and the association with coaches, players and fellow workers.

Nowadays you don't have the camaraderie with coaching staffs that you once did, such as we had in the days of Rex Enright.

I miss the association with the crew - Tommy Suggs was with me for 21 years, and people such as Todd Ellis, David Spence, Ree Hart, Clark Newsom, Liz McMillan, Carol Senn and Burt Smith were great to work with in my final seasons.

I worked with Don Williams on football and basketball for twelve years, and Homer Fesperman was my engineer for some twenty years.

At one time or another, on the network crews, were John and Cliff Terry, Charles Irick, Julian Gibbons, Johnny Evans and others. There were also the Carolina sports information directors, Don Barton, Bob Isbell, Tom Price and Kerry Tharpe.

I miss the excitement of being in the booth with the broadcast crew, doing the countdown to kickoff. To me that was total excitement.

I don't miss the people in the press box prior to the games, because Carol and I are still in there. That's good, because I don't think I could enjoy the game in the stands, where you stand the risk of sitting near someone who criticizes the coach or the team. I've always felt that, as far as fans are concerned, if you are negative toward the team or program, you are not part of the solution; you are part of the problem.

I still enjoy all the conveniences of the beautiful new press box, with the wonderful food and many courtesies. When I first started doing college sports, you were lucky to get a sandwich and a soft drink. Now it's like a banquet.

However, there's a difference when you're not actively involved in one way or another. You don't feel as much a part of what's going on. Following my retirement, I became a consultant with the athletics department and as such, I have had the opportunity to renew my relationships with many former Carolina athletes and the wonderful Gamecock fans.

Bob Fulton "My Career My Life"

~IN PARTING ~

Many people ask me if I'm enjoying my retirement. I am, although at times I'm busier than I would like to be. I continue to produce what I call my "fantasy CD's," which I described earlier and make people the hero of a Carolina football or basketball game. The CD's allow me to continue my play-by-play broadcasting, and they always have a happy ending!

I would be less than honest, if I said I didn't miss what I had been doing for 53 years. However, I have had the time to do things I was not able to do before.

One of these is tailgating, something I had never done until I retired. Now I know what I was missing all these years. Dr. Charlie Crews took me with a busload of Gamecock fans to Knoxville for the Carolina-Tennessee football game in 1995, and I learned first hand that despite the outcome of the game, a trip is great fun. Since then we have made many bus trips with tours sponsored by Don Weathers.

Quite a bit of my retirement time is spent following the fortunes of the Gamecocks. I'm firmly convinced that the best for our teams lies ahead.

My 53-year journey in broadcasting has allowed me to realize the dream I had as a youth. It has not always been easy, but I guarantee you that it has never been dull.

I had the opportunity to meet so many wonderful people who have played a very important part in any success I have achieved.

I have been asked to pick my all-this and all-that teams at Carolina, and that would be fun to try. However, I've had the pleasure of watching so many outstanding athletes here; it would be a disservice to those that I did not choose. On the other hand, I don't find it too difficult to select the person I feel was the most outstanding in each of the three major sports.

Football - George Rogers, the 1980 Heisman Trophy recipient.

Basketball - John Roche, who made the All-America teams in 1980 and 1981.

Baseball - Earl Bass, who won every game I saw him pitch, from Dixie Youth through college ball, until the championship game of the 1975 College World Series, when he took the mound in the championship game after only two days of rest.

I hesitate to speculate on the future of sports. Your guess is as good as mine. However, as far as college sports are concerned, you can play an important part in correcting the things you think are wrong, if you address your feelings to those who can do something about it.

Games are games - not wars. We all need to have patience and a good sense of humor.

My late brother-in-law, who was a psychologist, once told me that all of us, when we get up in the morning, should look at ourselves in the mirror and say, "I'm not as important as I think I am."

When I made out my "last will and testament," I wanted something carved on my gravestone that would bring a smile to someone who might happen by. At first I thought it would be, "I'll be back in a moment," a phrase I had used thousands of times in my broadcasting career.

After very serious consideration, I chose,
"WAIT TILL NEXT YEAR"

~THESE ARE THE NEXT YEARS~

Since my retirement we have had several changes in the Athletics Department at Carolina – or what else is new.

ERIC HYMAN

In July 2005, Eric Hyman began his tenure as Athletics Director at Carolina. Prior to coming to USC he had spent eight years as the Athletics Director at TCU where he was named the 2003-04 Street and Smith's Sports Business Journal National Athletics Director of the Year and honored as the Division 1-A West Regional Athletics Director of the Year by the National Assoc. of Collegiate Directors of Athletics.

Hyman has also served as Athletics Directors at Miami of Ohio and VMI and Associate Athletics Directors at both North Carolina State and Furman - he also was as Assistant Football Coach at Furman.

During his college years, Hyman was an outstanding football lineman at North Carolina, where he earned all ACC honors.

I feel certain that Eric Hyman is developing the strongest Athletics Department in the history of Carolina athletics.

LOU HOLTZ

Lou Holtz replaced Brad Scott as football's head coach. Lou was an assistant to Paul Dietzel in the '65 and '66 seasons – and although I was broadcasting Georgia Tech football in those years, I was still covering other sports at USC. On several occasions, Dietzel asked me to emcee Gamecock football banquets. All members of the coaching staff took their turn at the lectern. After the first banquet that I worked, my wife asked me which of the coaches did the best job. I said, "no, you give me your pick," and she quickly responded, "that little man sitting at the end of the dais who spoke last" – yes, it was Lou Holtz who spiked his presence at the table with some magic tricks. I agreed - it was no contest.

When Holtz was head football coach at NC State, his team received a bid to play in the Peach Bowl at Atlanta. Lou thought that the Wolfpack might play Florida State so he decided to scout the Seminoles when they played Carolina in Columbia. At the half time of that game he came to the top of the broadcast booth and asked me to join him, which I did. He had heard that Paul Dietzel would retire at the end of the current season and that he would like very much to be the coach to replace – in fact, he wouldn't mind if he received less money than he was making at NC State. He asked me to help him, and of course I told him I would. As a background to all this when Holtz was an assistant to Dietzel at Carolina maintained that Paul had told him that he would never be the head coach of a college football team. Dietzel denies that he ever said this. Years later, after having proven his ability to be a successful college coach and wanting Dietzel to eat his words, Lou returned to the place where all this began. As it turned out, Lou's trip to Columbia was still all for nil. Carolina upset Florida State and Dietzel decided not to resign.

Lou Holtz continued to climb the latter of success in his coaching career, and it took a great selling job by the A.D. Mike McGee to have him to return to Carolina replacing Brad Scott as head coach in 1999.

Ted Felker in the article he wrote on me in the publication, GAMECOCK ILLUSTRATED, asked me how I felt about Lou Holtz, and this was my reply: "When I look back on his career, I think it was tremendous. I feel that what the man did was unbelievable.

What happened to him, I have seen happen before. Lou's son, Skip, was a member of the coaching staff. I've seen too many examples of a father and son, where either the son is a player or the son is a coach. It just doesn't work in most cases - an exception would be father and son on Coach Spurrier' staff. However, I do think that had a lot to do with the downfall of Lou Holtz. I've talked to people at East Carolina and they love SKIP up there. They think he is doing a tremendous job. And it was especially unfortunate for Lou to have happen what happened at Clemson (the brawl). It was terrible and it wasn't his fault. It was a shame to see a man go out like that after the career he had. He had become very conservative and the people don't like that. When you're losing, if it's wide-open football it's not quite as bad. But when you are not winning and you are running quarterback draws, etc., you know they don't like it. It was a tough ending for him and I feel he deserved better than he got. I really do."

STEVE SPURRIER

The first time I saw Steve Spurrier as a player was in 1964 when he was on his way to winning the Heisman Trophy as an outstanding quarterback of the Florida Gators.

The Gamecocks under Coach Marvin Bass were in Gainesville, Florida, to take on the heavily favored Florida Gators. It was a miss-match. The Gators led by Steve Spurrier, who had an outstanding day, had built up a 28 to 0 lead at halftime – and jokingly at the second half, I told the engineer that I was going to use a four-letter word on the broadcast – and if we didn't get any calls, we could wrap up our equipment and go home.

Florida won the game 37 to 0, and the only plus for me was to watch Steve Spurrier as he convinced me – as he had many others – that he would be the recipient of the Heisman Trophy – that he was the best college quarterback I had ever seen.

I regret that my broadcasting career ended before Spurrier arrived at Carolina. Not only is his offense fun for the fans to watch but it is great for broadcasters to describe. Steve's offense has built-in excitement, and if the play-by-play broadcaster cannot hold his audience with Spurrier on the sideline, he should make a living elsewhere.

When you look at Spurrier's record in coaching Duke and Florida teams to a total of eight conference championships and one national title, is there any reason not to believe that Carolina will have one of the top football programs in the country.

Coach Spurrier is viewed as arrogant by the opponents – but great if he is on your side of the field. There is one area of his coaching career that probably does not receive the recognition due. He does a great job of public relations and does not tap-dance around expressing his thoughts on some very volatile situations.

Coach Joe Patrone, of Penn State, one who is not accustomed to tossing flowers at people, said that Steve Spurrier was the best game-day coach in college football.

I believe that as long a Steve Spurrier is the head football coach at Carolina the fans will experience what I like to call "Total Excitement."

When it comes to college football coaching, Steve Spurrier is in a class by himself.

RAY TANNER

At the conclusion of the 2007 season, Ray Tanner had compiled a record of performance which will probably never be matched again by any other Carolina baseball coach. The following are some of his accomplishments:

3 college World Series appearances

1 final World Series appearance

Total wins at Carolina – 500, losses – 222, .694%

Total career wins – 895, total losses – 393, - 3 ties,   win percentage of .694

8 times going to NCAA playoffS

One of only two teams in the nation to reach the NCAA Super Regional in 7 of the 8 years

Compiled 45 and 22 record in post season play

4th highest win total in Division 1 baseball in the last 8 years.

The winningest SEC team in SEC games in the last 8 years

The .694 winning % in games at Carolina is the second highest total among all SEC coaches.

It was no surprise to me and many Gamecock fans, that Ray Tanner would be so successful as head baseball coach at Carolina. Ray had nine successful seasons at his alma mater at N.C. State, along with affiliation with team U.S.A.

While head coach of the Wolfpack, Tanner led his team to seven appearances in NCAA post-season play. In 1990, he was voted the A.C.C. Coach of the Year.

While a four-year starter at third base and shortstop at N.C. State, he earned all A.C.C. honors in his senior year and still ranks among the Wolfpack's all-time leader in several categories.

During Tanner's first season as head baseball coach at Carolina, the Gamecocks made a tremendous comeback from their first losing season in 26 years, as they finished nine games over .500 and qualified for the S.C.C. post season tournament.

The following year, Tanner coached the Gamecocks to the Eastern Regional for the first time in five years and Ray was named the S.C.C. Coach of the Year.

Tanner's successful coaching career both in college and with U. S. Olympic teams goes on and on.

I have great respect and admiration of Ray Tanner, something I share with all Gamecock fans, and I am certain that my best chance to celebrate the Gamecocks winning a national championship will be with a Ray Tanner coached Carolina baseball team.

DAVE ODEM

The most I knew of Dave Odem before he came to Carolina was that he had been a successful coach at Wake Forest who had recruited a tremendous big man named Tim

Duncan. If you are not familiar with Tim Duncan, contact the Cleveland Cavaliers, who lost four in a row to the San Antonio Spurs who were led by Duncan in the NBA championship series which were concluded in June of 2007.

Although Odem had been a head coach at East Carolina where he had received his Master's Degree, his real success story began when he was appointed as head coach at Wake Forest in 1989, where he formerly had been an assistant coach.

In no time at all, Odem revived a losing program into championship basketball. Dave Odem earned National Coach of the Year honors in 1995. He led the Deacs to two ACC championships and three top national finishes, and his team appeared in seven straight NCAA tournaments involving the Elite Eight – and as a warm-up to what would happen a few years later, his Wake Forest team won the NIT championship in the 2000 season.

I believe that most Carolina fans in evaluating Dave Odem's coaching ability would name his leading the Gamecocks to two successive NIT championships; however his three games with the eventual national champions, Florida, proved to me that Dave Odem is an outstanding coach. In his first game that year the game with Billy Donovan's Florida Gators, the Gamecocks upset the Gators in Columbia. The next time that season they met was at Florida's home floor at Gainesville. I had broadcast there many times and would vote it one of the toughest places to play in the conference. The crowd is very close to the floor and the noise is unbelievable. After having upset the Gators in Columbia, I just did not think the Gamecocks could defeat Florida on their home court where they were heavily favored. But the Gamecocks made me and the oddsmakers look bad as Carolina took charge early and came off with a tremendous win.

That season Coach Odem's Gamecocks had their third encounter with Florida. Carolina without a day's rest fought their way to the SEC tournament game against a well-rested Florida team that had played one less game. With time running out the Gamecocks were clinging to a one point lead. Florida coach, Billy Donovan, set up a baseline screen – the shot was successful and Florida was on their way to the playoffs and a national championship while the Gamecocks were denied an opportunity to participate in the NCAA playoffs.

However you can't win games with only coaching ability, you have to have outstanding players to coach, and that is a problem Dave Odem and all college coaches face today.

~GOING UP THE HILL FOR WCOS~

Although I enjoyed the many other radio stations with whom I have been associated, none gave me the opportunity to help through programming ideas to move a station that was last in the market in ratings, and about to go under, to the number one station in the market.

After broadcasting many high school football games on WCOS, I joined the station on a full-time basis. Shortly after this happened, WCOS AM and FM were purchased by George Buck. George was a young man who had failing eye sight. When I met him, it marked the beginning of a long-time relationship which I still value today.

George Buck probably knew more about jazz than anyone in the country. He started a jazz club in Columbia which sponsored a jazz festival every year. George did not want to carry any sports – just play music. But I convinced him that I could sell high school football games and bring in the Mutual Game of the Day broadcasts. I did this and sold the whole package. Having just left the Game of the Day made it much easier to sell these broadcasts. We even got permission to recreate from Western Union, the New York Yankees games when Roger Maris was trying to break Mickey Mantles record of home runs for one season. Maris never broke the record, but he sure increased our listening audience – we were certainly on the road to replacing WNOK as the number one station in the Columbia market.

At this stage our station needed to change its music format, and George Buck had the answer. He came up with the "Top Sixty in Dixie." I suggested that to promote this move that the station play nothing but Dixie for 24 hours – which we did. Listeners found it difficult to complain. United Press gave us national publicity and we later won an advertising award.

I had been a disk jockey on three other stations so I decided to take over the morning show that had not been doing well. I sold the commercials which I would ad lib on the air and we did very well – not because of me, but rather as a result of featuring the Beatles. We also had our go-to guy, Jack Grant, visit the schools and tape the kids reading the lunch menu every day, plus a lot of other promotions.

When I was in Houston to broadcast the Blue Bonnet Bowl, I took a cab at the Houston Airport to the Shamrock Hotel. I asked the cab driver what was "hot" in the radio market. He told me that on station KLEE, they were selling totem poles. KLEE happened to be the originating station for the Blue Bonnet Network so the manager of the station told me it was a great promotion. He said that these totem poles came from Sausalito, just across the bay from San Francisco. I had previously visited that art colony and had seen gaily colored totem poles in front of many homes. KLEE had contracted with a man named West to deliver the poles if they were sold. KLEE played the commercials straight with background music, giving the pitch that was telling the listener he could have a status decoration for his front yard, and the price was $6,000. KLEE didn't sell any totem poles but everyone was talking about them. I carried this promotion back to WCOS – used the same approach that KLEE was doing – no we didn't sell any totem poles but it really had everyone in town talking about totem poles and WCOS.

Perhaps the most valuable idea that we carried out was to recreate election results. On election night I worked out of an office at the station with papers pasted over the glass entrance to give us privacy. We had three radios dialed to the other three stations in the market, and three members of our staff would tabulate the votes as they came in. I would take the station that had the latest poll count and put the results on the air. We did a couple of things that made it appear more authentic by not giving the exact count and to avoid suspicion, we would place a few staff members at the various polls. They really had nothing to do – we were doing it all at the station. We went from being the worst station in election coverage to the number one spot, and we did it for years with no one outside of our staff knowing our little secret. What we were doing was not illegal as what is broadcast is Public Domain.

Our morning drive time had become number one in the market but the afternoon segment was not doing as well. Woody Windham came in from Windham Corners to audition as a jockey for that time slot. George Buck thought Woody, who was eighteen years old, was too young for the job, but I was impressed with Woody and talked George into hiring him. We were lucky – Woody was an instant hit. Several days after he started, I walked into the control room and said to Woody that he had a great first name –"why don't you say this is Woody with the goodies" – he must have liked it as he still uses it today.

Woody and I put on a Twist-a-thon at the Township Auditorium – we had everyone who attended wear Beatle wigs. The place was packed – we held a twist contest on the stage – gave away prizes – and made some money. Incidentally, I was the best man at Woody's wedding at Windham Corners.

WCOS was on top in the Columbia market and I thought it was time for me to move on to something new. Before my going-away party, George Buck told me if it hadn't been for me the station would never have made it. If that be true, it was only because I had the help of so many hard-working and talented people. In the sales department, Dennis Waldrop, who also emceed a call-in show during those very volatile times. Bob Truere, our news director, and attorney Dave Fedor were excellent call-in hosts.

Announcers Leo Windham, Woody's brother; Pete Noce; Warren Moon; Chris Craft; Jack Brown; Ben Rast - all of whom were top-flight announcers - and the station owner George Buck, who ran a great jazz show every Sunday night. Jimmy Collins, former Carolina basketball star, was a great addition to our sales staff; and I talked Jess Plummer to leave WIS and join our staff as our commercial manager. And last, but certainly not least, all the wonderful gals in the office. I am sure I missed mentioning some people, and for that I apologize.

George Buck, at one time, offered to sell me the FM station for $75,000. FM just did not have many listeners at the time and I felt that it would not be wise for me to buy. When George Buck sold his FM station several years ago, he received thirteen million dollars. Well you can't win them all! George is now totally blind and manages a station in New Orleans, which is one of ten radio stations that he owns. I correspond with George on a regular basis. My stay with WCSO was a great ride and I will never forget it.

~THE AGENCIES~

My close friend Don Barton was associated with several others in one of the leading advertising agencies in Columbia. I told Don that I liked advertising and I would help him set up his own agency and I would join him as a part-time partner. Shortly thereafter, we decided to bring in John Terry, one of my clients and a long-time friend, as one of our partners. John was the owner of the Big T – Taylor Street Pharmacy. The advertising agency we had set up for Don Barton was doing very well, and although we were partners, Terry and I were not active in the day to day operation. Barton brought in two partners who represented profitable accounts, so John and I decided to step out. Don later bought the shares owned by Terry and me.

Since I still controlled several large accounts, I decided to open my own ad agency. I rented an office in Five Points and hired Margie Miles, a long time friend of mine, as my secretary. Margie for many years was the featured singer with many big bands in Columbia. The agency was doing very and Margie was doing such a great job that during the summer months we would often close shop at noontime and I would go home to my place at the lake and join my wife Dody and enjoy what amounted to "living in another world." Dody at the time had the summers off as a school librarian. We had hoped to spend many years at our place, which we loved, but that was not to be as she was diagnosed with breast cancer in 1975 and died nine months later in June of 1976. I not only had lost a wonderful wife but my best friend. Dody was a rare bird – her mother likened her to Peter Pan. She touched so many lives, not only as a friend but as a librarian at Hayward Gibbs and later at Dutch Fork elementary school where she had been honored as Teacher of the Year. She is sorely missed by all of us. My final resting place will be beside her. Her burial site is at Greenlawn Cemetery in Columbia.

Before my retirement I was continuing to broadcast football, baseball and basketball. I also became involved in other areas which included a morning sky watch on WSCQ. I liked this as it gave me a chance to operate our plane. My license had expired many years ago but my regular pilot let me take over the controls quite often and he allowed me to shoot some landings.

Bob Fulton "My Career My Life"

~TO MY READERS – FINAL THOUGHT~

So many people have asked me why I gave up a career in major league baseball at a better than average salary to come back to Columbia and continue my career here. The answer is very simple. My family and I love South Carolina, its people, and the University of South Carolina.

There is no way I could thank the many fans who over the years have given me such great support. I will be ever thankful.

~BOB FULTON - A PROFILE~

Native of Ridley Park, Pennsylvania, a suburb of Philadelphia.

Attended West Chester State Teachers College, West Chester, Pennsylvania, and the University of the Ozarks, Clarksville, Arkansas. Graduated with a major in speech.

Graduate work at Emile Kreide School of Speech in Philadelphia.

Began radio career with WCAM, Camden, New Jersey. Was program director for the station.

Sports director of KLRA and KXLR in Little Rock, Arkansas. For nine years originated broadcasts of University of Arkansas basketball and football on statewide networks.

Coached basketball and football in Little Rock school system and in Hartman, Arkansas.

Broadcast baseball for Pueblo, Colorado, of the Western League in 1950.

Broadcast baseball for Hornell, New York of Pony League in 1951.

Came to Columbia in 1952 and broadcast Columbia Reds baseball on WNOK-Radio and WNOK-TV every season that the club was in operation, except for 1954.

Began broadcasting University of South Carolina football in 1952, and served in that capacity through 1994, except for the 1965 and 1966 seasons, when he was announcer for the Georgia Tech network.

In 1954 joined the Mutual Broadcasting System Game of the Day staff, broadcasting major league baseball games over a nationwide network and the Armed Forces Network for overseas broadcasts.

In 1980 and 1981 broadcast baseball for the Columbia Mets.

In 1967 signed a long term contract to broadcast sporting events for Carolina on radio and television. Did Carolina TV basketball for five years and worked with TVS on regional and national telecasts.

Broadcast Carolina baseball games, beginning in 1974.

Did national radio play by play for Bluebonnet Bowl six times, Gator Bowl twice and Sun Bowl once.

Served as president of both the Columbia Tipoff Club and Columbia Touchdown Club.

~HONORS AND AWARDS~

Eight-time recipient of Outstanding Sportscaster Award for the state of South Carolina.

In 1973 he was honored by the South Carolina State legislature with a resolution commending him for many years of outstanding service to South Carolina as a broadcaster of sports.

In 1985 he received the Distinguished Service Award from the South Carolina Athletic Hall of Fame.

In 1986 he was the only media member honored by the Columbia Bicentennial Sports Awards Committee.

In 1990 he became the only non coach or athlete to be inducted into the South Carolina Athletic Hall of Fame.

In 1990 he became the first sports broadcaster to be presented the Masters Award by the South Carolina Broadcasters Association.

In 1993 he was inducted into the University of South Carolina Athletic Hall of Fame.

In 1994 he received the state's highest award, The Order of the Palmetto, from Governor Carroll Campbell.

January 18, 1995, was designated as Bob Fulton Day in Columbia by Mayor Bob Coble and the City Council.

On January 1, 1995, he was honored by CBS-TV during the telecast of the Carolina-West Virginia Carquest Bowl at Miami, Florida.

On March 12, 1995, he was honored by the Jefferson Pilot TV Network during the half-time intermission of the Southeastern Conference championship basketball game in Atlanta.

On March 12, 1995, he was honored at a banquet, sponsored by the University of South Carolina on behalf of his 43 years of service to the school.

In October 1995 he was honored with a Lifetime Membership in the University of South Carolina Alumni Association.

In May 2007 he was honored by the South Carolina Hall of Fame for his contributions to sports in the Palmetto State.

Bob Fulton "My Career My Life"

~PICTURE GALLERY~

Bob Fulton came to Columbia in 1952 to Broadcast Columbia Reds baseball games from this booth in Capital City Park.

Bob Fulton

Cowboy Bob in 1924.

In Jenkintown,
Pennsylvania, 1924.

This is how the well-dressed
eight-year-old looked in 1928.

225

Bob and Dody Terrel were married in Little Rock in 1948. She died of cancer in 1976.

Bob and fellow broadcaster Frank Page in Little Rock, Arkansas. Page later became host of the "Louisiana Hayride" radio show, on which Elvis Presley got his start.

In the early 1950s television sports shows didn't have the electronic marvels that are in use today, as evidenced by the above set. How do you spell Cin(n)cinnati?

Fulton and color announcer Bob Truere re-creating a
Columbia Gems baseball game from the window of
Taylor Street Pharmacy in downtown Columbia.

In 1956 Fulton spent 12 days on the roof of Capital City Park in a successful
effort to sell tickets to Columbia Gems baseball games. Lou Essick (right) of
WCOS-Radio is shown with Fulton prior to a home game.

Johnny Evans worked with Fulton on Carolina football broadcasts in the 1950s.

In 1965 and 1966 Fulton broadcast Georgia Tech football games, for which Atlanta's WGST was the originating station.

Fulton talks with members of the 1953 Carolina football team who received All-Atlantic Coast Conference honors. Left to right, end Clyde Bennett, guard Frank Mincevich, quarterback Johnny Gramling and center Leon Cunningham.

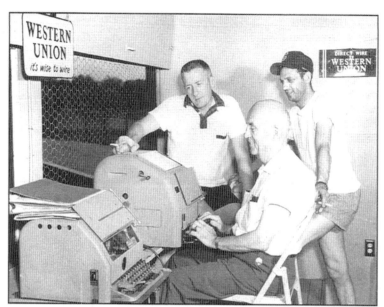

Baseball re-creations were done with information received from Western
Union operators, such as Doug Fleming of the Columbia office. Bob and Lou
Essick check his report that was being sent to another Sally League city.

Fulton was South Carolina Sportscaster of the Year eight times. He is shown
here receiving one of the awards from North Carolina Governor Terry
Sanford and Miss North Carolina in ceremonies at Salisbury, N.C.

A representative of the Savannah baseball club makes a presentation to the Mutual Game of the Day crew (left to right) Fulton, Al Helfer and Paul Jonas.

Members of the Mutual Game of the Day crew met with local representatives prior to broadcast of a South Atlantic League game in Charlotte. Among those pictured are Bob Quincy (left), sports editor of the Charlotte News, Dick Butler (second from left), president of the South Atlantic League, Al Helfer (fourth from left), Paul Jonas (third from right) and Fulton (far right).

The Mutual Game of the Day crew was welcomed with open arms everywhere they went.

Fulton broadcast all of Frank McGuire's 16 seasons of basketball games at Carolina.

Fulton broadcast Frank McGuire's 300th victory on March 9, 1967, when the Gamecocks defeated Maryland in the ACC tournament at Greensboro.
McGuire and his wife, Pat, are shown cutting a cake in honor of the occasion.

During the broadcast of Fulton's 1,000th Carolina basketball game, he received awards from (left to right) Athletics Director King Dixon, South Carolina Network director Tom Stevens and Gamecock basketball Coach Frank McGuire.

Spotter's boards are in place, as Bob prepares to broadcast a game from Williams-Brice Stadium.

Fulton with Carolina baseball Coach June Raines (center) and Leon Goodall, Columbia insurance executive and a sponsor of Gamecock baseball.

Broadcast conditions for college baseball games are not always ideal, as shown in this set-up for a game between Carolina and Virginia Tech in 1984.

Bob needed a booster seat for his broadcast of the 1984 Gator Bowl game between Carolina and Oklahoma State.

Mick Mixon of WIS-Radio worked with Bob on many Carolina broadcasts. Mixon is now analyst for the North Carolina Tar Heels network.

Bob interviews Mike Dunleavy, former Gamecock basketball star.
Dunleavy played in the NBA and coached the Los Angeles Lakers and
Milwaukee Bucks before becoming general manager of the Bucks.

Fulton and Gamecock basketball
Coach Bill Foster.

Casey Manning, former
Gamecock basketball player,
was analyst for the Gamecock
network during Fulton's final
season.

The South Carolina Network broadcast crew, before the 1994 Carolina-Clemson game at Clemson. On the left are (clockwise) Todd Ellis, David Spence, Tommy Suggs and Fulton. At right are (bottom to top) Liz McMillan, Burt Smith, Ree Hart, Julian Gibbons and Dan Radakovich.

Fulton's final broadcast in Williams-Brice Stadium took place on October 29, 1994. At halftime of the Carolina-Tennessee game the band spelled out his last name, as part of ceremonies honoring Fulton.

235

Don Barton (right) was the analyst on Carolina football broadcasts in 1956.

Fulton was installed in the South Carolina Athletic Hall of Fame in 1990.

Bob Fulton and longtime Carolina sports information director Tom Price with avid Gamecock fan Todd Morris of Turbeville, South Carolina.

Fulton and Gamecock football Coach Brad Scott.

Fulton with his friend, Tatum Gressette, Gamecock football star in the 1920s and a Gamecock Hall of Fame member.

Fulton confers with analyst Tommy Suggs prior to a game at Williams-Brice Stadium in Columbia.

Bob and daughters Robin Jensen (left) of Tustin, California, and Nancy Johnson of Morganton, North Carolina.

239

Carol and Bob with NBC-TV Today Show weatherman Willard Scott in 1996.

Fulton and Gamecock basketball Coach Eddie Fogler.

Bob received the first Brad Scott "Service to the University" award in 1995.
Carol accepted the award on behalf of her husband.

241

Columbia Mayor Bob Coble declared January 18, 1995, "Bob Fulton Day" in the city.

Bob was Grand Marshal of the Five Points St. Patrick's Day parade in 1994. The car is a 1930 Ford, complete with rumble seat.

George Rogers, 1980
Heisman Trophy winner,
was one of the speakers
at a tribute dinner for
Bob in 1995.

Bob bids farewell to Carolina fans at halftime of the Carolina-Tennessee
game on October 29, 1994, in Williams-Brice Stadium.

At WWHG, Hornell, New York, in 1951.

Fulton was honored by Clemson University at halftime of his final Carolina-Clemson football broadcast at Clemson. Cocky and Clemson broadcaster Jim Phillips are shown, as Bob displays a plaque he received.

Peggy Peattie

Bob and Carol Fulton were marshals of the 1994 Carolina homecoming parade.

Bob and Cocky.

Carol and Bob stand beside a framed replica of the jersey that was hung among retired jerseys in Carolina Coliseum on March 4, 1995, at halftime of the Carolina-Tennessee basketball game.